ENCYCLOPAEDIA OF
CYBER LAWS AND CRIME

ENCYCLOPAEDIA OF CYBER LAWS AND CRIME

Vol. 5

Indian Legislation on Cyber Crime

Edited by

S.R. Sharma

ANMOL PUBLICATIONS PVT. LTD.
NEW DELHI - 110 002 (INDIA)

ANMOL PUBLICATIONS PVT. LTD.
4374/4B, Ansari Road, Daryaganj
New Delhi - 110 002
Ph.: 23261597, 23278000
Visit us at: www.anmolpublications.com

Encyclopaedia of Cyber Laws and Crime

First Edition, 2003

ISBN 81-261-1432-0 (Set)

PRINTED IN INDIA

Published by J.L. Kumar for Anmol Publications Pvt. Ltd., New Delhi - 110 002 and Printed at Mehra Offset Press, Delhi.

CONTENTS

PREFACE

In the last years of the twentieth century a phenomenon has been witnessed which is likely to change the shape of human civilization. This is the explosion which has taken place in electronics and as a result of which there has been infinite expansion of knowledge that is commonly described as information explosion. The most astounding development in this area has been the geometric expansion of trade commerce entertainment and information jointly known as the internet or the web. The web accepts no restrictions of the country, race religion or country and has been totally responsible as a decisive factor in taking the world into what is now known as globalisation.

It is generally believed that a website is created every minute and along with its positive aspect it also brings about a new sense of responsibility. The free trade and commerce available through website in what is known as cyber space has also given birth to a mobile population where intent may be basically criminal. Thus we have hachers, virus carriers, sleepers and moles, who may constitute a real threat to the creativity of the web. There is, therefore, the eternal question of intellectual copyright and the policing of vast cyber space to protect and maintain what manhood can truly achieve.

Consequently the TRAI Act 1997 has been enacted by the Indian parliament in the 48th year of Republic of India on 28th March 1997 to provide for the establishment of the Telecom Regulatory Authority of India (TRAI) to regulate the telecommunication services and for matters connected therewith are incidental thereto.

As per Section 11 (2) of the TRAI Act TRAI is empowered to fix/revise tariff for various telecom services provided in India and service providers including the Department service provisions have to implement the tariffs, notified by the TRAI as per provisions of law.

. The TRAI has been mandated to fix/revise tariff for various telecom services by virtue of section 11 (2) of TRAI Act.

The Encyclopaedia tries to cover as many laws as possible, promulgated by various countries and unions of countries like the European Union in this area to give a comprehensive and comparative view of CYBER Law.

The editor has no claims to originality and has simply compiled and edited the material collected from various sources. In view of the English language being the medium most of the material has been collected from American, British and Indian sources.

The editor is grateful to the Librarians of the library of the Supreme Court, the Indian Law Institute and the Ministry of Law, Justice and Company Affairs, for their kind assistance in locating the material from various sources.

The editor is specifically grateful to Shri Jawahar Lal Kumar, Managing Director, Anmol Publications Pvt. Ltd., New Delhi for venturing to publish the Encyclopaedia on Cyber Laws.

—Dr. S.R. Sharma

1 THE INFORMATION TECHNOLOGY ACT, 2000

An Act to provide legal recognition for transactions carried out by means of electronic data interchange and other means of electronic communication, commonly referred to as "electronic commerce", which involve the use of alternatives to paper-based methods of communication and storage of information, to facilitate electronic filing of documents with the Government agencies and further to amend the Indian Penal Code, the Indian Evidence Act, 1872, the Banker's Book Evidence Act, 1891 and the Reserve Bank of India Act, 1934 and for matters connected therewith or incidental thereto.

WHEREAS the General Assembly of the United Nations by resolution A/RES/51/162 dated the 30th January, 1997 has adopted the Model Law on Electronic Commerce adopted by the United Nations Commission on International Trade Law;

AND WHEREAS the said resolution recommends inter alia *that all states give favourable consideration to the said Model Law when they enact or revise their laws, in view of the need for uniformity of the law applicable to alternatives to paper based methods of communication and storage of information;*

AND WHEREAS it is considered necessary to give

effect to the said resolution and to promote efficient delivery of Government services by means of reliable electronic records;

BE it enacted by Parliament in the Fifty-first Year of the Republic of India as follows:—

I

PRELIMINARY

1. Short title, extent, commencement and application

(1) This Act may be called the Information Technology Act, 2000.

(Note: The Act has come into force on 17-10-2000)

(2) It shall extend to the whole of India and, save as otherwise provided in this Act, it applies also to any offence or contravention thereunder committed outside India by any.person.

(3) It shall come into force on such date as the Central Government may, by notification, appoint and different dates may be appointed for different provisions of this Act and any reference in any such provision to the commencement of this Act shall be construed as a reference to the commencement of that provision.

(4) Nothing in this Act shall apply to,--

(a) a negotiable instrument as defined in Section 13 of the Negotiable Instruments Act, 1881 (26 of 1881);

(b) a power-of-attorney as defined in Section 1A of the Powers-of-Attorney Act, 1882 (7 of 1882);

(c) a trust as defined in Section 3 of the Indian Trusts Act, 1882 (2 of 1882);

(d) a will as defined in clause (h) of Section 2 of the Indian Succession Act, 1925 (39 of 1925) including any other testamentary disposition by whatever name called;

(e) any contract for the sale or conveyance of immovable property or any interest in such property;

(f) any such class of documents or transactions as may be notified by the Central Government in the Official Gazette.

2. Definitions

(1) In this Act, unless the context otherwise requires,—

(a) "access" with its grammatical variations and cognate expressions means gaining entry into, instructing or communicating with the logical, arithmetical, or memory function resources of a computer, computer system or computer network;

(b) "addressee" means a person who is intended by the originator to receive the electronic record but does not include any intermediary;

(c) "adjudicating officer" means an adjudicating officer appointed under sub-section (1) of Section 46;

(d) "affixing digital signature" with its grammatical variations and cognate expressions means adoption of any methodology or procedure by a person for the purpose of authenticating an electronic record by means of digital signature;

(e) "appropriate Government" means as respects any matter,—

(i) enumerated in List II of the Seventh Schedule to the Constitution;

(ii) relating to any State law enacted under List III of the Seventh Schedule to the Constitution,

the State Government and in any other case, the Central Government;

(f) "asymmetric crypto system" means a system of a secure key pair consisting of a private key for creating a digital signature and a public key to verify the digital signature;

(g) "Certifying Authority" means a person who has been granted a licence to issue a Digital Signature Certificate under Section 24;

(h) "certification practice statement" means a statement issued by a Certifying Authority to specify the practices that the Certifying Authority employs in issuing Digital Signature Certificates;

(i) "computer" means any electronic magnetic, optical or other high-speed data processing device or system which performs logical, arithmetic, and memory functions by manipulations of electronic, magnetic or optical impulses, and includes all input, output, processing, storage, computer software, or communication facilities which are connected or related to the computer in a computer system or computer network;

(j) "computer network" means the interconnection of one or more computers through—

(i) the use of satellite, microwave, terrestrial line or other communication media; and

(ii) terminals or a complex consisting of two or more interconnected computers whether or not the interconnection is continuously maintained;

(k) "computer resource" means computer, computer system, computer network, data, computer database or software;

(l) "computer system" means a device or collection of devices, including input and output support devices and excluding calculators which are not programmable and capable of being used in conjunction with external files, which contain computer programmes, electronic instructions, input data, and output data, that performs logic, arithmetic, data storage and retrieval, communication control and other functions;

(m) "Controller" means the Controller of Certifying Authorities appointed under sub-section (1) of Section 17;

(n) "Cyber Appellate Tribunal" means the Cyber Regulations Appellate Tribunal established under sub-section (1) of Section 48;

(o) "data" means a representation of information, knowledge, facts, concepts or instructions which are being prepared or have been prepared in a formalised manner, and is intended to be processed, is being processed or has been processed in a computer system or computer network, and may be in any form (including computer printouts magnetic or optical storage media, punched cards, punched tapes) or stored internally in the memory of the computer;

(p) "digital signature" means authentication of any electronic record by a subscriber by means of an electronic method or procedure in accordance with the provisions of Section 3;

(q) "Digital Signature Certificate" means a Digital Signature Certificate issued under sub-section (4) of Section 35;

(r) "electronic form" with reference to information means any information generated, sent, received or stored in media, magnetic, optical, computer memory, microfilm, computer generated micro fiche or similar device;

(s) "electronic Gazette" means Official Gazette published in the electronic form;

(t) "electronic record" means data, record or data generated, image or sound stored, received or sent in an electronic form or microfilm or computer generated micro fiche;

(u) "function", in relation to a computer, includes logic, control, arithmetical process, deletion, storage and retrieval and communication or telecommunication from or within a computer;

(v) "information" includes data, text, images, sound, voice, codes, computer programmes, software and databases or micro film or computer generated micro fiche;

(w) "intermediary" with respect to any particular electronic message means any person who on behalf of another person receives, stores or transmits that message or provides any service with respect to that message;

(x) "key pair", in an asymmetric crypto system, means a private key and its mathematically related public key, which are so related that the public key can verify a digital signature created by the private key;

(y) "law" includes any Act of Parliament or of a State Legislature, Ordinances promulgated by the President or a Governor, as the case may be, Regulations made by the President under article 240, Bills enacted as President's Act under sub-clause (a) of clause (l) of article 357 of the Constitution and includes rules, regulations, bye-laws and orders issued or made thereunder;

(z) "licence" means a licence granted to a Certifying Authority under Section 24;

(za) "originator" means a person who sends, generates, stores or transmits any electronic message or causes any electronic message to be sent, generated, stored or transmitted to any other person but does not include an intermediary;

(zb) "prescribed" means prescribed by rules made under this Act;

(zc) "private key" means the key of a key pair used to create a digital signature;

(zd) "public key" means the key of a key pair used to verify a digital signature and listed in the Digital Signature Certificate;

(ze) "secure system" means computer hardware, software, and procedure that —

(a) are reasonably secure from unauthorised access and misuse;

(b) provide a reasonable level of reliability and correct operation;

(c) are reasonably suited to performing the intended functions; and

(d) adhere to generally accepted security procedures;

(zf) "security procedure" means the security procedure prescribed under Section 16 by the Central Government;

(zg) "subscriber" means a person in whose name the Digital Signature Certificate is issued;

(zh) "verify" in relation to a digital signature, electronic record or public key, with its grammatical variations and cognate expressions means to determine whether—

(a) the initial electronic record was affixed with the digital signature by the use of private key corresponding to the public key of the sub-scriber;

(b) the initial electronic record is retained intact or has been altered since such electronic record was so affixed with the digital signature.

(2) Any reference in this Act to any enactment or any provision thereof shall, in relation to an area in which such enactment or such provision is not in force, be construed as a reference to the corresponding law or the relevant provision of the corresponding law, if any, in force in that area.

II

DIGITAL SIGNATURE

3. Authentication of electronic records

(1) Subject to the provisions of this section any subscriber

may authenticate an electronic record by affixing his digital signature.

(2) The authentication of the electronic record shall be effected by the use of asymmetric crypto system and hash function which envelop and transform the initial electronic record into another electronic record.

Explanation.—For the purposes of this sub-section, "hash function" means an algorithm mapping or translation of one sequence of bits into another, generally smaller, set known as 'hash result" such that an electronic record yields the same hash result every time the algorithms executed with the same electronic record as its input making it computationally infeasible—

(a) to derive or reconstruct the original electronic record from the hash result produced by the algorithm;

(b) that two electronic records can produce the same hash result using the algorithm.

(3) Any person by the use of a public key of the subscriber can verify the electronic record.

(4) The private key and the public key are unique to the subscriber and constitute a functioning key pair.

III

ELECTRONIC GOVERNANCE

4. Legal recognition of electronic records

Where any law provides that information or any other matter shall be in writing or in the typewritten or printed form, then, notwithstanding anything contained in such law, such requirement shall be deemed to have been satisfied if such information or matter is—-

(a) rendered or made available in an electronic form; and

(b) accessible so as to be usable for a subsequent reference.

5. Legal recognition of digital signatures

Where any law provides that information or any other matter shall be authenticated by affixing signature or any document shall be signed or bear the signature of any person then, withstanding anything contained in such law, such requirement shall be deemed to have been satisfied, if such information or matter is authenticated by means of digital signature affixed in such manner as may be prescribed by the Central Government.

Explanation.—For the purposes of this section, "signed", with its grammatical variations and cognate expressions, shall, with reference to a person, mean affixing of his hand written signature or any mark on any document and the expression "signature" shall be construed accordingly.

6. Use of electronic records and digital signatures in Government and its agencies

(1) Where any law provides for—

(a) the filing of any form, application or any other document with any office, authority, body or agency owned or controlled by the appropriate Government in a particular manner;

(b) the issue or grant of any licence, permit, sanction or approval by whatever named called in a particular manner;

(c) the receipt or payment of money in a particular manner,

then, notwithstanding anything contained in any other law for the time being in force, such requirement shall be deemed to have been satisfied if such filing, issue, grant, receipt or payment, as the case may be, is effected by means of such electronic form as may be prescribed by the appropriate Government.

(2) The appropriate Government may, for the purposes of sub-section (1), by rules, prescribe—

(a) the manner and format in which such electronic records shall be filed, created or issued;

(b) the manner or method of payment of any fee or charges for filing, creation or issue any electronic record under clause (a).

7. Retention of electronic records

(1) Where any law provides that documents, records or information shall be retained for any specific period, then, that requirement shall be deemed to have been satisfied if such documents, records or information are retained in the electronic form, if—

(a) the information contained therein remains accessible so as to be usable for a subsequent reference;

(b) the electronic record is retained in the format in which it was originally generated, sect or received or in a format which can be demonstrated to represent accurately the information originally generated, sent or received;

(c) the details which will facilitate the identification of the origin, destination, date and time of despatch or receipt of such electronic record are available in the electronic record:

Provided that this clause does not apply to any information which is automatically generated solely for the purpose of enabling an electronic record to be despatched or received.

(2) Nothing in this section shall apply to any law that expressly provides for the retention of documents, records or information in the form of electronic records.

8. Publication of rules, regulation, etc., in Electronic Gazette

Where any law provides that any rule, regulation, order, bye-law, notification or any other matter shall be published in the Official Gazette, then, such requirement shall be deemed to have been satisfied if such rule, regulation, order, bye-law, notification or any other matter is published in the Official Gazette or electronic Gazette:

Provided that where any rule, regulation, order, bye-law, notification or any other matters is published in the Official Gazette or Electronic Gazette, the date of publication shall be deemed to be the date of the Gazette which was first published in any form.

9. Sections 6, 7 and 8 not to confer right to insist document should be accepted in electronic form

Nothing contained in Sections 6, 7 and 8 shall confer a right upon any person to insist that any Ministry or Department of the Central Government or the State Government or any authority or body established by or under any law or controlled or funded by the Central or State Government should accept, issue, create, retain and preserve any document in the form of electronic records or effect any monetary transaction in the electronic form.

10. Power to make rules by Central Government in respect of digital signature

The Central Government may, for the purposes of this Act, by rules, prescribe —

(a) the type of digital signature;

(b) the manner and format in which the digital signature shall be affixed;

(c) the manner or procedure which facilitates identification of the person affixing the digital signature;

(d) control processes and procedures to ensure adequate integrity, security and confidentiality of electronic records or payments; and

(e) any other matter which is necessary to give legal effect to digital signatures.

ATTRIBUTION, ACKNOWLEDGEMENT AND DESPATCH OF ELECTRONIC RECORDS

11. Attribution of electronic records

An electronic record shall be attributed to the originator—

(a) if it was sent by the originator himself;

(b) by a person who had the authority to act on behalf of the originator in respect of that electronic record; or

(c) by an information system programmed by or on behalf of the originator to operate automatically.

12. Acknowledgement of receipt

(1) Where the originator has not agreed with the addressee that the acknowledgement of receipt of electronic record be given in a particular form or by a particular method, an acknowledgement may be given by—

(a) any communication by the addressee, automated or otherwise; or

(b) any conduct of the addressee, sufficient to indicate to the originator that the electronic record has been received.

(2) Where the originator has stipulated that the electronic record shall be binding only on receipt of an acknowledgement of such electronic record by him, then unless acknowledgement has been so received, the electronic record shall be deemed to have been never sent by the originator.

(3) Where the originator has not stipulated that the electronic record shall be binding only on receipt of such acknowledgement, and the acknowledgement has not been received by the originator within the time specified or agreed or, if no time has been specified or agreed to within a reasonable time, then the originator may give notice to the addressee stating that no acknowledgement has been received by him and specifying a reasonable time by which the acknowledgement must be received by him and if no acknowledgement is received within the aforesaid time limit he may after giving notice to the addressee, treat the electronic record as though it has never been sent.

13. Time and place of despatch and receipt of electronic record

(1) Save as otherwise agreed to between the originator and the addressee, the despatch of an electronic record occurs when it enters a computer resource outside the control of the originator.

(2) Save as otherwise agreed between the originator and the addressee, the time of receipt of an electronic record shall be determined as follows, namely:—

(a) if the addressee has designated a computer resource for the purpose of receiving electronic records,—

(i) receipt occurs at the time when the electronic record enters the designated computer resource; or

(ii) if the electronic record is sent to a computer resource of the addressee that is not the designated computer resource, receipt occurs at the time when the electronic record is retrieved by the addressee;

(b) if the addressee has not designated a computer resource along with specified timings, if any, receipt occurs when the electronic record enters the computer resource of the addressee.

(3) Save as otherwise agreed to between the originator and the addressee, an electronic record is deemed to be despatched at the place where the originator has his place of business, and is deemed to be received at the place where the addressee has his place of business.

(4) The provisions of sub-section (2) shall apply notwithstanding that the place where the computer resource is located may be different from the place where the electronic record is deemed to have been received under sub-section (3).

(5) For the purposes of this section,—

(a) it the originator or the addressee has more than one place of business, the principal place of business, shall be the place of business;

(b) if the originator or the addressee does not have a place of business, his usual place of residence shall be deemed to be the place of business;

(c) "usual place of residence", in relation to a body corporate, means the place where it is registered.

V

SECURE ELECTRONIC RECORDS AND SECURE DIGITAL SIGNATURES

14. Secure electronic record

Where any security procedure has been applied to an electronic record at a specific point of time then such record shall be deemed to be a secure electronic record from such point of time to the time of verification.

15. Secure digital signature

If, by application of a security procedure agreed to by the parties concerned, it can be verified that a digital signature, at the time it was affixed, was—

(a) unique to the subscriber affixing it;
(b) capable of identifying such subscriber;
(c) created in a manner or using a means under the exclusive control of the subscriber and is linked to the electronic record to which it relates in such a manner that if the electronic record was altered the digital signature would be invalidated,

then such digital signature shall be deemed to be a secure digital signature.

16. Security procedure

The Central Government shall for the purposes of this Act prescribe the security procedure having regard to commercial circumstances prevailing at the time when the procedure was used, including—

(a) the nature of the transaction;

(b) the level of sophistication of the parties with reference to their technological capacity;

(c) the volume of similar transactions engaged in by other parties;

(d) the availability of alternatives offered to but rejected by any parly,

(e) the cost of alternative procedures; and

(f) the procedures in general use for similar types of transactions or communications.

VI

REGULATION OF CERTIFYING AUTHORITIES

17. Appointment of Controller and other officers

(1) The Central Government may, by notification in the Official Gazette, appoint a Controller of Certifying Authorities for the purposes of this Act and may also by the same or subsequent notification appoint such number of Deputy Controllers and Assistant Controllers as it deems fit.

(2) The Controller shall discharge his functions under this Act subject to the general control and directions of the Central Government.

(3) The Deputy Controllers and Assistant Controllers shall perform the functions assigned to them by the Controller under the general superintendence and control of the Controller.

(4) The qualifications, experience and terms and conditions of service of Controller, Deputy Controllers and Assistant Controllers shall be such as may be prescribed by the Central Government;

(5) The Head Office and Branch Office of the office of the Controller shall be at such places as the Central Government may specify, and these may be established as such places at the Central Government may think fit.

(6) There shall be a seal of the Office of the Controller.

18. Functions of Controller

The Controller may perform all or any of the following functions, namely:—

(a) exercising supervision over the activities of the Certifying Authorities;

(b) certifying public keys of the Certifying Authorities;

(c) laying down the standards to be maintained by the Certifying Authorities;

(d) specifying the qualifications and experience which employees of the Certifying Authorities should possess;

(e) specifying the conditions subject to which the Certify Authorities shall conduct their business;

(f) specifying the contents of written, printed or visual materials and advertisements that may be distributed or used in respect of a Digital Signature Certificate and the public key;

(g) specifying the form and content of a Digital Signature Certificate and the key;

(h) specifying the form and manner in which accounts shall be maintained by the Certifying Authorities;

(i) specifying the terms and conditions subject to which auditors may be appointed and the remuneration to be paid to them;

(j) facilitating the establishment of any electronic system by a Certifying Authority either solely or jointly with other Certifying Authorities and regulation of such systems;

(k) specifying the manner in which the Certifying Authorities shall conduct their dealings with the subscribers;

(l) resolving any conflict of interests between the Certifying Authorities and the subscribers;

(m) laying down the duties of the Certifying Authorities;

(n) maintaining a database containing the disclosure record of every Certifying Authority containing such particulars as may be specified by regulations, which shall be accessible to public.

19. Recognition of foreign certifying Authorities

(1) Subject to such conditions and restrictions as may be specified by regulations, the Controller may with the previous approval of the Central Government, and by notification in the Official Gazette, recognise any foreign Certifying Authority as a Certifying Authority for the purposes of this Act.

(2) Where any Certifying Authority is recognised under sub-section (1), the Digital Signature Certificate issued by such Certifying Authority shall be valid for the purposes of this Act.

(3) The Controller may if he is satisfied that any Certifying Authority has contravened any of the conditions and restrictions subject to which it was granted recognition under sub-section (1) he may, for reasons to be recorded in writing, by notification in the Official Gazette, revoke such recognition.

20. Controller to act as repository

(1) The Controller shall be the repository of all Digital Signature Certificates issued under this Act.

(2) The Controller shall—

(a) make use of hardware, software and procedures that are secure from intrusion and misuse;

(b) observe such other standards as may be prescribed by the Central Government, to ensure that the secrecy and security of the digital signatures are assured.

(3) The Controller shall maintain a computerised database of all public keys in such a manner that such database and the public keys are available to any member of the public.

21. Licence to issue Digital Signature Certificates

(1) Subject to the provisions of sub-section (2), any person may make an application, to the Controller, for a licence to issue Digital Signature Certificates.

(2) No licence shall be issued under sub-section (1), unless the applicant fulfils such requirements with respect to qualification, expertise, manpower, financial resources and other infrastructure facilities, which are necessary to issue Digital Signature Certificates as may be prescribed by the Central Government.

(3) A licence granted under this section shall—

(a) be valid for such period as may be prescribed by the Central Government;

(b) not be transferable or heritable;

(c) be subject to such terms and conditions as may be specified by the regulations.

22. Application for licence

(1) Every application for issue of a licence shall be in such form as may be prescribed by the Central Government.

(2) Every application for issue of a licence, shall be accompanied by—

(a) a certification practice statement;

(b) a statement including the procedures with respect to identification of the applicant;

(c) payment of such fees, not exceeding twenty-five thousand rupees as may be prescribed by the Central Government;

(d) such other documents, as may be prescribed by the Central Government.

23. Renewal of licence

An application for renewal of a licence shall be—

(a) in such form;

(b) accompanied by such fees, not exceeding five thousand rupees,

as may be prescribed by the Central Government and shall be made not less than forty-five days before the date of expiry of the period of validity of the licence.

24. Procedure for grant or rejection of licence

The Controller may, on receipt of an application under sub-section (1) of Section 21, after considering the documents accompanying the application and such other factors, as he deems fit grant the licence or reject the application:

Provided that no application shall be rejected under this section unless the applicant has been given a reasonable opportunity of presenting his case.

25. Suspension of licence

(1) The Controller may, if he is satisfied after making such inquiry, as he may think fit, that a Certifying Authority has—

(a) made a statement in, or in relation to, the application for the issue or renewal of the licence, which is incorrect or false in material particulars;

(b) failed to comply with the terms and conditions subject to which the licence was granted;

(c) failed to maintain the standards specified under clause (b) of sub-section (2) of Section 20;

(d) contravened any provisions of this Act, rule, regulation or order made thereunder,

revoke the licence:

Provided that no licence shall be revoked unless the Certifying Authority has been given a reasonable opportunity of showing cause against the proposed revocation.

(2) The Controller may, if he has reasonable cause to believe that there is any ground for invoking a licence under sub-section (1), by order suspend such licence pending the completion of any inquiry ordered by him:

Provided that no licence shall be suspended for a period exceeding ten days unless the Certifying Authority has been given a reasonable opportunity of showing cause against the proposed suspension.

(3) No Certifying Authority whose licence has been suspended shall issue any Digital Signature Certificate during such suspension.

26. Notice of suspension or revocation of licence

(1) Where the licence of the Certifying Authority is suspended or revoked, the Controller shall publish notice of such suspension or revocation, as the case may be, in the database maintained by him.

(2) Where one or more repositories are specified, the Controller shall publish notices of such suspension or revocation, as the case may be, in all such repositories:

Provided that the database containing the notice of such suspension or revocation, as the case may be, shall be made available through a web site which shall be accessible round the clock:

Provided further that the Controller may, if he considers necessary, publicise the contents of database in such electronic or other media, as he may consider appropriate.

27. Power to delegate

The Controller may, in writing, authorise the Deputy Controller, Assistant Controller or any officer to exercise any of the powers of the Controller under this Chapter.

28. Power to investigate contraventions

(1) The Controller or any officer authorised by him in this behalf shall take up for investigation any contravention of the provisions of this Act, rules or regulations made thereunder.

(2) The Controller or any officer authorised by him in this behalf shall exercise the like powers which are conferred on Income-tax authorities under Chapter XIII of the Income-tax Act, 1961 (43 of 1961) and shall exercise such powers, subject to such limitations laid down under that Act.

29. Access to computers and data

(1) Without prejudice to the provisions of sub-section (1) of Section 68, the Controller or any person authorised by him shall, if he has reasonable cause to suspect that any contravention of the provisions of this Act, rules or regulations made thereunder has been committed, have access to any computer system, any apparatus, data or any other material connected with such system. for the purpose of searching or causing a search to be made for obtaining any information or data contained in or available to such computer system.

(2) For the purposes of sub-section (1), the Controller or any person authorised by him may by order, direct any person incharge of, or otherwise concerned with the operation of the computer system, data apparatus or material, to provide him with such reasonable technical and other assistance as he may consider necessary.

30. Certifying authority to follow certain procedures

Every Certifying authority shall,—

(a) make use of hardware, software, and procedures that are secure from intrusion and misuse;

(b) provide a reasonable level of reliability in its services which are reasonably suited to the performance of intended functions;

(c) adhere to security procedures to ensure that the secrecy and privacy of the digital signatures are assured; and

(d) observe such other standards as may be specified by regulations.

31. Certifying Authority to ensure compliance of the Act, etc.

Every Certifying Authority shall ensure that every person employed or otherwise engaged by it complies, in the course of his employment or engagement, with the provisions of this Act, rules, regulations and orders made thereunder.

32. Display of licence

Every Certifying Authority shall display its licence at a conspicuous place of the premises in which it carries on its business.

33. Surrender of licence

(1) Every Certifying Authority whose licence is suspended or revoked shall immediately after such suspension or revocation, surrender the licence to the Controller.

(2) Where any certifying authority fails to surrender a licence under sub-section (1), the person. In whose favour a licence is issued, shall be guilty of an offence and shall be punished with imprisonment which may extent upto six months or a fine which may extend upto ten thousand rupees or with both.

34. Disclosure

(1) Every Certifying Authority shall disclose in the manner specified by regulations—

(a) its Digital Signature Certificate which contains the public key corresponding to the private key used by that Certifying Authority to digitally sign another Digital Signature Certificate;

(b) any certification practice statement relevant thereto;

(c) notice of the revocation or suspension of its Certifying Authority certificate, if any; and

(d) any other fact that materially and adversely affects

either the reliability of a Digital Signature Certificate, which that Authority has issued, or the Authority's ability to perform its services.

(2) Where in the opinion of the Certifying Authority any event has occurred or any situation has arisen which may materially and adversely affect the integrity of its computer system or the conditions subject to which a Digital Signature Certificate was granted, then, the Certifying Authority shall—

(a) use reasonable efforts to notify any person who is likely to be affected by that occurrence; or

(b) act in accordance with the procedure specified in its certification practice statement to deal with such event or situation.

VII

DIGITAL SIGNATURE CERTIFICATES

35. Certifying authority to issue Digital Signature Certificate

(1) Any person may make an application to the Certifying Authority for the issue of a Digital Signature Certificate in such form as may be prescribed by the Central Government.

(2) Every such application shall be accompanied by such fee not exceeding twenty-five thousand rupees as may be prescribed by the Central Government, to be paid to the Certifying Authority:

Provided that while prescribing fees under sub-section (2) different fees may be prescribed for different classes of applicants.

(3) Every such application shall be accompanied by a certification practice statement or where there is no such statement, a statement containing such particulars, as may be specified by regulations.

(4) On receipt of an application under sub-section (1), the Certifying Authority may, after consideration of the certification practice statement or the other statement under sub-section (3) and after making such enquiries as it may deem fit, grant the Digital Signature Certificate or for reasons to be recorded in writing, reject the application:

Provided that no Digital Signature Certificate shall be granted unless the Certifying Authority is satisfied that—

(a) the applicant holds the private key corresponding to the public key to be listed in the Digital Signature Certificate;

(b) the applicant holds a private key, which is capable of creating a digital signature;

(c) the public key to be listed in the certificate can be used to verify a digital signature affixed by the private key held by the applicant:

Provided further that no application shall be rejected unless the applicant has been given a reasonable opportunity of showing cause against the proposed rejection.

36. Representations upon issuance of Digital Signature Certificate

A Certifying Authority while issuing a Digital Signature Certificate shall certify that—

(a) it has complied with the provisions of this Act and the rules and regulations made thereunder;

(b) it has published the Digital Signature Certificate

or otherwise made it available to such person relying on it and the subscriber has accepted it;

(c) the subscriber holds the private key corresponding to the public key, listed in the Digital Signature Certificate;

(d) the subscriber's public key and private key constitute a functioning key pair;

(e) the information contained in the Digital Signature Certificate is accurate; and

(f) it has no knowledge of any material fact, which if it had been included in the Digital Signature Certificate would adversely affect the reliability of the representations made in clauses (a) to (d).

37. Suspension of Digital Signature Certificate

(1) Subject to the provisions of sub-section (2), the Certifying Authority which has issued a Digital Signature Certificate may suspend such Digital Signature Certificate,—

(a) on receipt of a request to that effect from—

(i) the subscriber listed in the Digital Signature Certificate; or

(ii) any person duly authorised to act on behalf of that subscriber;

(b) if it is of opinion that the Digital Signature Certificate should be suspended in public interest.

(2) A Digital Signature Certificate shall not be suspended for a period exceeding fifteen days unless the subscriber has been given an opportunity of being heard in the matter.

(3) On suspension of a Digital Signature Certificate under this section, the Certifying Authority shall communicate the same to the subscriber.

38. Revocation of Digital Signature Certificate

(1) A Certifying Authority may revoke a Digital Signature Certificate issued by it—

(a) Where the subscriber or any other person authorised by him makes a request to that effect; or

(b) upon the death of the subscriber; or

(c) upon the dissolution of the firm or winding up of the company where the subscriber is a firm or a company.

(2) Subject to the provisions of sub-section (3) and without prejudice to the provisions of sub-section (1), a Certifying Authority may revoke a Digital Signature Certificate which has been issued by it at any time, if it is of opinion that—

(a) a material fact represented in the Digital Signature Certificate is false or has been concealed;

(b) a requirement for issuance of the Digital Signature Certificate was not satisfied;

(c) the Certifying Authority's private key or security system was compromised in a manner materially affecting the Digital Signature Certificate's reliability;

(d) the subscriber has been declared insolvent or dead or where a subscriber is a firm or a company, which has been dissolved, wound-up or otherwise ceased to exist.

(3) A Digital Signature Certificate shall not be revoked unless the subscriber has been given an opportunity of being heard in the matter.

(4) On revocation of a Digital Signature Certificate under this section, the Certifying Authority shall communicate the same to the subscriber.

39. Notice of suspension or revocation

(1) Where a Digital Signature Certificate is suspended or revoked under Section 37 or Section 38, the Certifying Authority shall publish a notice of such suspension or revocation, as the case may be, in the repository specified in the Digital Signature Certificate for publication of such notice.

(2) Where one or more repositories are specified, the Certifying Authority shall publish notices of such suspension or revocation, as the case may be, in all such repositories.

VIII

DUTIES OF SUBSCRIBERS

40. Generating key pair

Where any Digital Signature Certificate, the public key of which corresponds to the private key of that subscriber which is to be listed in the Digital Signature Certificate has been accepted by a subscriber, then, the subscriber shall generate the key pair by applying the security procedure.

41. Acceptance of Digital Signature Certificate

(1) A subscriber shall be deemed to have accepted a Digital Signature Certificate if he publishes or authorises the publication of a Digital Signature Certificate—

(a) to one or more persons;

(b) in a repository, or

otherwise demonstrates his approval of the Digital Signature Certificate in any manner.

(2) By accepting a Digital Signature Certificate the subscriber certifies to all who reasonably rely on the information contained in the Digital Signature Certificate that—

(a) the subscriber holds the private key corresponding to the public key listed in the Digital Signature Certificate and is entitled to hold the same;

(b) all representations made by the subscriber to the Certifying Authority and all material relevant to the information contained in the Digital Signature Certificate are true;

(c) all information in the Digital Signature Certificate that is within the knowledge of the subscriber is true.

42. Control of private key

(1) Every subscriber shall exercise reasonable care to retain control of the private key corresponding to the public key listed in his Digital Signature Certificate and take all steps to prevent its disclosure to a person not authorised to affix the digital signature of the subscriber.

(2) If the private key corresponding to the public key listed in the Digital Signature Certificate has been compromised, then, the subscriber shall communicate the same without any delay to the Certifying Authority in such manner as may be specified by the regulations.

Explanation.—For the removal of doubts, it is hereby declared that the subscriber shall be liable till he has informed the Certifying authority that the private key has been compromised.

IX

PENALTIES AND ADJUDICATION

43. Penalty for damage to computer, computer system, etc.

If any person without permission of the owner or any other person who is incharge of a computer, computer system or computer network,—

(a) accesses or secures access to such computer, computer system or computer network;

(b) downloads, copies or extracts any data, computer database or information from such computer, computer system or computer network including information or data held or stored in any removable storage medium;

(c) introduces or causes to be introduced any computer contaminant or computer virus into any computer, computer system or computer network;

(d) damages or causes to be damaged any computer, computer system or computer network, data, computer data base or any other programmes residing in such computer, computer system or computer network;

(e) disrupts or causes disruption of any computer, computer system or computer network;

(f) denies or causes the denial of access to any person authorised to access any computer, computer system or computer network by any means;

(g) provides any assistance to any person to facilitate access to a computer, computer system or computer network in contravention of the provisions of this Act, rules or regulations made thereunder;

(h) charges the services availed of by a person to the account of another person by tampering with or manipulating any computer, computer system, or computer network,

he shall be liable to pay damages by way of compensation not exceeding one crore rupees to the person so affected.

Explanation.—For the purposes of this section,—

(i) "computer contaminant" means any set of computer instructions that are designed—

(a) to modify, destroy, record, transmit data or programme residing within a computer, computer system or computer network; or

(b) by any means to usurp the normal operation of the computer, computer system, or computer network;

(ii) "computer database" means a representation of information, knowledge, facts, concepts or instructions in text, image, audio, video that are being prepared or have been prepared in a formalised manner or have been produced by a computer, computer system or computer network and are intended for use in a computer, computer system or computer network;

(iii) "computer virus" means any computer instruction, information, data or programme that destroys, damages, degrades or adversely affects the performance of a computer resource or attaches itself to another computer resource and operates when a programme, data or instruction is executed or some other event takes place in that computer resource;

(*iv*) "damage" means to destroy, alter, delete, add, modify or rearrange any computer resource by any means.

44. Penalty for failure to furnish information, return, etc

If any person who is required under this Act or any rules or regulations made thereunder to—

(a) furnish any document, return or report to the Controller or the Certifying Authority fails to furnish the same, he shall be liable to a penalty not exceeding one lakh and fifty thousand rupees for each such failure;

(b) file any return or furnish any information, books or other documents within the time specified therefore in the regulations fails to file return or furnish the same within the time specified therefore in the regulations, he shall be liable to a penalty not exceeding five thousand rupees for every day during which such failure continues;

(c) maintain books of account or records fails to maintain the same, he shall be liable to a penalty not exceeding ten thousand rupees for every day during which the failure continues.

45. Residuary penalty

Whoever contravenes any rules or regulations made under this Act, for the contravention of which no penalty has been separately provided, shall be liable to pay a compensation not exceeding twenty-five thousand rupees to the person affected by such contravention or a penalty not exceeding twenty-five thousand rupees.

46. Power to adjudicate

(1) For the purpose of adjudging under this Chapter whether any person has committed a contravention of any of the provisions of this Act or of any rule, regulation, direction or order made thereunder the Central Government shall, subject to the provisions of sub-section (3), appoint any officer not below the rank of a Director to the Government of India or an equivalent officer of a State Government to be an adjudicating officer for holding an inquiry in the manner prescribed by the Central Government.

(2) The adjudicating officer shall after giving the person referred to in sub-section (1) a reasonable opportunity for making representation in the matter and if, on such inquiry, he is satisfied that the person has committed the contravention, he may impose such penalty or award such compensation as he thinks fit in accordance with the provisions of that section.

(3) No person shall be appointed as an adjudicating officer unless he possesses such experience in the field of Information Technology and legal or judicial experience as may be prescribed by the Central Government.

(4) Where more than one adjudicating officers are appointed, the Central Government shall specify by order the matters and places with respect to which such officers shall exercise their jurisdiction.

(5) Every adjudicating officer shall have the powers of a civil court which are conferred on the Cyber Appellate Tribunal under sub-section (2) of Section 58, and —

(a) all proceedings before it shall be deemed to be judicial proceedings within the meaning of Sections 193 and 228 of the Indian Penal Code (45 of 1860);

(b) shall be deemed to be a civil court for the purposes of Sections 345 and 346 of the Code of Criminal Procedure, 1973 (2 of 1974).

47. Factors to be taken account by the, adjudicating officer

While adjudging the quantum of compensation under this Chapter, the adjudicating officer shall have due regard to the following factors, namely: —

(a) the amount of gain of unfair advantage; wherever quantifiable, made as a result of the default;

(b) the amount of loss caused to any person as a result of the default;

(c) the repetitive nature of the default.

X

THE CYBER REGULATIONS APPELLATE TRIBUNAL

48. Establishment of Cyber Appellate Tribunal

(1) The Central Government shall, by notification, establish one or more appellate tribunals to be known as the Cyber Regulations Appellate Tribunal.

(2) The Central Government shall also specify, in the notification referred to in sub-section (1), the matters and places in relation to which the Cyber Appellate Tribunal may exercise jurisdiction.

49. Composition of Cyber Appellate Tribunal

A Cyber Appellate Tribunal shall consist of one person only (hereinafter referred to as the Presiding Officer of the Cyber Appellate Tribunal) to be appointed, by notification, by the Central Government.

50. Qualifications for appointment as Presiding Officer of the Cyber Appellate Tribunal

A person shall not be qualified for appointment as the Presiding Officer of a Cyber Appellate Tribunal unless he—

(a) is, or has been, or is qualified to be, a Judge of a High Court; or

(b) is or has been a member of the Indian Legal Service and is holding or has held a post in Grade I of that Service for at least three years.

51. Term of office

The Presiding Officer of a Cyber Appellate Tribunal shall hold office for a term of five years from the date on which he enters upon his office or until he attains the age of sixty five years, whichever is earlier.

52. Salary, allowances and other terms and conditions of service of Presiding Officer

The salary and allowances payable to, and the other terms and conditions of service including pension, gratuity and other retirement benefits of, the Presiding Officer of a Cyber Appellate Tribunal shall be such as may be prescribed:

Provided that neither the salary and allowances nor the other terms and conditions of service of the Presiding Officer shall be varied to his disadvantage after appointment.

53. Filling up of vacancies

If, for reason other than temporary absence, any vacancy occurs in the office of the Presiding Officer of a Cyber Appellate Tribunal, then the Central Government shall appoint another person in accordance with the provisions of this Act to fill the vacancy and the proceedings may be continued before the Cyber Appellate Tribunal from the stage at which the vacancy is filled.

54. Resignation and removal

(1) The Presiding Officer of a Cyber Appellate Tribunal may, by notice in writing under his hand addressed to the Central Government, resign his office:

Provided that the said Presiding Officer shall, unless he is permitted by the Central Government to relinquish his office sooner, continue to hold office until the expiry of three months from the date of receipt of such notice or until a person duly appointed as his successor enters upon his office or until the expiry of his term of office, whichever is the earliest.

(2) The Presiding Officer of a Cyber Appellate Tribunal shall not be removed from his office except by an order by the Central Government on the ground of proved misbehaviour or incapacity after an inquiry made by a Judge of the Supreme Court in which the Presiding Officer concerned has been informed of the charges against him and given a reasonable opportunity of being heard in respect of these charges.

(3) The Central Government may, by rules, regulate the procedure for the investigation of misbehaviour or incapacity of the aforesaid Presiding Officer.

55. Orders constituting Appellate Tribunal to be final and not to invalidate its proceedings

No order of the Central Government appointing any person as the Presiding Officer of a Cyber Appellate Tribunal shall be called in question in any manner and no act or proceeding before a Cyber Appellate Tribunal shall be called in question in any manner on the ground merely of any defect in the constitution of a Cyber Appellate Tribunal.

56. Staff of the Cyber Appellate Tribunal

(1) The Central Government shall provide the Cyber

Appellate Tribunal with such officers and employees as that Government may think fit.

(2) The officers and employees of the Cyber Appellate Tribunal shall discharge their functions under general superintendence of the Presiding Officer.

(3) The salaries and allowances and other conditions of service of the officers and employees of the Cyber Appellate Tribunal shall be such as may be prescribed by the Central Government.

57. Appeal to Cyber Regulations Appellate Tribunal

(1) Save as provided in sub-section (2), any person aggrieved by an order made by Controller or an adjudicating officer under this Act may prefer an appeal to a Cyber Appellate Tribunal having jurisdiction in the matter.

(2) No appeal shall lie to the Cyber Appellate Tribunal from an order made by an adjudicating officer with the consent of the parties.

(3) Every appeal under sub-section (1) shall be filed within a period of forty-five days from the date on which a copy of the order made by the Controller or the adjudicating officer is received by the person aggrieved and it shall be in such form and be accompanied by such fee as may be prescribed:

Provided that the Cyber Appellate Tribunal may entertain an appeal after the expiry of the said period of forty-five days if it is satisfied that there was sufficient cause for not filing it within that period.

(4) On receipt of an appeal under sub-section (1), the Cyber Appellate Tribunal may, after giving the parties to the appeal, an opportunity of being heard, pass such orders thereon as it thinks fit, confirming, modifying or setting aside the order appealed against.

(5) The Cyber Appellate Tribunal shall send a copy of every order made by it to the parties to the appeal and to the concerned Controller or adjudicating officer.

(6) The appeal filed before the Cyber Appellate Tribunal under sub-section (1) shall be dealt with by it as expeditiously as possible and endeavour shall be made by it to dispose of the appeal finally within six months from the date of receipt of the appeal.

58. Procedure and powers of the Cyber Appellate Tribunal

(1) The Cyber Appellate Tribunal shall not be bound by the procedure laid down by the Code of Civil Procedure, 1908 (5 of 1908) but shall be guided by the principles of natural justice and, subject to the other provisions of this Act and of any rules, the Cyber Appellate Tribunal shall have powers to regulate its own procedure including the place at which it shall have its sittings.

(2) The Cyber Appellate Tribunal shall have, for the purposes of discharging its functions under this Act, the same powers as are vested in a civil court under the Code of Civil Procedure, 1908 (5 of 1908), while trying a suit, in respect of the following matters, namely:—

(a) summoning and enforcing the attendance of any person and examining him on oath:

(b) requiring the discovery and production of documents or other electronic records;

(c) receiving evidence on affidavits;

(d) issuing commissions for the examination of witnesses or documents;

(e) reviewing its decisions;

(f) dismissing an application for default or deciding it *ex parte;*

(g) any other matter which may be prescribed.

(3) Every proceeding before the Cyber Appellate Tribunal shall be deemed to be a judicial proceeding within the meaning of Sections 193 and 228, and for the purposes of Section 196 of the Indian Penal Code (45 of 1860) and the Cyber Appellate Tribunal shall be deemed to be a civil court for the purposes of Section 195 and Chapter XXVI of the Code of Criminal Procedure, 1973 (2 of 1974).

59. Right to legal representation

The appellant may either appear in person or authorise one or more legal practitioners or any of its officers to present his or its case before the Cyber Appellate Tribunal.

60. Limitation

The provisions of the Limitation Act, 1963 (36 of 1963), shall, as far as may be, apply to an appeal made to the Cyber Appellate Tribunal.

61. Civil Court not to have Jurisdiction

No court shall have jurisdiction to entertain any suit or proceeding in respect of any matter which an adjudicating officer appointed under this Act or the Cyber Appellate Tribunal constituted under this Act is empowered by or under this Act to determine and no injunction shall be granted by any court or other authority in respect of any action taken or to be taken in pursuance of any power conferred by or under this Act.

62. Appeal to High Court

Any person aggrieved by any decision or order of the Cyber Appellate Tribunal may file an appeal to the High Court within sixty days from the date of communication of the decision or order of the Cyber Appellate Tribunal to him on any question of fact or law arising out of such order:

Provided that the High Court may, if it is satisfied that the appellant was prevented by sufficient cause from filing the appeal within the said period, allow it to be filed within a further period not exceeding sixty days.

63. Compounding of contraventions

(1) Any contravention under this Chapter may, either before or after the institution of adjudication proceedings, be compounded by the Controller or such other officer as may be specially authorised by him in this behalf or by the adjudicating officer, as the case may be, subject to such conditions as the Controller or such other officer or the adjudicating officer may specify:

Provided that such sum shall not, in any case, exceed the maximum amount of the penalty which may be imposed under this Act for the contravention so compounded.

(2) Nothing in sub-section (1) shall apply to a person who commits the same or similar contravention within a period of three years from the date on which the first contravention, committed by him, was compounded.

Explanation.—For the purposes of this sub-section, any second or subsequent contravention committed after the expiry of a period of three years from the date on which the contravention was previously compounded shall be deemed to be a first contravention.

(3) Where any contravention has been compounded under sub-section (1), no proceeding or further proceeding, as the case may be, shall be taken against the person guilty of such contravention in respect of the contravention so compounded.

64. Recovery of penalty

A penalty imposed under this Act, if it is not paid,

shall be recovered as an arrear of land revenue and the licence or the Digital Signature Certificate, as the case may be, shall be suspended till the penalty is paid.

XI

OFFENCES

65. Tampering with computer source documents

Whoever knowingly or intentionally conceals, destroys or alters or intentionally or knowingly causes another to conceal, destroy or alter any computer source code used for a computer, computer programme, computer system or computer network, when the computer source code is required to be kept or maintained by law for the time being in force, shall be punishable with imprisonment up to three years, or with fine which may extend up to two lakh rupees, or with both.

Explanation.—For the purposes of this section, "computer source code" means the listing of programmes, computer commands, design and layout and programme analysis of computer resource in any form.

66. Hacking with Computer System

(1) Whoever with the intent to cause or knowing that he is likely to cause wrongful loss or damage to the public or any person destroys or deletes or alters any information residing in a computer resource or diminishes its value or utility or affects it injuriously by any means, commits hacking.

(2) Whoever commits hacking shall be punished with imprisonment up to three years, or with fine which may extend upto two lakh rupees, or with both.

67. Publishing of information which is obscene in electronic form

Whoever publishes or transmits or causes to be published in the electronic form, any material which is lascivious or appeals to the prurient interest or if its effect is such as to tend to deprave and corrupt persons who are likely, having regard to all relevant circumstances, to read, see or hear the matter contained or embodied in it, shall be punished on first conviction with imprisonment of either description for a term which may extend to five years and with fine which may extend to one lakh rupees and in the event of a second or subsequent conviction with imprisonment of either description for a term which may extend to ten years and also with fine which may extend to two lakh rupees.

68. Power of the Controller to give directions

(1) The Controller may, by order, direct a Certifying Authority or any employee of such Authority to take such measures or cease carrying on such activities as specified in the order if those are necessary to ensure compliance with the provisions of this Act, rules or any regulations made thereunder.

(2) Any person who fails to comply with any order under sub-section (1) shall be guilty of an offence and shall be liable on conviction to imprisonment for a term not exceeding three years or to a fine not exceeding two lakh rupees or to both.

69. Directions of Controller to a subscriber to extend facilities to decrypt information

(1) If the Controller is satisfied that it is necessary or expedient so to do in the interest of the sovereignty or integrity of India, the security of the State, friendly relations with foreign States or public order or for preventing

incitement to the commission of any cognizable offence, for reasons to be recorded in writing, by order, direct any agency of the Government to intercept any information transmitted through any computer resource.

(2) The subscriber or any person in charge of the computer resource shall, when called upon by any agency which has been directed under sub-section (I), extend all facilities and technical assistance to decrypt the information.

(3) The subscriber or any person who fails to assist the agency referred to in sub-section *(2)* shall be punished with an imprisonment for a term which may extend to seven years.

70. Protected system

(1) The appropriate Government may, by notification in the Official Gazette, declare that any computer, computer system or computer network to be a protected system.

(2) The appropriate Government may, by order in writing, authorise the persons who are authorised to access protected systems notified under sub-section (1).

(3) Any person who secures access or attempts to secure access to a protected system in contravention of the provisions of this section shall be punished with imprisonment of either description for a term which may extend to ten years and shall also be liable to fine.

71. Penalty for misrepresentation

Whoever makes any misrepresentation to, or suppresses any material fact from, the Controller or the Certifying Authority for obtaining any licence or Digital Signature Certificate, as the case may be, shall be punished with imprisonment for a term which may extend to two years, or with fine which may extend to one lakh rupees, or with both.

72. Breach of confidentiality and privacy

Save as otherwise provided in this Act or any other law for the time being in force, any person who, in pursuance of any of the powers conferred under this Act, rules or regulations made thereunder, has secured access to any electronic record, book, register, correspondence, information, document or other material without the consent of the person concerned discloses such electronic record, book, register, correspondence, information, document or other material to any other person shall be punished with imprisonment for a term which may extend to two years, or with fine which may extend to one lakh rupees, or with both.

73. Penalty for publishing Digital Signature Certificate false in certain particulars

(1) No person shall publish a Digital Signature Certificate or otherwise make it available to any other person with the knowledge that — (a) the Certifying Authority listed in the certificate has not issued it; or (b) the subscriber listed in the certificate has not accepted it; or (c) the certificate has been revoked or suspended, unless such publication is for the purpose of verifying in digital signature created prior to such suspension or revocation.

(2) Any person who contravenes the provisions of sub-section (1) shall be punished with imprisonment for a term which may extend to two years, or with fine which may extend to one lakh rupees, or with both.

74. Publication for fraudulent purpose

Whoever knowingly creates, publishes or otherwise makes available a Digital Signature Certificate for any fraudulent or unlawful purpose shall be punished with imprisonment for a term which may extend to two years, or with fine which may extend to one lakh rupees, or with both.

75. Act to apply for offence or contravention committed outside India

(1) Subject to the provisions of sub-section (2), the provisions of this Act shall apply also to any offence or contravention committed outside India by any person irrespective of his nationality.

(2) For the purposes of sub-section (1), this Act shall apply to an offence or contravention committed outside India by any person if the act or conduct constituting the offence or contravention involves a computer, computer system or computer network located in India.

76. Confiscation

Any computer, computer system, floppies, compact disks, tape drives or any other accessories related thereto, in respect of which any provision of this Act, rules, orders or regulations made thereunder has been or is being contravened, shall be liable to confiscation:

Provided that where it is established to the satisfaction of the court adjudicating the confiscation that the person in whose possession, power or control of any such computer, computer system, floppies, compact disks, tape drives or any other accessories relating thereto is found is not responsible for the contravention of the provisions of this Act, rules, orders or regulations made thereunder, the court may, instead of making an order for confiscation of such computer, computer system, floppies, compact disks, tape drives or any other accessories related thereto, make such other order authorised by this Act against the person contravening of the provisions of this Act, rules, orders or regulations made thereunder as it may think fit.

77. Penalties and confiscation not to interfere with other punishments

No penalty imposed or confiscation made under this Act shall prevent the imposition of any other punishment to which the person affected thereby is liable under any other law for the time being in force.

78. Power to investigate offences

Notwithstanding anything contained in the Code of Criminal Procedure, 1973 (2 of 1974), a police officer not below the rank of Deputy Superintendent of Police shall investigate any offence under this Act.

XII

NETWORK SERVICE PROVIDERS NOT TO BE LIABLE IN CERTAIN CASES

79. Network service providers not to be liable in certain cases

For the removal of doubts, it is hereby declared that no person providing any service as a network service provider shall be liable under this Act, rules or regulations made thereunder for any third party information or data made available by him if he proves that the offence or contravention was committed without his knowledge or that he had exercised all due diligence to prevent the commission of such offence or contravention.

Explanation.—For the purposes of this section,—

(a) "network service provider" means an intermediary;

(b) "third party information" means any information dealt with by a network service provider in his capacity as an intermediary.

XIII

MISCELLANEOUS

80. Power of police officer and other officers to enter, search, etc

(1) Notwithstanding anything contained in the Code of Criminal Procedure, 1973 (2 of 1974) any police officer; not below the rank of a Deputy Superintendent of Police, or any other officer of the Central Government or a State Government authorised by the Central Government in this behalf may enter any public place and search and arrest without warrant any person found therein who is reasonably suspected or having committed or of committing or of being about to commit any offence under this Act.

Explanation.—For the purposes of this sub-section, the expression "public place" includes any public conveyance, any hotel, any shop or any other place intended for use by, or accessible to the public.

(2) Where any person is arrested under sub-section (1) by an officer other than a police officer, such officer shall, without unnecessary delay, take or send the person arrested before a magistrate having jurisdiction in the case or before the officer-in-charge of a police station.

(3) The provisions of the Code of Criminal Procedure, 1973 (2 of 1974) shall, subject to the provisions of this section, apply, so far as may be, in relation to any entry, search or arrest, made under this section.

81. Act to have overriding effect

The provisions of this Act shall have effect notwithstanding anything inconsistent therewith contained in any other law for the time being in force.

82. Controller, Deputy Controller and Assistant Controllers to be public servants

The Presiding Officer and other officers and employees of a Cyber Appellate Tribunal, the Controller, the Deputy Controller and the Assistant Controllers shall be deemed to be public servants within the meaning of Section 21 of the Indian Penal Code (45 of 1860).

83. Power to give directions

The Central Government may give directions to any State Government as to the carrying into execution in the State of any of the provisions of this Act or of any rule, regulation or order made thereunder.

84. Protection of action taken in good faith

No suit, prosecution or other legal proceeding shall lie against the Central Government, the State Government, the Controller or any person acting on behalf of him, the Presiding Officer, adjudicating officers and the staff of the Cyber Appellate Tribunal for anything which is in good faith done or intended to be done in pursuance of this Act or any rule, regulation or order made thereunder.

85. Offences by companies

(1) Where a person committing a contravention of any of the provisions of this Act or of any rule, direction or order made thereunder is a company, every person who, at the time the contravention was committed, was in charge of, and was responsible to, the company for the conduct of business of the company as well as the company, shall be guilty of the contravention and shall be liable to be proceeded against and punished accordingly:

Provided that nothing contained in this sub-section shall render any such person liable to punishment if he proves that the contravention took place without his knowledge or that he exercised all due diligence to prevent such contravention.

(2) Notwithstanding anything contained in sub-section (1), where a contravention of any of the provisions of this Act or of any rule, direction or order made thereunder has been committed by a company and it is proved that the contravention has taken place with the consent or connivance of, or is attributable to any neglect on the part of, any director, manager, secretary or other officer of the company, such director, manager, secretary or other officer shall also be deemed to be guilty of the contravention and shall be liable to be proceeded against and punished accordingly.

Explanation.—For the purposes of this section,—

(i) "company" means any body corporate and includes a firm or other association of individuals; and

(ii) "director" in relation to a firm, means a partner in the firm.

86. Removal of difficulties

(1) If any difficulty arises in giving effect to the provisions of this Act, the Central Government may, by order published in the Official Gazette, make such provisions not inconsistent with the provisions of this Act as appear to it to be necessary or expedient for removing the difficulty:

Provided that no order shall be made under this section after the expiry of a period of two years from the commencement of this Act.

(2) Every order made under this section shall be laid, as soon as may be after it is made, before each House of Parliament.

87. Power of Central Government to make rules

(1) The Central Government may, by notification in the Official Gazette and in the Electronic Gazette make rules to carry out the provisions of this Act.

(2) In particular, and without prejudice to the generality of the foregoing power, such rules may provide for all or any of the following matters, namely:—

(a) the manner in which any information or matter may be authenticated by means of digital signature under Section 5;

(b) the electronic form in which filing, issue, grant or payment shall be effected under subsection (1) of Section 6;

(c) the manner and format in which electronic records shall be filed, or issued and the method of payment under sub-section (2) of Section 6;

(d) the matters relating to the type of digital signature, manner and format in which it may be affixed under Section 10;

(e) the security procedure for the purpose of creating secure electronic record and secure digital signature under Section 16;

(f) the qualifications, experience and terms and conditions of service of Controller, Deputy Controllers and Assistant Controllers under Section 17;

(g) other standards to be observed by the Controller under clause (b) of sub-section (2) of Section 20;

(h) the requirements which an applicant must fulfil under sub-section (2) of Section 21;

(i) the period of validity of licence granted under clause (a) of sub-section (3) of Section 21;

(j) the form in which an application for licence may be made under sub-section (1) of Section 22;

(k) the amount of fees payable under clause (c) of sub-section (2) of Section 22;

(l) such other documents which shall accompany an application for licence under,clause (d) of sub-section (2) of Section 22;

(m) the form and the fee for renewal of a licence and the fee payable thereof under Section 23;

(n) the amount of late fee payable under the proviso to Section 23;

(o) the form in which application for issue of a Digital Signature Certificate may be made under sub-section (1) of Section 35;

(p) the fee to be paid to the Certifying Authority for issue of a Digital Signature Certificate under sub-section (2) of Section 35;

(q) the manner in which the adjudicating officer shall hold inquiry under sub-section (1) of Section 46;

(r) the qualification and experience which the adjudicating officer shall possess under subsection (2) of Section 46;

(s) the salary, allowances and the other terms and conditions of service of the Presiding Officer under Section 52;

(t) the procedure for investigation of misbehaviour or incapacity of the Presiding Officer under sub-section (3) of Section 54;

(u) the salary and allowances and other conditions of service of other officers and employees under sub-section (3) of Section 56;

(v) the form in which appeal may be filed and the fee thereof under sub-section (3) of Section 57;

(w) any other power of a civil court required to be prescribed under clause (g) of subsection (2) of Section 58; and

(x) any other matter which is required to be, or may be, prescribed.

(3) Every notification made by the Central Government under clause (f) of sub-section (4) of Section 1 and every rule made by it shall be laid, as soon as may be after it is made, before each House of Parliament, while it is in session, for a total period of thirty days which may be comprised in one session or in two or more successive sessions, and if, before the expiry of the session immediately following the session or the successive sessions aforesaid, both Houses agree in making any modification in the notification or the rule or both Houses agree that the notification or the rule should not be made, the notification or the rule shall thereafter have effect only in such modified form or be of no effect, as the case may be; so, however, that any such modification or annulment shall be without prejudice to the validity of anything previously done under that notification or rule.

88. Constitution of Advisory Committee

(1) The Central Government shall, as soon as may be after the commencement of this Act, constitute a Committee called the Cyber Regulations Advisory Committee.

(2) The Cyber Regulations Advisory Committee shall consist of a Chairperson and such number of other official and non-official members representing the interests principally affected or having special knowledge of the subject-matter as the Central Government may deem fit.

(3) The Cyber Regulations Advisory Committee shall advise—

(a) the Central Government either generally as regards any rules or for any other purpose connected with this Act;

(b) the Controller in framing the regulations under this Act.

(4) There shall be paid to the non-official members of such Committee such travelling and other allowances as the Central Government may fix.

89. Power of Controller to make regulations

(1) The Controller may, after consultation with the Cyber Regulations Advisory Committee and with the previous approval of the Central Government, by notification in the Official Gazette, make regulations consistent with this Act and the rules made thereunder to carry out the purposes of this Act.

(2) In particular, and without prejudice to the generality of the foregoing power, such regulations may provide for all or any of the following matters, namely:—

(a) the particulars relating to maintenance of database containing the disclosure record of every Certifying Authority under clause (m) of Section 18;

(b) the conditions and restrictions subject to which the Controller may recognise any foreign Certifying Authority under sub-section (1) of Section 19;

(c) the terms and conditions subject to which a licence may be granted under clause (c) *of* sub-section (3) of Section 21;

(d) other standards to be observed by a Certifying Authority under clause (d) of Section 30;

(e) the manner in which the Certifying Authority shall disclose the matters specified in subsection (1) of Section 34;

(f) the particulars of statement which shall accompany an application under sub-section (3) of Section 35;

(g) the manner by which the subscriber communicate the compromise of private key to the Certifying Authority under sub-section (2) of Section 42.

(3) Every regulation made under this Act shall be laid, as soon as may be after it is made, before each House of Parliament, while it is in session, for a total period of thirty days which may be comprised in one session or in two or more successive sessions, and if, before the expiry of the session immediately following the session or the successive sessions aforesaid, both Houses agree in making any modification in the regulation or both Houses agree that the regulation should not be made, the regulation shall thereafter have effect only in such modified form or be of no effect, as the case may be; so, however, that any such modification or annulment shall be without prejudice to the validity of anything previously done under that regulation.

90. Power of State Government to make rules

(1) The State Government may, by notification in the Official Gazette, make rules to carry out the provisions of this Act.

(2) In particular, and without prejudice to the generality of the foregoing power, such rules may provide for all or any of the following matters, namely:—

(a) the electronic form in which filing, issue, grant receipt or payment shall be effected under sub-section (1) of Section 6;

(b) for matters specified in sub-section (2) of Section 6;

(c) any other matter which is required to be provided by rules by the State Government.

(3) Every rule made by the State Government under this section shall be laid, as soon as may be after it is made, before each House of the State Legislature where it consists of two Houses, or where such Legislature consists of one House, before that House.

91. Amendment of Act 45 of 1860

The Indian Penal Code shall be amended in the manner specified in the First Schedule to this Act.

92. Amendment of Act 1 of 1872

The Indian Evidence Act, 1872 shall be amended in the manner specified in the Second Schedule to this Act.

93. Amendment of Act 18 of 1891

The Bankers' Books Evidence Act, 1891 shall be amended in the manner specified in the Third Schedule to this Act.

94. Amendment of Act 2 of 1934

The Reserve Bank of India Act, 1934 shall be amended in the manner specified in the Fourth Schedule to this Act.

THE FIRST SCHEDULE

(*See* Section 90)

AMENDMENTS TO THE INDIAN PENAL CODE
[45 OF 1860]

1. After Section 29, the following section shall be inserted, namely:—

"29A. *Electronic record.*—The words "electronic record" shall have the meaning assigned to them in clause (s) of sub-section (1) of Section 2 of the Information Technology Act, 1999."

2. In Section 167, for the words "such public servant, charged with the preparation or translation of any document, frames or translates that document", the words "such public servant, charged with the preparation or translation of any document or electronic record, frames, prepares or translates that document or electronic record" shall be substituted.

3. In Section 172, for the words "produce a document in a Court of Justice", the words "produce a document or an electronic record in a Court of Justice" shall be substituted.

4. In Section 173, for the words "to produce a document in a Court of Justice", the words "to produce a document or electronic record in a Court of Justice" shall be substituted.

5. In Section 175, for the word "document" at both the places where it occurs, the words "document or electronic record" shall be substituted.

6. In Section 192, for the words "makes any false entry in any book or record, or makes any document containing a false statement", the words, "makes any false entry in any book or record, or electronic record or makes any document or electronic record containing a false statement" shall be substituted.

7. In Section 204 for the word "document" at both the places where it occurs, the words "document or electronic record" shall be substituted.

8. In Section 463, for the words "Whoever makes any false documents or part of a document with intent to cause

damage or injury", the words "Whoever makes any false documents or false electronic record or part of a document or electronic record, with intent to cause injury" shall be substituted.

9. In Section 464,—

(a) for the portion beginning with the words "A person is said to make a false document" and ending with the words "by reason of deception practised upon him, he does not know the contents of the document or the nature of the alteration", the following shall be substituted, namely:—

"A person is said to make a false document or false electronic record—

First—Who dishonestly or fraudulently—

(a) makes, signs, seals or executes a document or part of a document;

(b) makes or transmits any electronic record or part of any electronic record;

(c) affixes any digital signature on any electronic record;

(d) makes any mark denoting the execution of a document or the authenticity of the digital signature,

with the intention of causing it to be believed that such document or part of document, electronic record or digital signature was made, signed, sealed executed, transmitted or affixed by or by the authority of a person by whom or by whose authority he knows that it was not made, signed, sealed, executed or affixed; or

Secondly—Who, without lawful authority, dishonestly or fraudulently, by cancellation or otherwise, alters a document or an electronic record in any material part thereof, after it has been made, executed or affixed with digital signature either by himself or by any other person, whether such person be living or dead at the time of such alteration; or

Thirdly—Who dishonestly or fraudulently causes any person to sign, seal, execute or alter a document or an electronic record, or to affix his digital signature on any electronic record knowing that such person by reason of unsoundness of mind or intoxication cannot, or that by reason of deception practised upon him, he does not know the contents of the document or electronic record or the nature of the alteration.";

(b) after *Explanation* 2, the following *Explanation* shall be inserted at the end, namely:—

'*Explanation* 3.—For the purposes of this section, the expression "affixing digital signature" shall have the meaning assigned to it in clause (d) of sub-section (1) of Section 2 of the Information Technology Act, 1999.'

10. In Section 466,-

(a) for the words "Whoever forges a document", the words "Whoever forges a document or an electronic record" shall be substituted;

(b) the following *Explanation* shall be inserted at the end, namely:—

Explanation.—For the purposes of this section, "register" includes any list, data or record of any entries maintained in the electronic form as defined in clause (r) of sub-section (1) of Section 2 of the Information Technology Act, 1999.'

11. In Section 468, for the words "document forged", the words "document or electronic record forged" shall be substituted.

12. In Section 469, for the words "intending that the document forged", the words "intending that the document or electronic record forged" shall be substituted.

13. In Section 470, for the word "document" in both the places where it occurs, the words "document or electronic record" shall be substituted.

14. In Section 471, for the word "document" wherever it occurs, the words "document or electronic record" shall be substituted.

15. In Section 474, for the portion beginning with the words "Whoever has in his possession any document" and ending with the words "if the document is one of the description mentioned in Section 466 of this Code", the following shall be substituted, namely:—

> "Whoever has in his possession any document or electronic record, knowing the same to be forged and intending that the same shall fraudulently or dishonestly be used as a genuine, shall, if the document or electronic record is one of the description mentioned in Section 466 of this Code."

16. In Section 476, for the words "any document", the words "any document or electronic record" shall be substituted.

17. In Section 477A, for the words "book, paper, writing"

at both the places where they occur, the words "book, electronic record, paper, writing" shall be substituted.

THE SECOND SCHEDULE

(*See* Section 91)

AMENDMENTS TO THE INDIAN EVIDENCE ACT, 1872 (1 OF 1872)

1. In Section 3,—

(a) in the definition of "Evidence", for the words "all documents produced for the inspection of the Court", the words "all documents including electronic records produced for the inspection of the Court" shall be substituted;

(b) after the definition of "India", the following shall be inserted, namely:—

'the expressions "Certifying Authority", "digital signature", "Digital Signature Certificate", "electronic form", "electronic records", "information", "secure electronic record", "secure digital signature" and "subscriber" shall have the meanings respectively assigned to them in the Information Technology Act, 1999.'

2. In Section 17, for the words "oral or documentary", the words "oral or documentary or contained in electronic form" shall be substituted.

3. After Section 22, the following section shall be inserted, namely:—

"22A. *When oral admission as to contents of electronic records are relevant,*—Oral admissions as to the contents of electronic records are not relevant, unless the genuineness of the electronic record produced is in question."

4. In Section 34, of the words "Entries in the books of account", the words "Entries in the books of account, including those maintained in an electronic form" shall be substituted.

5. In Section 35, for the word "record", in both the places where it occurs, the words "record or an electronic record" shall be substituted.

6. For Section 39, the following section shall be substituted, namely:—

"39. *What evidence to be given when statement forms part of a conversation, document, electronic record, book or series of letters or papers.*—When any statement of which evidence is given forms part of a longer statement, or of a conversation or part of an isolated document, or is contained in a document which forms part of a book, or is contained in part of electronic record or of a connected series of letters or papers, evidence shall be given of so much and no more of the statement, conversation, document, electronic record, book or series of letters or papers as the Court considers necessary in that particular case to the full understanding of the nature and effect of the statement, and of the circumstances under which it was made."

7. After Section 47, the following section shall be inserted, namely:—

"47A. *Opinion as to digital signature when relevant.*—When the Court has to form an opinion as to the digital signature of any person, the opinion of the Certifying Authority which has issued the Digital Signature Certificate is a relevant fact."

8. In Section 59, for the words "contents of documents", the words "contents of documents or electronic records" shall be substituted.

9. After Section 65, the following sections shall be inserted, namely:—

'65A. *Special provisions as to evidence relating to electronic record.*—The contents of electronic records may be proved in accordance with the provisions of Section 65B.

65B. *Admissibility of electronic records.*—(1) Notwithstanding anything contained in this Act, any information contained in an electronic record which is printed oh a paper, stored, recorded or copied in optical or magnetic media produced by a computer (hereinafter referred to as the computer output) shall be deemed to be also a document, if the conditions mentioned in this section are satisfied in relation to the information and computer in question and shall be admissible in any proceedings, without further proof or production of the original, as evidence of any contents of the original or of any fact stated therein of which direct evidence would be admissible.

(2) The conditions referred to in sub-section (1) in respect of a computer output shall be the following, namely:—

(a) the computer output containing the information was produced by the computer during the period over which the computer was used regularly to store or process information for the purposes of any activities regularly carried on over that period by the person having lawful control over the use of the computer;

(b) during the said period, information of the kind contained in the electronic record or of the kind from which the information so contained is derived was regularly fed into the computer in the ordinary course of the said activities;

(c) throughout the material part of the said period, the computer was operating properly or, if not, then in respect of any period in which it was not operating properly or was out of operation during that part of the period, was not such as to affect the electronic record or the accuracy of its contents; and

(d) the information contained in the electronic record reproduces or is derived from such information fed into the computer in the ordinary course of the said activities.

(3) Where over any period, the function of storing or processing information for the purposes of any activities regularly carried on over that period as mentioned in clause (a) of sub-section (2) was regularly performed by computers, whether—

(a) by a combination of computers operating over that period; or

(b) by different computers operating in succession over that period; or

(c) by different combinations of computers operating in succession over that period; or

(d) in any other manner involving the successive operation over that period, in whatever order, of one or more computers and one or more combinations of computers,

all the computers used for that purpose during that period shall be treated for the purposes of this section as constituting a single computer; and references in this section to a computer shall be construed accordingly.

(4) In any proceedings where it is desired to give a statement in evidence by virtue of this section, a certificate doing any of the following things, that is to say,—

(a) identifying the electronic record containing the statement and describing the manner in which it was produced;

(b) giving such particulars of any device involved in the production of that electronic record as may be appropriate for the purpose of showing that the electronic record was produced by a computer,

(c) dealing, with any of the matters to which the conditions mentioned in subsection (2) relate,

and purporting to be signed by a person occupying a responsible official position in relation to, the operation of the relevant device or the management of the relevant activities (whichever is appropriate) shall be evidence of any matter stated in the certificate: and for the purposes of this sub-section it shall be sufficient for a matter to be stated to the best of the knowledge and belief of the person stating it.

(5) For the purposes of this section,—

(a) information shall be taken to be supplied to a

computer if it is supplied thereto in any appropriate form and whether it is so supplied directly or (with or without human intervention) by means of any appropriate equipment;

(b) whether in the course of activities carried on by any official, information is supplied with a view to its being stored or processed for the purposes of those activities by a computer operated otherwise than in the course of those activities, that information, if duly supplied to that computer, shall be taken to be supplied to it in the course of those activities;

(c) a computer output shall be taken to have been produced by a computer whether it was produced by it directly or (with or without human intervention) by means of any appropriate equipment.

Explanation.—For the purposes of this section any reference to information being derived from other information shall be a reference to its being derived therefrom by calculation, comparison or any other process.'

10. After Section 67, the following section shall be inserted, namely:—

"67A. *Proof as to, digital, signature.* — Except in the case of a secure digital signature, if the digital signature of any subscriber is alleged to have been affixed to an electronic record the fact that such digital signature is the digital signature of the subscriber must be proved."

11. After Section 73, the following section shall be inserted, namely:—

"73A. *Proof as to verification of digital signature.* — In order to ascertain whether a digital signature is that of the person by whom it purports to have been affixed, the Court may direct —

(a) that person or the Controller or the Certifying Authority to produce the Digital . Signature Certificate;

(b) any other person to apply the public key listed in the Digital Signature Certificate and verify the digital signature purported to have been affixed by that person."

Explanation— for the purposes of this section, "Controller" means the Controller appointed under sub-section (1) of Section 17 of the Information Technology Act, 1999.

12. After Section 81, the following, section shall be inserted, namely: —

"81A. *Presumption as to Gazettes in electronic forms.* — The Court shall presume the genuineness of every electronic record purporting to be the Official Gazette, or purporting to be electronic record directed by any law to be kept by any person, if such electronic record is kept substantially in the form required by law and is produced from proper custody."

13. After Section 85, the following sections shall be inserted, namely: —

"85A. *Presumption as to electronic agreements.* — The Court shall presume that every electronic record purporting to be an agreement containing the digital signatures of the parties was so concluded by affixing the digital signature of the parties.

85B. *Presumption as to electronic records and digital signatures.* — (1) In any proceedings involving a secure electronic record, the Court shall presume unless contrary is proved, that the secure electronic record has not been altered since the specific point of time to which the secure status relates.

(2) In any proceedings, involving secure digital signature, the Court shall presume unless the contrary is proved that—

(a) the secure digital signature is affixed by subscriber with the intention of signing or approving the electronic record;

(b) except in the case of a secure electronic record or a secure digital signature, nothing in this section shall create any presumption relating to authenticity and integrity of the electronic record or any digital signature.

85C. *Presumption as to Digital Signature Certificates.*— The Court shall presume, unless contrary is proved, that the information listed in a Digital Signature Certificate is correct, except for information specified as sub-scriber information which has not been verified, if the certificate was accepted by the subscriber."

14. After Section 88, the following section shall be inserted, namely:—

'88A. *Presumption as to electronic messages.*—The Court may presume that an electronic message forwarded by the originator through an electronic mail server to the addressee to whom the message purports to be addressed corresponds with the message as fed into his computer for transmission; but the Court shall not make any presumption as to the person by whom such message was sent.

Explanation.—For the purposes of this section, the expressions "addressee" and "originator" shall have the same meanings respectively assigned to them in clauses (b) and (z) of sub-section (1) of Section 2 of the Information Technology Act, 1999'.

15. After Section 90, the following section shall be inserted, namely:—

"90A. *Presumption as to electronic records five years old.*—Where any electronic record, purporting or proved to be five years old, is produced from any custody which the Court in the particular case considers proper, the Court may presume that the digital signature which purports to be the digital signature of any particular person was so affixed by him or any person authorised by him in this behalf.

Explanation.—Electronic records are said to be in proper custody if they are in the place in which, and under the care of the person with whom, they naturally be; but no custody is improper if it is proved to have had a legitimate origin, or the circumstances of the particular case are such as to render such an origin probable.

This *Explanation* applies also to Section 81 A."

16. For Section 131, the following section shall be substituted, namely:—

"131. *Production of documents or electronic records which another person, having possession, could refuse to produce.*—No one shall be compelled to produce documents in his possession or electronic records under his control, which any other person would be entitled to refuse to produce if they were in his possession or control, unless such last-mentioned person consents to their production."

THE THIRD SCHEDULE

(*See* Section 92)

AMENDMENTS TO THE BANKERS' BOOKS EVIDENCE ACT, 1891

(18 of 1891)

1. In Section 2—

(a) for clause (3), the following clause shall be substituted, namely:—

'(3) "bankers' books" include ledgers, day-books, cash-books, account-books and all other books used in the ordinary business of a bank whether kept in the written form or as printouts of data stored in a floppy, disc, tape or any other form of electro-magnetic dala storage device;

(b) for clause (8), the following clause shall be substituted, namely:—

'(8) "certified copy" means when the books of a bank,—

(a) are maintained in written form, a copy of any entry in such books together with a certificate written at the foot of such copy that it is a true copy of such entry, that such entry is contained in one of the ordinary books of the bank and was made in the usual and ordinary course of business and that such book is still in the custody of the bank, and where the copy was obtained by a mechanical or other process which in itself ensured the accuracy of the copy, a further certificate to that effect, but where the book from which such copy was prepared has been destroyed in the usual course of the bank's business after the date on which the copy had been so prepared, a further certificate to that effect, each such certificate being dated and subscribed by the principal accountant or manager of the bank with his name and official title; and

(b) consist of printouts of data stored in a floppy, disc, tape or any other electromagnetic data storage device, a printout of such entry or a copy of such printout together with such statements certified in accordance with the provisions of Section 2A.'

2. After Section 2 the following section shall be inserted namely:—

"2A. *Conditions in the printout.*—A printout of entry or a copy of printout referred to in sub-section (8) of Section 2 shall be accompanied by the following, namely:—

(a) a certificate to the effect that it is a printout of such entry or a copy of such printout by the principal accountant or branch manager; and

(b) a certificate by a person in-charge of computer system containing a brief description of the computer system and the particulars of —

(A) the safeguards adopted by the system to ensure that data is entered or any other operation performed only by authorised persons;

(B) the safeguards adopted to prevent and detect unauthorised change of data;

(C) the safeguards available to retrieve data that is lost due to systemic failure or any other reasons;

(D) the manner is which data is transferred from the system to removable media like floppies, discs, tapes or other electro-magnetic data storage devices;

(E) the mode of verification in order to ensure that data has been accurately transferred to such removable media;

(F) the mode of identification of such data storage devices;

(G) the arrangements for the storage and custody of such storage devices;

(H) the safeguards to prevent and detect any tampering with the system; and

(I) any other factor which will vouch for the integrity and accuracy of the system.

(c) a further certificate from the person in-charge of the computer system to the effect that to the best of his knowledge and belief, such computer system operated properly at the material time, he was provided with all the relevant data and the printout in question represents correctly, or is appropriately derived from, the relevant data."

THE FOURTH SCHEDULE

(*See* Section 93)

AMENDMENT TO THE RESERVE BANK OF INDIA ACT, 1934 (2 OF 1934)

In the Reserve Bank of India Act, 1934, in Section 58, in sub-section (2), after clause (p), the following clause shall be inserted, namely: —

"*(pp)* the regulation of fund transfer through electronic means between the banks or between the banks and other financial institutions referred to in clause (c) of Section 45-1, including the laying down of the conditions subject to which banks and other financial institutions shall participate in such fund transfers, the manner of such fund transfers and the rights and obligations of the participants in such fund transfers;"

THE CYBER REGULATIONS APPELLATE TRIBUNAL (PROCEDURE) RULES, 2000

G.S.R. 791 (E). In exercise of the powers conferred by Section 87 of the Information Technology Act, 2000 (21 of 2000), the Central Government hereby makes the following rules, namely:—

1. *Short title and commencement.*—(1) These rules may be called the Cyber Regulations Appellate Tribunal (Procedure) Rules, 2000.

(2) They shall come into force on the date of publication in the Official Gazette.

2. *Definitions.*—In these rules, unless the context otherwise requires.—

(a) "Act" means the Information Technology Act, 2000; (21 of 2000);

(b) "agent" means a person duly authorised by a party to present an application or reply on its behalf before the Tribunal; '

(c) "application" means an application made to the Tribunal under Section 57;

(d) "legal practitioner" shall have the same meaning

as is assigned to it in the Advocates Act, 1961 (25 of 1971);

(e) "Presiding Officer" means the Presiding Officer of the Tribunal;

(f) "Registrar" means the Registrar of the Tribunal and includes any officer to whom the powers and functions of the Registrar may be delegated;

(g) "registry" means the Registry of the Tribunal;

(h) "section" means a section of the Act;

(i) "transferred application" means the suit or other proceeding which has been transferred to the Tribunal under sub-section (1) of Section 29;

(j) "Tribunal" means the Cyber Regulations Appellate Tribunal established under Section 48.

3. *Procedure for filing applications.*—(I) An application to the Tribunal shall be presented in Form-1 annexed to these rules by the applicant in person or by an agent or by a duly authorized legal practitioner, to the Registrar or sent by registered post addressed to the Registrar.

(2) The application under sub-rule (1) shall be presented in six complete sets in a paper-book form along with one empty file size envelope bearing full address of the respondent. Where the number of respondents is more than one, sufficient number of extra paper-books together with required number of empty file size envelopes bearing the full address of each respondent shall be furnished by the applicant.

(3) The applicant may attach to and present with his application a receipt slips as in Form No. 1 which shall be signed by the Registrar or the

officer receiving the applications on behalf of the Registrar in acknowledgement of the receipt of the application.

(4) Notwithstanding anything contained in sub-rules (1), (2) and (3), the Tribunal may permit:—

(a) more than one person to join together and file a single application if it is satisfied, having regard to the cause of action and the nature of relief prayed for, that they have the same interest in the service matter; or

(b) an Association representing the persons desirous of joining in a single application provided, however, that the application shall disclose the names of all the persons on whose behalf it has been filed.

4. *Presentation and scrutiny of applications.*—(1) The Registrar, or the officer authorised by the Registrar shall endorse on every application the date on which it is presented or deemed to have been presented under that rule and shall sign the endorsement.

(2) If, on scrutiny, the application is found to be in order, it shall be duly registered and given a serial number.

(3) If the application, on scrutiny, is found to be defective, and the defect noticed is formal in nature, the Registrar may allow the party to rectify the same in his presence, and if the said defect is not formal in nature, the Registrar may allow the applicant such time to rectify the defect as he may deem fit.

(4) If the applicant fails to rectify the defect within the time allowed under sub-rule (3), the Registrar may, by order and for reasons to be recorded in writing, decline to register the application.

(5) An appeal against the order of the Registrar under sub-rule (4) shall be made within 15 days of the making of such order to the Tribunal whose decision thereon shall be final.

5. *Place of filing application.*—The applicant shall file application with the Registrar.

6. *Application fee.*—Every application filed with the Registrar shall be accompanied by a fee of Rs. 2,000/- (Rupees two thousand only) which shall be either in the form of a crossed demand draft or a pay order drawn on a Scheduled Bank in favour of the Registrar and payable at New Delhi.

7. *Contents of application.*—(1) Every application filed under rule 3 shall set forth concisely under distinct heads, the grounds for such application and such grounds shall be numbered consecutively and typed in double space on one side of the paper.

(2) It shall not be necessary to present a separate application to seek an interim order or direction if the application contains a prayer seeking an interim order or direction pending final disposal of the application.

(3) An application may, subsequent to the filing of application under Section 57 of the Act, apply for an interim order or direction. Such an application shall, as far as possible, be in the same form as is prescribed for on application under Section 57 and shall be accompanied by a fee of Rs. 5/- (Rupees five only) which shall be payable in court fee stamps affixed on such application.

8. *Paper book, etc. to accompany the application.*—(1) Every

application shall be accompanied by a paper book containing:—

(i) a certified copy of the order against which the application has been filed;

(ii) copies of the documents relied upon by the applicant and referred to in the application; and

(iii) an index of documents.

(2) The documents referred to in sub-rule (1) may be attested by an advocate or by a Gazetted Officer.

(3) Where an application is filed by an agent, documents authorising him to act as such agent shall also be appended to the application:

Provided that where an application is filed by an advocate it shall be accompanied by a duly executed 'vakalatnama'.

9. *Plural remedies.* — An application shall be based upon a single cause of action and may seek one or more reliefs provided they are consequential to one another.

10. *Service of notice of application on the respondents.* — (1) A copy of the application in the paper-book shall ordinarily be served on each of the respondents by the Registrar in one of the following modes: —

(i) hand delivery (dasti) through the applicant or through a process server; or

(ii) through registered post with acknowledgement due.

(2) Notwithstanding anything contained in sub-rule (1), the Registrar may, taking into account the number of respondents and their places of residence or work and other circumstances direct

that notice of the application shall be served upon the respondents in any other manner including any manner of substituted service, as it appear to the Registrar just and convenient.

(3) Every applicant shall pay a fee for the service or execution of processes, in respect of an application where the number of respondents exceeds five, as under: —

(i) a sum of Rs. 50 (Rupees fifty) for each respondent in excess of five respondents; or

(ii) where the service is in such manner as the Registrar may direct under sub-rule (2), a sum not exceeding the actual charges incurred in effecting the service as may be determined by the Registrar.

(4) The fee for the service or execution of processes under sub-rule (3) shall be remitted by the applicant either in the form of a crossed Demand Draft drawn on a Scheduled Bank in favour of the Registrar and payable at the station where Registrar's office is situated or remitted through a crossed Indian Postal Order drawn in favour of the Registrar and payable in General Post Office of the station where the Tribunal is located.

(5) Notwithstanding anything contained in sub-rules (1), (2), (3) and (4), if the Tribunal is satisfied that it is not reasonably practicable to serve notice of application upon all the respondents, if may for reasons to be recorded in writing, direct that the application shall be heard notwithstanding that some of the respondents have not been served with notice of the application, provided that no application shall be heard unless: —

(i) notice of the application has been served on the Government, if Government is respondent;

(ii) notice of the application has been served on the authority which passed the order against which the application has been filed; and

(iii) the Tribunal is satisfied that the interests of the respondents on whom notice of the application has not been served are adequately and sufficiently represented by the respondents on whom notice of the application has been served.

11. *Filing of reply and other documents by the respondent.*— (1) The respondent shall file six complete sets containing the reply to the application alongwith the documents in a paper-book form with the Registrar within one month of the date of service of the notice of the application on him.

(2) The respondent shall also serve a copy of the reply along with copies of documents as mentioned in sub-rule (1) to the applicant or his advocate, if any, and file proof of such service with the Registrar. The Tribunal may, on application by the respondent, allow filing of the reply after the expiry of the period of one month.

12. *Date and place of hearing to be notified.* — The Tribunal shall notify to the parties the date and the place of hearing of the application.

13. *Sittings of the Tribunal.* — The Tribunal shall ordinarily hold its sittings at New Delhi:

Provided that, if at any time, the Presiding Officer of the Tribunal is satisfied that circumstances exist which render it necessary to have sittings of the Tribunal at any place other than New Delhi the Presiding Officer may direct to hold the sittings at any such appropriate place.

14. *Decision on applications.* — (1) Tribunal shall draw up a calendar for the hearing of transferred cases and as far as possible hear and decide the cases according to the calendar.

(2) Every application shall be heard and decided, as far as possible, within six months of the date of its presentation.

(3) For purposes of sub-rule (1) and (2), the Tribunal shall have the power to decline an adjournment and to limit the time for oral arguments.

15. *Action on application for applicant's default.* — (1) Where on the date fixed for hearing of the application or on any other date to which such hearing may be adjourned, the applicant does not appear when the application is called on for hearing, the Tribunal may, in its discretion, either dismiss the application for default or hear and decide it on merit.

(2) Where an application has been dismissed for default and the applicant appears afterwards and satisfies the Tribunal that there was sufficient cause for his non-appearance when the application was called on for hearing, the Tribunal shall make an order setting aside the order dismissing the application and restore the same.

16. *Hearing on application ex-parte.* — (1) Where on the date fixed for hearing the application or on any other date to which hearing is adjourned, the applicant appears and the respondent does not appear when the application is called on for hearing, the Tribunal may, in its discretion, adjourn or hear and decide the application *ex-parte*.

(2) Where an application has been heard *ex-parte* against a respondent or respondents, such respondent or respondents may apply to the Tribunal for an order to set it aside and if such respondent or respondents satisfy the Tribunal that the notice was not duly served, or that he or they were prevented by any sufficient cause from appearing when the application was called on for hearing, the Tribunal may make an order setting aside the *ex-parte* hearing as against him or them upon such terms as it thinks fit, and shall appoint a day for proceeding with the application:

Provided that where the *ex-parte* hearing of the application is of such nature that it cannot be set aside as against one respondent only, it may be set aside as against all or any of the other respondents also:

Provided further that Tribunal shall not set aside *ex-parte* hearing of an application merely on the ground that there has been an irregularity in the service of notice, if it is satisfied that the respondent had notice of the date of hearing and had sufficient time to appear and answer the applicant's claim.

17. *Adjournment of application.* — The Tribunal may on such terms as it deems fit and at any stage of the proceedings adjourn the hearing of the application.

18. *Order to be signed and dated.* — Every order of the Tribunal shall be in writing and shall be signed and dated by the Presiding Officer.

19. *Publication of orders.*— Such of the orders of the Tribunal as are deemed fit for publication in any report or the press may be released for such publication on such terms and conditions as the Tribunal may lay down.

20. *Communication of orders to parties.* — Every order passed on an application shall be communicated to the applicant and to the respondent either in person or by registered post free of cost.

21. *No fee for inspection of records.*—No fee shall be charged for inspecting the records of a pending application by a party thereto.

22. *Orders and directions in certain cases.*—The Tribunal may make such orders or give such directions as may be necessary or expedient to give effect or in relation to its orders or to prevent abuse of its process or to secure the ends of justice.

23. *Registration of legal practitioners clerks.*—(1) A clerk employed by a legal practitioner and permitted as such to have access to the records and to obtain copies of the orders of the Tribunal in which the legal practitioner ordinarily practices shall be known as a "registered clerk".

(2) A legal practitioner desirous of registering his clerk shall make an application to the Registrar in Form 2.

(3) A legal practitioner shall have at a time not more than two registered clerks unless the Registrar by general or special order otherwise permits.

(4) A register of all the registered clerks shall, be maintained in the office of the Registrar and after registration of the clerk, the Registrar shall direct the issue of an identity card to him which shall be non transferable and shall be produced by the holder upon request by an officer or any other employee of the Tribunal.

(5) The identity card mentioned in sub-rule (4) shall

be issued under the signatures of the Registrar of the Tribunal.

(6) Whenever a legal practitioner ceases to employ a registered clerk, he shall notify the fact at once to the Registrar by means of a letter enclosing therewith the identity card issued to his clerk and on receipt of such letter the name of the said registered clerk shall be struck off from the register.

24. *Working hours of the Tribunal.*—Except on Saturday, Sundays and other holidays, the offices of the Tribunal shall, subject to any order made by the Presiding Officer, remain open daily from 10.00 a.m. to 5.00 p.m. but no work, unless it is of an urgent nature, shall be admitted after 4.30 p.m. on any working day.

25. *Sitting hours of the Tribunal.*—The sitting hours of the Tribunal shall ordinarily be from 10.30 a.m. to 1.00 p.m. and 2.00 p.m. to 5.00 p.m. subject to any order made by the Chairman.

26. *Powers and functions of the Registrar.*—(1) The Register shall have the custody of the records of the Tribunal and shall exercise such other functions as may be assigned to him under these rules or by the Presiding Officer.

(2) The Registrar may, with the approval of the Presiding Officer, delegate to another officer of the Tribunal any functions required by these rules to be exercised by the Registrar.

(3) In the absence of the Registrar, officer of the Tribunal authorised in writing by the Presiding Officer in his behalf may perform or exercise all or any of the functions and powers of the Registrar.

(4) The Registrar shall keep in his custody the official seal of the Tribunal.

(5) The Registrar shall, subject to any general or special direction by the Presiding Officer, affix the official seal of the Tribunal on any order, notice or other process.

(6) The Registrar shall have the power to authorise in writing the affixing of the seal of the Tribunal on a certified copy of any order of the Tribunal.

27. *Additional powers and duties of Registrar.*—In addition to the powers conferred elsewhere in these rules, the Registrar shall have the following powers and duties subject to any general or special order of the Presiding Officer namely:

(i) to receive all applications and other documents including transferred applications;

(ii) to decide all questions arising out of the scrutiny of the applications before they are registered;

(iii) to require any application presented to the Tribunal to be amended in accordance with the Act and the rules;

(iv) subject to the directions of the Tribunal to fix dates of hearing of the applications or other proceedings and issue notices thereof;

(v) to direct any formal amendment of records;

(vi) to order grant of copies of documents to parties to the proceedings;

(vii) to dispose of all matters, relating to the service of notices of other processes, applications for the issue of fresh notices or for extending the time therefore;

(viii) to requisition records from the custody of any court or other authority;

(ix) to receive applications for the substitution of legal representatives of the deceased parties, during the pendency of the application;

(x) to receive and dispose of applications for substitution, except where the substitution would involve setting aside an order or abatement; and

(xi) to receive and dispose of application by parties for return of documents.

28. *Seal and emblem.*—The official seal and emblem of the Tribunal shall be such as the Government may specify.

FORM-1

(*See* rule 4)

APPLICATION UNDER SECTION 57 OF THE INFORMATION TECHNOLOGY ACT, 2000

For use in Tribunal's Office

Date of Filing ....

OR

Date of Receipt By post ....

Registration No. ....

Signature of Registrar

IN THE CYBER REGULATIONS APPELLATE TRIBUNAL

....

....

BETWEEN

A	B	APPLICANT
	AND	
C	D	RESPONDENT

Details of Application:

1. Particulars of the applicant:—
   - (i) Name of the applicant
   - (ii) Name of Father/Husband
   - (iii) Designation and office in which employed
   - (iv) Office Address
   - (v) Address for service of all notice
2. Particulars of the respondent:—
   - (i) Name and/or designation of the respondent
   - (ii) Office address of the respondent
   - (iii) Address for service of all notices
3. Particulars of the Order against which application is made:

   The application is against the following order:—
   - (i) Order No.
   - (ii) Date
   - (iii) Passed by
   - (iv) Subject in brief
4. Jurisdiction of the Tribunal:—

   The applicant declares that the subject matter of the order against which he wants re-dressal is within the jurisdiction of the Tribunal.
5. Limitation:—

The applicant further declares that the application is within the limitation prescribed in Section 57 of the Information Technology Act, 2000.

6. Fact of the case:—

The facts of the case are given below:—

(Give here a concise statement of facts in a chronological order, each paragraph containing as nearly as possible a separate issue, fact or otherwise).

7. Relief(s) sought:—

In view of the facts mentioned in para 6 above, the applicant prays for the following relief(s):—

[Specify below the relief(s) sought explaining the ground for the relief(s) and the legal provisions (if any) relied upon].

8. Interim order, if prayed for:—

Pending final decision on the application, the applicant seeks issue of the following interim order:—

(Give here the nature of the interim order prayed for with reasons).

9. Details of the remedies exhausted:—

The applicant declares that he has availed of all the remedies available to him under the relevant service rules, etc. -

(Give here chronologically the details of representations made and the outcome of such representation).

10. Matter not pending with any other court, etc.:—

The applicant further declares that the matter regarding which this application has been made is not pending before any court of law or any other authority or has not been rejected by any court of law or other authority.

11. Details of Index:—

    An index in duplicate containing the details of the documents to be relied upon is enclosed.

12. List of enclosures:—

Verification:

I, ______________ (name of the applicant), S/o, D/o, W/o____________ age ______ working as____________ resident of__________ hereby verify that the contents from 1 to 13 are true to my personal knowledge and belief and that I have not suppressed any material facts.

Place:

Date: Signature of applicant

To
The Registrar,
Cyber Regulation Appellate Tribunal
New Delhi

RECEIPT SLIP

Receipt of the application filed in the Cyber Regulation Appellate Tribunal by Shri/Smt. _________ working as_______________ in the Office of _______________ residing ________ acknowledged.

FORM - 2
(*See* Rule 24)

APPLICATION FOR THE REGISTRATION OF A CLERK

1. Name of legal practitioner on whose be registered.
2. Particulars of the clerk to be registered.
   (i) Full Name (in capitals)
   (ii) Father's name
   (iii) Age and date of birth
   (iv) Place of birth
   (v) Nationality
   (vi) Educational qualifications
   (vii) Particulars of previous employment if any.

   I, __________ (clerk above named) do hereby affirm that the particulars relating to me are true.
3. Whether the legal practitioner has a clerk already registered in his employ and whether the clerk sought to be registered is in lieu of or in addition to the clerk already registered.
4. Whether the clerk sought to be registered is already registered as a clerk of any other legal practitioner and if so, the name of such practitioner.

   I,__________(legal practitioner) certify that the particulars given above are true to the best of my information and belief and that I am not aware of any facts which would render undesirable the registration of the said __________ (name) as a clerk.

Date:

To   Signature of legal practitioner

The Registrar of the Tribunal

____

____

THE INFORMATION TECHNOLOGY (CERTIFYING AUTHORITIES) RULES, 2000

G.S.R.789 (E). In exercise of the powers conferred by Section 87 of the Information Technology Act, 2000 (21 of 2000), the Central Government hereby makes the following rules regulating the application and other guidelines for Certifying Authorities, namely: —

1. Short title and commencement.— (1) These Rules may be called Information Technology (Certifying Authorities) Rules, 2000.

(2) They shall come into force on the date of their publication in the Official Gazette.

2. Definitions.— In these Rules, unless the context otherwise requires, —

(a) "Act" means the Information Technology Act, 2000 (21 of 2000);

(b) "applicant" means Certifying Authority applicant;

(c) "auditor" means any internationally accredited computer security professional or agency appointed by the Certifying Authority and recognized by the Controller for conducting technical audit of operation of Certifying Authority;

(d) "Controller" means Controller of Certifying Authorities appointed under sub-section (1) of Section 17 of the Act;

(e) "Digital Signature Certificate" means Digital Signature Certificate issued under sub-section (4) of Section 3 5 of the Act;

(f) "information asset" means all information

resources utilized in the course of any organisation's business and includes all information, applications (software developed or purchased), and technology (hardware, system software and networks);

(g) "licence" means a .licence granted to Certifying Authorities for the issue of Digital Signature Certificates under these rules;

(h) "licensed Certifying Authority" means Certifying Authority who has been granted a licence to issue Digital Signature Certificates;

(i) "person" shall include an individual; or a company or association or body of individuals; whether incorporated or not; or Central Government or a State Government or any of the Ministries or Departments, Agencies or Authorities of such Governments;

(j) "Schedule" means a schedule annexed to these rules;

(k) "subscriber identity verification method" means the method used to verify and authenticate the identity of a subscriber;

(l) "trusted person" means any person who has:

(i) direct responsibilities for the day-to-day operations, security and performance of those business activities that are regulated under the Act or these Rules in respect of a Certifying Authority; or

(ii) duties directly involving the issuance, renewal, suspension, revocation of Digital Signature Certificates (including the identification of any person requesting a Digital Signature Certificate from a licensed Certifying

Authority), creation of private keys or administration of a Certifying Authority's computing facilities.

(m) words and expressions used herein and not defined but defined in Schedule-IV shall have the meaning respectively assigned to them in that schedule.

3. The manner in which information be authenticated by means of Digital Signature.—A Digital Signature shall,—

(a) be created and verified by cryptography that concerns itself with transforming electronic record into seemingly unintelligible forms and back again;

(b) use what is known as "Public Key Cryptography", which employs an algorithm using two different but mathematical related "keys"—one for creating a Digital Signature or transforming data into a seemingly unintelligible form, and another key for verifying a Digital Signature or returning the electronic record to original form,

the process termed as hash function shall be used in both creating and verifying a Digital Signature.

Explanation: Computer equipment and software utilizing two such keys are often termed as "asymmetric cryptography".

4. Creation of Digital Signature.— To sign an electronic record or any other item of information, the signer shall first apply the hash function in the signer's software; the hash function shall compute a hash result of standard length which is unique (for all practical purposes) to the electronic record; the signer's software transforming the hash result into a Digital Signature using signer's private key; the resulting Digital Signature shall be unique to both electronic record and private key used to create it; and the Digital Signature shall be attached to its electronic record and stored or transmitted with its electronic record.

5. Verification of Digital Signature.— The verification of a Digital Signature shall be accomplished by computing a new hash result of the original electronic record by means of the hash function used to create a Digital Signature and by using the public key and the new hash result, the verifier shall check—

(i) if the Digital Signature was created using the corresponding private key; and

(ii) if the newly computed hash result matches the original result which was transformed into Digital Signature during the signing process. The verification software will confirm the Digital Signature as verified if:—

(a) the signer's private key was used to digitally sign the electronic record, which is known to be the case if the signer's public key was used to verify the signature because the signer's public key will verify only a Digital Signature created with the signer's private key; and

(b) the electronic record was unaltered, which is known to be the case if the hash result computed by the verifier is identical to the hash result extracted from the Digital Signature during the verification process.

6. Standards.— The Information Technology (IT) architecture for Certifying Authorities may support open standards and accepted de facto standards; the most important standards that may be considered for different activities associated with the Certifying Authority's functions are as under:

The product	*The standard*
Public Key Infrastructure	PKIX
Digital Signature Certificates and Digital Signature Revocation list	X.509. version 3 certificates as specified in ITU RFC 1422
Directory (DAP and LDAP)	X.500 for publication of certificates and Certification Revocation Lists (CRLs)
Database Management Operations	Use of generic SQL
Public Key algorithm	DSA and RSA
Digital Hash Function	MD5 and SHA-l
RSA Public Key Technology	PKCS#1 RSA Encryption Standard (512, 1024, 2048 bit)
	PKCS#5 Password Based Encryption Standard
	PKCS#7 Cryptographic Message Syntax Standard
	PKCS#8 Private Key Information Syntax Standard
	PKCS#9 Selected Attribute Types
	PKCS#10 RSA Certification Request
	PKCS#12 Portable format for storing/transporting a user's private keys and certificates
Distinguished name	X.520
Digital Encryption and Digital Signature	PKCS#7
Digital Signature Request Format	PKCS#10

7. Digital Signature Certificate Standard.— All Digital Signature has indicates issued by the Certifying Authorities shall conform to *ITU X.509 version 3 standard* as per rule 6 and shall *inter alia* contain the following data, namely:—

(a) Serial Number (assigning of serial number to the Digital Signature Certificate by Certifying Authority to distinguish it from other certificate);

(b) Signature Algorithm Identifier (which identifies the algorithm used by Certifying Authority to sign the Digital Signature Certificate);

(c) Issuer Name (name of the Certifying Authority who issued the Digital Signature Certificate);

(d) Validity period of the Digital Signature Certificate;

(e) Name of the subscriber (whose public key the Certificate identifies); and

(f) Public Key information of the subscriber.

8. Licensing of Certifying Authorities.— (1) The following persons may apply for grant of a licence to issue Digital Signature Certificates, namely:—

(a) an individual, being a citizen of India and having a captain of five crores of rupees or more of this business or profession;

(b) a company having—

(i) paid up capital of not less than five crores of rupees; and

(ii) net worth of not less than fifty crores of rupees:

Provided that no company in which the equity share capital held in aggregate by the Non-resident Indians, Foreign Institutional Investors, or foreign companies, exceeds forty-nine per cent of its capital, shall be eligible for grant of licence:

Provided further that in a case where the company has been registered under the Companies Act, 1956 (1 to 1956) during the preceding financial year or in the financial year during which it applies for grant of licence under the Act and whose main object is to act as Certifying Authority, the net worth referred to in sub-clause (ii) of this clause shall be the aggregate net worth of its majority shareholders holding at least 51% of paid equity capital, being the Hindu Undivided Family, firm or company:

Provided also that the majority shareholders referred to in the second proviso shall not include Nonresident Indian, foreign national, Foreign Institutional Investor and foreign company:

Provided also that the majority shareholders of a company referred to in the second proviso whose net worth has been determined on the basis of such majority shareholders, shall not sell or transfer its equity shares held in such company—

(i) unless such a company acquires or has its own net worth of not less than fifty crores of rupees:

(ii) without prior approval of the Controller;

(c) a firm having—

(i) capital subscribed by all partners of not less than five crores of rupees; and

(ii) net worth of not less than fifty crores of rupees:

Provided that no firm, in which the capital held in aggregate by any Non-resident Indian, and foreign national, exceeds forty-nine per cent of its capital, shall be eligible for grant of licence:

Provided further that in a case where the firm has been registered under the Indian Partnership Act, 1932 (9 of 1932) during the preceding financial year or in the financial year during which it applies for grant of licence under the Act and whose main object is to act as Certifying Authority, the net worth referred to in sub-clause (ii) of this clause shall be the aggregate net worth of all of its partners:

Provided also that the partners referred to in the second proviso shall not include Non-resident Indian and foreign national:

Provided also that the partners of a firm referred to in the second proviso whose net worth has been determined on the basis of such partners, shall not sell or transfer its capital held in such firm—

(i) unless such firm has acquired or has its own net worth of not less than fifty crores of rupees;

(ii) without prior approval of the Controller;

(d) Central Government or a State Government or any of the Ministries or Departments, Agencies or Authorities of such Governments.

Explanation.—For the purpose of this rule,—

(i) "company" shall have the meaning assigned to it in clause 17 of Section 2 of the Income-tax Act, 1961 (43 of 1961);

(ii) "firm", "partner" and "partnership" shall have the meanings respectively assigned to them in the Indian Partnership Act, 1932 (9 of 1932); but the expression "partner" shall also include any person who, being a minor has been admitted to the benefits of partnership;

(iii) "foreign company" shall have the meaning assigned to it in clause (23 A) of Section 2 of the Income-tax Act, 1961 (43 of 1961);

(iv) "net worth" shall have the meaning assigned to it in clause (ga) of sub-section (1) of Section 3 of the Sick Industrial Companies (Special Provisions) Act, 1985 (1 of 1986);

(v) "Non-resident" shall have the meaning assigned to it as in clause 26 of Section 2 of the Income-tax Act, 1961 (43 of 1961).

(2) The applicant being an individual, or a company, or a firm under sub-rule (1), shall submit a performance bond or furnish a banker's guarantee from a scheduled bank in favour of the Controller in such form and in such manner as may be approved by the Controller for an amount of not less than five crores of rupees and the performance bond or banker's guarantee shall remain valid for a period of six years from the date of its submission:

Provided that the company and firm referred to in the second proviso to clause (b) and the second proviso to clause (c) of sub-rule (1) shall submit a performance bond or furnish a banker's guarantee for ten crores of rupees:

Provided further that nothing in the first proviso shall apply to the company or firm after it has acquired or has its net worth of fifty crores of rupees.

(3) Without prejudice to any penalty which may be imposed or prosecution may be initiated for any offence under the Act or any other law for the time being in force, the performance bond or banker's guarantee may be invoked—

(a) when the Controller has suspended the licence under sub-section (2) of Section 25 of the Act; or

(b) for payment of an offer of compensation made by the Controller; or

(c) for payment of liabilities and rectification costs attributed to the negligence of the Certifying Authority, its officers or employees; or

(d) for payment of the costs incurred in the discontinuation of transfer of operations of the licensed Certifying Authority, if the Certifying Authority's licence or operations is discontinued; or

(e) any other default made by the Certifying Authority in complying with the provisions of the Act or rules made thereunder.

Explanation.—"transfer of operation" shall have the meaning assigned to it in clause (47) of Section 2 of the Income-tax Act, 1961 (43 of 1961).

9. Location of the Facilities.—The infrastructure associated with all functions of generation, issue and management of Digital Signature Certificate as well as maintenance of Directories containing information about the status, and validity of Digital Signature Certificate shall be installed at any location in India.

10. Submission of Application.—Every application for a licensed Certifying Authority shall be made to the Controller,—

(i) in the form given at Schedule-I; and

(ii) in such manner as the Controller may, from time to time, determine, supported by such documents and information as the Controller may require and it shall *inter alia* include—

(a) a Certification Practice Statement (CPS);

(b) a statement including the procedures with respect to identification of the applicant;

(c) a statement for the purpose and scope of anticipated Digital Signature Certificate technology, management, or operations to be outsourced;

(d) certified copies of the business registration documents of Certifying Authority that intends to be licensed;

(e) a description of any event, particularly current or past insolvency, that could materially affect the applicant's ability to act as a Certifying Authority;

(f) an undertaking by the applicant that to its best knowledge and belief it can and will comply the requirements of its Certification Practice Statement;

(g) an undertaking that the Certifying Authority's operation would not commence until its operation and facilities associated with the functions of generation, issue and management of Digital Signature Certificate are audited by the auditors and approved by the Controller in accordance with rule 20;

(h) an undertaking to submit a performance bond or. banker's guarantee in accordance with sub-rule (2) of rule 8 within one month of Controller indicating his approval for the grant of licence to operate as a Certifying Authority;

(i) any other information required by the Controller.

11. Fee.— (1) The application for the grant of a licence shall be accompanied by a non-refundable fee of twenty-five thousand rupees payable by a bank draft or by a pay order drawn in the name of the Controller.

(2) The application submitted to the Controller for renewal of Certifying Authority's licence shall be accompanied by a non-refundable fee of five thousand rupees payable by a bank draft or by a pay order drawn in the name of the Controller.

(3) Fee or any part thereof shall not be refunded if the licence is suspended or revoked during its validity period.

12. Cross Certification.— (1) The licensed Certifying Authority shall have arrangement for cross certification with other licensed Certifying Authorities within India which shall be submitted to the Controller before the commencement of their operations as per rule 20:

Provided that any dispute arising as a result of any such arrangement between the Certifying Authorities; or between Certifying Authorities or Certifying Authority and the Subscriber shall be referred to the Controller for arbitration or resolution.

(2) The arrangement for Cross Certification by the licensed Certifying Authority with a Foreign Certifying Authority along with the application, shall be submitted to the Controller in such form and in such manner as may be provided in the regulations made by the Controller; and the licensed Certifying Authority shall not commence cross certification operations unless it has obtained the written or digital signature approval from the Controller.

13. Validity of licence.— (1) A licence shall be valid for a period of five years from the date of its issue.

(2) The licence shall not be transferable.

14. Suspension of Licence.— (1) The Controller may by order suspend the licence in accordance with the provisions contained in sub-section (2) of Section 25 of the Act.

(2) The licence granted to the persons referred to in clauses (a) to (c) of sub-rule (1) of rule 8 shall stand suspended when the performance bond submitted or the banker's guarantee furnished by such persons is invoked under sub-rule (2) of that rule.

15. Renewal of licence.— (1) The provisions of rule 8 to rule 13, shall apply in the case of an application for renewal of a licence as it applies to a fresh application for licensed Certifying Authority.

(2) A Certifying Authority shall submit an application for the renewal of its licence not less than forty-five days before the date of expiry of the period of validity of licence.

(3) The application for renewal of licence may be submitted in the form of electronic record subject to such requirements as the Controller may deem fit.

16. Issuance of Licence.— (1) The Controller may, within four weeks from the date of receipt of the application, after considering the documents accompanying the application and such other factors, as he may deem fit, grant or renew the licence or reject the application:

Provided that in exceptional circumstances and for reasons to be recorded in writing, the period of four weeks may be extended to such period, not exceeding eight weeks in all as the Controller may deem fit.

(2) If the application for licensed Certifying Authority is approved, the applicant shall—

(a) submit a performance bond or furnish a banker's guarantee within one month from the date of such approval to the Controller in accordance with sub-rule (2) of rule 8; and

(b) execute an agreement with the Controller binding himself to comply with the terms and conditions of the licence and the provisions of the Act and the rules made thereunder.

17. Refusal of Licence.— The Controller may refuse to grant or renew a licence if—

(i) the applicant has not provided the Controller with such information relating to its business, and to any circumstances likely to affect its method of conducting business, as the Controller may require; or

(ii) the applicant is in the course of being wound up or liquidated; or

(iii) a receiver has, or a receiver and manager have, been appointed by the court in respect of the applicant; or

(iv) the applicant or any trusted person has been convicted, whether in India or out of India, of an offence the conviction for which involved a finding that it or such trusted person acted fraudulently or dishonestly, or has been convicted of an offence under the Act or these rules; or

(v) the Controller has invoked performance bond or banker's guarantee; or

(vi) a Certifying Authority commits breach of, or fails to observe and comply with, the procedures and practices as per the Certification Practice Statement; or

(vii) a Certifying Authority fails to conduct, or does not submit, the returns of the audit in accordance with rule 31; or

(viii) the audit report recommends that the Certifying Authority is not worthy of continuing Certifying Authority's operation; or

(ix) a Certifying Authority fails to comply with the directions of the Controller.

18. Governing Laws.— The Certification Practice Statement of the Certifying Authority shall comply with, and be governed by, the laws of the country.

19. Security Guidelines for Certifying Authorities.— (1) The Certifying Authorities shall have the sole responsibility of integrity, confidentiality and protection of information and information assets employed in its operation, considering classification, declassification, labeling, storage, access and destruction of information assets according to their value, sensitivity and importance of operation.

(2) Information Technology Security Guidelines and Security Guidelines for Certifying Authorities aimed at protecting the integrity, confidentiality and availability of service of Certifying Authority are given in Schedule-II and Schedule-III respectively.

(3) The Certifying Authority shall formulate its Information Technology and Security Policy for operation complying with these guidelines and submit it to the Controller before commencement of operation:

Provided that any change made by the Certifying Authority in the Information Technology and Security Policy shall be submitted by it within two weeks to the Controller.

20. Commencement of Operation by Licensed Certifying Authorities.— The licensed Certifying Authority shall commence its commercial operation of generation and issue of Digital Signature only after—

(a) it has confirmed to the Controller the adoption of Certification Practice Statement;

(b) it has generated its key pair, namely, private and corresponding public key, and submitted the public key to the Controller;

(c) the installed facilities and infrastructure associated with all functions of generation, issue and management of Digital Signature Certificate have been audited by the accredited auditor in accordance with the provisions of rule 31; and

(d) it has submitted the arrangement for cross certification with other licensed Certifying Authorities within India to the Controller.

21. Requirements Prior to Cessation as Certifying Authority.— Before ceasing to act as a Certifying Authority, a Certifying Authority shall,—

(a) give notice to the Controller of its intention to cease acting as a Certifying Authority:

Provided that the notice shall be made ninety days before ceasing to act as a Certifying Authority or ninety days before the date of expiry of licence;

(b) advertise sixty days before the expiry of licence or ceasing to act as Certifying Authority, as the case may be, the intention in such daily newspaper or newspapers and in such manner as the Controller may determine;

(c) notify its intention to cease acting as a Certifying Authority to the subscriber and Cross Certifying Authority of each unrevoked or unexpired Digital Signature Certificate issued by it:

Provided that the notice shall be given sixty days before ceasing to act as a Certifying Authority or sixty days before the date of expiry of unrevoked or unexpired Digital Signature Certificate, as the case may be;

(d) the notice shall be sent to the Controller, affected subscribers and Cross Certifying Authorities by digitally signed e-mail and registered post;

(e) revoke all Digital Signature Certificates that remain unrevoked or unexpired at the end of the ninety days notice period, whether or not the subscribers have requested revocation;

(f) make a reasonable effort to ensure that discontinuing its certification services causes minimal disruption to its subscribers and to persons duly needing to verify digital signatures by reference to the public keys contained in outstanding Digital Signature Certificates;

(g) make reasonable arrangements for preserving the records for a period of seven years;

(h) pay reasonable restitution (not exceeding the

cost involved in obtaining the new Digital Signature Certificate) to subscribers for revoking the Digital Signature Certificates before the date of expiry;

(i) after the date of expiry mentioned in the licence, the Certifying Authority shall destroy the certificate-signing private key and confirm the date and time of destruction of the private key to the Controller.

22. Database of Certifying Authorities.—The Controller shall maintain a database of the disclosure record of every Certifying Authority, Cross Certifying Authority and Foreign Certifying Authority, containing *inter alia* the following details:

(a) the name of the person/names of the Directors, nature of business, Income-tax Permanent Account Number, web address, if any office and residential address, location of facilities associated with functions of generation of Digital Signature Certificate, voice and facsimile telephone numbers, . electronic mail address(es), administrative contacts and authorized representatives;

(b) the public key(s), corresponding to the private key(s) used by the Certifying Authority and recognized foreign Certifying Authority to digitally sign Digital Signature Certificate;

(c) current and past versions of Certification Practice Statement of Certifying Authority;

(d) time stamps indicating the date and time of—

(i) grant of licence;

(ii) confirmation of adoption of Certification

Practice Statement and its earlier versions by Certifying Authority;

(iii) commencement of commercial operations of generation and issue of Digital Signature Certificate by the Certifying Authority;

(iv) revocation or suspension of licence of Certifying Authority;

(v) commencement of operation of Cross Certifying Authority;

(vi) issue of recognition of foreign Certifying Authority;

(vii) revocation or suspension of recognition of foreign Certifying Authority.

23. Digital Signature Certificate.— The Certifying Authority shall, for issuing the Digital Signature Certificates, while complying with the provisions of Section 35 of the Act, also comply will the following, namely:—

(a) the Digital Signature Certificate shall be issued only after a Digital Signature Certificate application in the form provided by the Certifying Authority has been submitted by the subscriber to the Certifying Authority and the same has been approved by it:

Provided that the application Form contains, *inter alia,* the particulars given in the modal Form given in Schedule-IV;

(b) no interim Digital Signature Certificate shall be issued;

(c) the Digital Signature Certificate shall be generated by the Certifying Authority upon receipt of an authorised and validated request for:—

(i) new Digital Signature Certificates;

(ii) Digital Signature Certificates renewal;

(d) the Digital Signature Certificate must contain or incorporate, by reference such information, as is sufficient to locate or identify one or more repositories in which revocation or suspension of the Digital Signature Certificate will be listed, if the Digital Signature Certificate is suspended or revoked;

(e) the subscriber identity verification method employed for issuance of Digital Signature Certificate shall be specified in the Certification Practice Statement and shall be subject to the approval of the Controller during the application for a licence;

(f) where the Digital Signature Certificate is issued to a person (referred to in this clause as a New Digital Signature Certificate) on the basis of another valid Digital Signature Certificate held by the said person (referred in this clause as an Originating Digital Signature Certificate) and subsequently the originating Digital Signature Certificate has been suspended or revoked, the Certifying Authority that issued the new Digital Signature Certificate shall conduct investigations to determine whether it is necessary to suspend or revoke the new Digital Signature Certificate;

(g) the Certifying Authority shall provide a reasonable opportunity for the subscriber to verify, the contents of the Digital Signature Certificate before it is accepted;

(h) if the subscriber accepts the issued Digital Signature Certificate, the Certifying Authority shall publish a signed copy of the Digital Signature Certificate in a repository;

(i) where the Digital Signature Certificate has been issued by the licensed Certifying Authority and accepted by the subscriber, and the Certifying Authority comes to know of any fact, or otherwise, that affects the validity or reliability of such Digital Signature Certificate, it shall notify the same to the subscriber immediately;

(j) all Digital Signature Certificates shall be issued with a designated expiry date.

24. Generation of Digital Signature Certificate.— The generation of the Digital Signature Certificate shall involve:

(a) receipt of an approved and verified Digital Signature Certificate request;

(b) creating a new Digital Signature Certificate;

(c) binding the key pair associated with the Digital Signature Certificate to a Digital Signature Certificate owner;

(d) issuing the Digital Signature Certificate and the associated public key for operational use;

(e) a distinguished name associated with the Digital Signature Certificate owner; and

(f) a recognized and relevant policy as defined in Certification Practice Statement.

25. Issue of Digital Signature Certificate.— Before the issue of the Digital Signature Certificate, the Certifying Authority shall:—

(i) confirm that the user's name does not appear in its list of compromised users;

(ii) comply with the procedure as defined in his Certification practice Statement including verification of identification and/or employment;

(iii) comply with all privacy requirements;

(iv) obtain a consent of the person requesting the Digital Signature Certificate, that the details of such Digital Signature Certificate can be published on a directory service.

26. Certificate Lifetime.— (1) A Digital Signature Certificate,—

(a) shall be issued with a designated expiry date;

(b) which is suspended shall return to the operational use, it the suspension is withdrawn in accordance with the provisions of Section 37 of the Act;

(c) shall expire automatically upon reaching the designated expiry date at which time the Digital Signature Certificate shall be archived;

(d) on expiry, shall not be re-used.

(2) The period for which a Digital Signature Certificate has been issued shall hot be extended, but a new Digital Signature Certificate may be issued after the expiry of such period.

27. Archival of Digital Signature Certificate.— A Certifying Authority shall archive—

(a) applications for issue of Digital Signature Certificates;

(b) registration and verification documents of generated Digital Signature Certificates;

(c) Digital Signature Certificates;

(d) notices of suspension;

(e) information of suspended Digital Signature Certificates;

(f) information of revoked Digital Signature Certificates;

(g) expired Digital Signature Certificates,

for a minimum period of seven years or for a period in accordance with legal requirement.

28. Compromise of Digital Signature Certificate.— Digital Signature Certificates in operational use that become compromised shall be revoked in accordance with the procedure defined in the Certification Practice Statement of Certifying Authority.

Explanation: Digital Signature Certificates shall,-

(a) be deemed to be compromised where the integrity of: —

(i) the private key associated with the Digital Signature Certificate is in doubt;

(ii) the Digital Signature Certificate owner is in doubt, as to the use, or attempted use of his key pairs, or otherwise, for malicious or unlawful purposes;

(b) remain in the compromised state for only such time as it takes to arrange for revocation.

29. Revocation of Digital Signature Certificate.— (1) Digital Signature Certificate shall be revoked and become invalid for any trusted use, where—

(a) there is a compromise of the Digital Signature Certificate owner's private key;

(b) there is a misuse of the Digital Signature Certificate;

(c) there is a misrepresentation or errors in the Digital Signature Certificate;

(d) the Digital Signature Certificate is no longer required.

(2) The revoked Digital Signature Certificate shall be added to the Certificate Revocation List (CRL).

30. Fees for issue of Digital Signature Certificate.— (1) The Certifying Authority shall charge such fee for the issue of Digital Signature Certificate as may be prescribed by the Central Government under sub-section (2) of Section 35 of the Act.

(2) Fee may be payable in respect of access to Certifying Authority's X.500 directory for certificate downloading. Where fees are payable, Certifying Authority shall provide an up-to-date fee schedule to all its subscribers and users, this may be done by publishing fee schedule on a nominated website.

(3) Fees may be payable in respect of access to Certifying Authority's X.500 directory service for certificate revocation or status information. Where fees are payable, Certifying Authority shall provide an up-to-date fee schedule to all its subscribers and users, mis may be done by publishing the fee schedule on a nominated website.

(4) No fee is to be levied for access to Certification Practice Statement via Internet. A fee may be charged by the Certifying Authority for providing printed copies of its Certification Practice Statement.

31. Audit.— (1) The Certifying Authority shall get its operations audited annually by an auditor and such audit shall include *inter alia*,—

(i) security policy and planning;

(ii) physical security;

(iii) technology evaluation;

(iv) Certifying Authority's services administration;

(v) relevant Certification Practice Statement;

(vi) compliance to relevant Certification Practice Statement;

(vii) contracts/agreements;

(viii) regulations prescribed by the Controller;

(ix) policy requirements of Certifying Authorities Rules, 2000.

(2) The Certifying Authority shall conduct,—

(a) half yearly audit of the Security Policy, physical security and planning of its operation;

(b) a quarterly audit of its repository.

(3) The Certifying Authority shall submit copy of each audit report to the Controller within four weeks of the completion of such audit and where irregularities are found, the Certifying Authority shall take immediate appropriate action to remove such irregularities.

32. Auditor's relationship with Certifying Authority.— (1) The auditor shall be independent of the Certifying Authority being audited and shall not be a software or hardware vendor which is, or has been providing services or supplying equipment to the said Certifying Authority.

(2) The auditor and the Certifying Authority shall not have any current or planned financial, legal or other relationship, other than that of an auditor and the audited party.

33. Confidential Information.— The following information shall be confidential namely:—

(a) Digital Signature Certificate application, whether approved or rejected;

(b) Digital Signature Certificate information collected from the subscriber or elsewhere as part of the registration and verification record but not included in the Digital Signature Certificate information;

(c) subscriber agreement.

34. Access to Confidential Information.— (1) Access to confidential information by Certifying Authority's operational staff shall be on a "need-to-know" and "need-to-use" basis.

(2) Paper based records, documentation and backup data containing all confidential information as prescribed in rule 33 shall be kept in secure and locked container or filing system, separately from all other records.

(3) The confidential information shall not be taken out of the country except in a case where a properly constitutional warrant or other legally enforceable document is produced to the Controller and he permits to do so.

SCHEDULE-I

[SEE RULE 10]

Form for Application for Grant of Licence to be a Certifying Authority

For Individual

1. Full Name*

Last Name/Surname ______________________

First Name ______________________

Middle Name ______________________

2. Have you ever been known by any other name? If Yes,

Last Name/Surname	____________
First Name	____________
Middle Name	____________

3. Address

A. Residential Address*

Flat/Door/Block No.	____________
Name of Premises/ Building/Village	____________
Road/Street/Lane/Post Office	____________
Area/Locality/Taluka/ Sub-Division	____________
Town/City/District	________ Pin: ________
State/Union Territory	____________
Telephone No.	____________
Fax	____________
Mobile Phone No.	____________

B. Office Address*

Name of Office	____________
Flat/Door/Block No.	____________
Name of Premises/ Building/Village	____________
Road/Street/Lane/ Post Office	____________
Area/Locality/Taluka/ Sub-Division	____________
Town/City/District	____________
State/Union Territory	________ Pin: ________
Telephone No.	____________
Fax	____________

4. Address for Communication* Tick ✓ As applicabel A ☐ or B ☐

5. Father's Name*

Last Name/Surname	____________

First Name ______________

Middle Name ______________

6. Sex * (For individual Applicant only) — Tick ✓ As applicabel Male/Female

7. Date of Birth(dd/mm/yyyy)* ___/ ___/ ___

8. Nationality * ______________

9. Credit Card Details

Credit Card Type ______________

Credit Card No. ______________

Issued By ______________

10. E-mail Address ______________

11. Web URL address ______________

12. Passport Details #

Passport No. ______________

Passport issuing authority ______________

Passport expiry date (dd/mm/yyyy) ___/ ___/ ___

13. Voter's Identity Card No. ______________

14. Income Tax PAN no. # ______________

15. ISP Details

ISP Name * ______________

ISP's Website Address, if any ______________

Your User Name at ISP, if any ______________

16. Personal Web page

URL address, if any ______________

17. Capital in the business or profession * (Attach documentary proof) Rs.______________

For Company/Firm/Body of Individuals/Association of Persons/ Local Authority

18. Registration Number * ______________

19. Date of Incorporation/Agreement/Partnership * ___/___/___

20. Particulars of Business, if any: *

Head Office ______________________

Name of Office ______________________

Flat/Door/Block No. ______________________

Name of Premises/Building/ Village ______________________

Road/Street/Lane/Post Office

Area/Locality/Taluka/Sub-Division ______________________

Town/City/District ______________ Pin: __________

State/Union Territory ______________________

Telephone No. ______________________

Fax ______________________

Web page URL address, if any ______________________

No. of Branches ______________________

Nature of Business ______________________

21. Income Tax PAN No. * ______________________

22. Turnover in the last financial year Rs. ______________________

23. Net worth * Rs. ______________________
(Attach documentary proof)

24. Paid up Capital * Rs. ______________________
(Attach documentary proof)

25. Insurance Details

Insurance Policy No.* Rs. ______________________

Insurer Company * Rs. ______________________

26. Names, Addresses etc. of Partners/Members/Directors (For Information about more persons, please ad separate sheet(s) in the format given in the next page) *

No. of Partners/Members/ Directors Details of Partners/ Members/Directors ______________________

A. Full Name

Last Name/Surname ______________________

First Name ______________________

Middle Name ______________________

B. Address

Flat/Door/Block No. ____________

Name of Premises/Building/Village ____________

Road/Street/Lane/Post Office ____________

Area/Locality/Taluka/Sub-Division ____________

Town/City/District ____________

State/Union Territory Pin: ____________

Telephone No. ____________

Fax No. ____________

Mobile Phone No. ____________

C Nationality

In case of foreign national. Visa details ____________

D. Passport Details #

Passport No. ____________

Passport issuing authority ____________

Passport expiry date ____________

E. Voter's identity Card No. # ____________

F. Income Tax PAN no. # ____________

G. E-mail Address ____________

H. Personal Web page URL, if any ____________

27. Authorised Representative *

Name ____________

Flat/Door/Block No. ____________

Name of Premises/Building/Village____________

Road/Street/Lane/Post Office ____________

Area/Locality/Taluka/Sub-Division____________

Town/City/District Pin: ____________

State/Union Territory ____________

Telephone No. ____________

Fax ____________

Nature of Business ____________

For Government Ministry/Department/Agency/Authority

28. Particulars of Organisation: *

Name of Organisation ____________________

Administrative Ministry/Department____________________

Under State/Central Government ____________________

Flat/Door/Block No. ____________________

Name of Premises/Building/Village____________________

Road/Street/Lane/Post Office ____________________

Area/Locality/Taluka/Sub-Division ____________________

Town/City/District __________ Pin: __________

State/Union Territory ____________________

Telephone No. ____________________

Fax No. ____________________

Web page URL Address

Name of the Head of Organisation ____________________

Designation ____________________

E-mail Address ____________________

---

29. Bank Details

Bank Name * ____________________

Branch * ____________________

Bank Account No. * ____________________

Type of Bank Account * ____________________

30. Whether bank draft/pay order for licence fee enclosed *: Y / N

If yes,

Name of Bank ____________________

Draft/pay order No. ____________________

Date of Issue ____________________

Amount ____________________

31. Location of facility in India for generation of Digital Signature Certificate* ____________________

32. Public Key @

33. Whether undertaking for Bank Guarantee/Performance Bond attached *: Y/N

    (Not applicable if the applicant is a Government Ministry/ Department/Agency/Authority)

34. Whether Certification Practice Statement is enclosed *: Y/N

35. Whether certified copies of business registration document are enclosed: Y/N (For Company/Firm/Body of Individuals/ Association of Persons/Local Authority) If yes, the documents attached:

    i) ....

    ii) ....

    iii) ....

36. Any other information ______________________

____

____

Date

Signature of the Applicant

Instructions:

1. Columns marked with * are mandatory.
2. For the columns marked with #, details for at least one is mandatory.
3. Column No. 1 to 17 are to be filled up by individual applicant.
4. Column No. 18 to 27 are to be filled up if applicant is a Company/ Firm/Body of Individuals/Association of Persons/Local Authority.
5. Column No. 28 is to be filled up if applicant is a Government organisation.
6. Column No. 29,30,31 and 34 are to be filled up by all applicants.
7. @ Column No. 32 is applicable only for application for renewal of licence.
8. Column No. 33 is not applicable if the applicant is a Government organisation.

SCHEDULE-II

[See rule 19(2)]

Information Technology (IT) Security Guidelines

Introduction

This document provides guidelines for the implementation and management of information Technology Security. Due to the inherent dynamism of the security requirements, this document does not provide an exact template for the organizations to follow. However, appropriate suitable samples of security process are provided for guidelines. It is the responsibility of the organizations to develop internal processes that meet the guidelines set forth in this document.

The following words used in the Information Technology Security Guidelines shall be interpreted as follows:

- shall: The guideline defined is a mandatory requirement, and therefore must be complied with.
- should: The guideline defined is a recommended requirement. Non-compliance shall be documented and approved by the management. Where appropriate, compensating controls shall be implemented.
- must: The guideline defined is a mandatory requirement, and therefore must be complied with.
- may: The guideline defined is an optional requirement. The implementation of this guideline is determined by the organisation's requirement.

Implementation of an Information Security Programme

Successful implementation of a meaningful Information Security Programme rests with the support of the top management. Until and unless the senior managers of the organization understand and concur with the objectives of the information security programme its ultimate success is in question.

The Information Security Programme should be broken down into specific stages as follows:

(a) Adoption of a security policy;

(b) Security risk analysis;

(c) Development and implementation of a information classification system;

(d) Development and implementation of the security standards manual;

(e) Implementation of the management security self-assessment process;

(f) On-going security programme maintenance and enforcement; and

(g) Training.

The principal task of the security implementation is to define the responsibilities of persons within the organization. The implementation should be based on the general principle that the person who is generating the information is also responsible for its security. However, in order to enable him to carry out his responsibilities in this regard, proper tools, and environment need to be established.

When different pieces of information at one level are integrated to form higher value information, the responsibility for its security needs also should go up in the hierarchy to the integrator and should require higher level of authority for its access. It should be absolutely clear with respect to each information as to who is its owner, its custodian, and its users. It is the duty of the owner to assign the right classification to the information so that the required level of security can be enforced. The custodian of information is responsible for the proper implementation of security guidelines and making the information available to the users on a need to know basis.

Information Classification

Information assets must be classified according to their sensitivity and their importance to the organization. Since it is unrealistic to expect managers and employees to maintain absolute control over all information within the boundaries of the organization, it is necessary to advise them on which types of information are considered more sensitive, and how the organization would like the sensitive information handled and protected. Classification, declassification, labeling, storage, access, destruction and reproduction of classified data and the administrative overhead this process will create must be considered. Failure to maintain a balance between the value of the information classified and the administrative burden the classification system places on the organization will result in long-term difficulties in achieving success.

Confidential is that classification of information of which unauthorized disclosure/use could cause serious damage to the organization, e.g. strategic planning documents.

Restricted is that classification of information of which unauthorized disclosure/use would not be in the best interest of the organization and/or its customers, e.g. design details, computer software (programs, utilities), documentation, organization personnel data, budget information.

Internal use is that classification of information that does not require any degree of protection against disclosure within the company, e.g. operating procedures, policies and standards inter office memorandums.

Unclassified is that classification of information that requires no protection against disclosure e.g. published annual reports, periodicals.

While the above classifications are appropriate for a general organization view point, the following classifications may be considered:

Top Secret: It shall be applied to information unauthorized disclosure of which could be expected to cause exceptionally grave damage to the national security or national interest. This category is reserved for Nation's closest secrets and to be used with great reserve.

Secret: This shall be applied to information unauthorized disclosure of which could be expected to cause serious damage to the national security or national interest or cause serious embarrassment in its functioning. This classification should be used for highly important information and is the highest classification normally used.

Confidentiality: This shall be applied to information unauthorized disclosure of which could be expected to cause damage to the security of the organisation or could be prejudicial to the interest of the organisation, or could affect the organisation in its functioning. Most information will on proper analysis be classified no higher than confidential.

Restricted: This shall be applied to information which is essentially meant for official use only and which would not be published or communicated to anyone except for official purpose.

Unclassified: This is the classification of information that requires no protection against disclosure.

Physical and Operational Security

1. Site Design

(1) The site shall not be in locations that are prone to natural or man-made disasters, like flood, fire, chemical contamination and explosions.

(2) As per nature of the operations, suitable floor structuring, lighting, power and water damage protection requirements shall be provided.

(3) Construction shall comply with all applicable building and safety regulations as laid down by the relevant Government agencies. Further, the construction must be tamper-evident.

(4) Materials used for the construction of the operational site shall be fire-resistant and free of toxic chemicals.

(5) External walls shall be constructed of brick or reinforced concrete of sufficient thickness to resist forcible attack. Ground level windows shall be fortified with sturdy mild steel grills or impact-resistant laminated security glass. All internal walls must be from the floor to the ceiling and must be tamper-evident.

(6) Air-conditioning system, power supply system and uninterrupted power supply unit with proper backup shall be installed depending upon the nature of operation. All ducting holes of the air-conditioning system must be designed so as to prevent intrusion of any kind.

(7) Automatic fire detection, fire suppression systems and equipment in compliance with requirement specified by the Fire Brigade or any other agencies

of the Central or State Government shall be installed at the operational site.

(8) Media library, electrical and mechanical control rooms shall be housed in separate isolated areas, with access granted only to specific, named individuals on a need basis.

(9) Any facility that supports mission-critical and sensitive applications must be located and designed for repairability, relocation and reconfiguration. The ability to relocate, reconstitute and reconfigure these applications must be tested as part of the business continuity/ disaster recovery plan.

2. ***Fire Protection***

(1) Combustible materials shall not be stored within hundred meters of the operational site.

(2) Automatic fire detection, fire suppression systems and audible alarms as prescribed by the Fire Brigade or any other agency of the Central or State Government shall be installed at the operational site.

(3) Fire extinguishers shall be installed at the operational site and their locations clearly marked with appropriate signs.

(4) Periodic testing, inspection and maintenance of the fire equipment and fire suppression systems shall be carried out.

(5) Procedures for the safe evacuation of personnel in an emergency shall be visibly pasted/displayed at prominent places at the operational site. Periodic training and fire drills shall be conducted.

(6) There shall be no eating, drinking or smoking in the operational site. The work areas shall be kept clean at all times.

3. Environmental Protection

(1) Water detectors shall be installed under the raised floors throughout the operational site and shall be connected to audible alarms.

(2) The temperature and humidity condition in the operational site shall be monitored and controlled periodically.

(3) Personnel at the operational site shall be trained to monitor and control the various equipment and devices installed at the operational site for the purpose of fire and environment protection.

(4) Periodic inspection, testing and maintenance of the equipment and systems shall be scheduled.

4. Physical Access

(1) Responsibilities round the clock, seven days a week, three hundred sixty five days a year for physical security of the systems used for operation and also actual physical layout at the site of operation shall be defined and assigned to named individuals.

(2) Biometric physical access security systems shall be installed to control and audit access to the operational site.

(3) Physical access to the operational site at all times shall be controlled and restricted to authorised personnel only. Personnel authorized for limited physical access shall not be allowed to gain unauthorized access to restricted area within operational site.

(4) Dual control over the inventory and issue of access cards/keys during normal business hours to the Data Centre shall be in place. An up-to-date list of personnel who possess the cards/

keys shall be regularly maintained and archived for a period of three years.

(5) Loss of access cards/keys must be immediately reported to the security supervisor of the operational site who shall take appropriate action to prevent unauthorised access.

(6) All individuals, other than operations staff, shall sign in and sign out of the operational site and shall be accompanied by operations staff.

(7) Emergency exits shall be tested periodically to ensure that the access security systems are operational.

(8) All opening of the Data Centre should be monitored round the clock by surveillance video cameras.

5. Information Management

1. System Administration

(1) Each organization shall designate a properly trained "System Administrator" who will ensure that the protective security measures of the system are functional and who will maintain its security posture. Depending upon the complexity and security needs of a system or application, the System Administrator may have a designated System Security Administrator who will assume security responsibilities and provide physical, logical and procedural safeguards for information.

(2) Organisations shall ensure that only a properly trained System Security Administrator is assigned the system security responsibilities.

(3) The responsibility to create, classify, retrieve, modify, delete or archive information must rest only with the System Administrator.

(4) Any password used for the system administration and operation of trusted services must not be written down (in paper or electronic form) or shared with any one. A system for password management should be put in place to cover the eventualities such as forgotten password or changeover to another person in case of System Administrator (or System Security Administrator) leaving the organisation. Every instance of usage of administrator's passwords must be documented.

(5) Periodic review of the access rights of all users must be performed.

(6) The System Administrator must promptly disable access to a user's account if the user is identified as having left the Data Centre, changed assignments, or is no longer requiring system access. Reactivation of the user's account must be authorized in writing by the System Administrator (Digitally signed e-mail may be acceptable).

(7) The System Administrator must take steps to" safeguards classified information as prescribed by its owner.

(8) The System Administrator must authorize privileged access to users only on a need-to-know and need-to-do basis and also only after the authorization is documented.

(9) Criteria for the review of audit trails/access logs, reporting of access violations and procedures to ensure timely management action/response shall be established and documented.

(10) All security violations must be recorded, investigated, and periodic status reports compiled for review by the management.

(11) The System Administrator together with the system support staff, shall conduct a regular analysis of problems reported to and identify any weaknesses in protection of the information.

(12) The System Administrator shall ensure that the data, file and Public Key Infrastructure (PKI) servers are not left unmonitored while these systems are powered on.

(13) The System Administrator should ensure that no generic user is enabled or active on the system.

2. ***Sensitive Information Control***

(1) Information assets shall be classified and protected according to their sensitivity and criticality to the organization.

(2) Procedures in accordance with para 8.3 of these Guidelines must be in place to handle the storage media, which has sensitive and classified information.

(3) All sensitive information stored in any media shall bear or be assigned an appropriate security classification.

(4) All sensitive material shall be stamped or labeled accordingly.

(5) Storage media (i.e. floppy diskettes, magnetic tapes, portable hard disks, optical disks, etc.) containing sensitive information shall be secured according to their classification.

(6) Electronic communication systems, such as router, switches, network device and computers, used for transmission of sensitive information should be equipped or installed with suitable security software .and if necessary with an encryptor or encryption software. The appropriate procedure in this regard should be documented.

(7) Procedures shall be in place to ensure the secure disposal of sensitive information assets on all corrupted/damaged or affected media both internal (e.g. hard disk/optical disk) and external (e.g. diskette, disk drive, tapes etc.) to the system. Preferably such affected/corrupted/damaged media both internal and external to the system shall be destroyed.

3. Sensitive Information Security

(1) Highly sensitive information assets shall be stored on secure removable media and should be in an encrypted format to avoid compromise by unauthorized persons.

(2) Highly sensitive information shall be classified in accordance with para 5.

(3) Sensitive information and data, which are stored on the fixed disk of a computer shared by more than one person; must be protected by access control software (e.g., password). Security packages must be installed which partition or provide authorization to segregated directories/files.

(4) Removable electronic storage media must be removed from the computer and properly secured at the end of the work session or workday.

(5) Removable electronic storage media containing sensitive information and data must be clearly labeled and secured.

(6) Hard disks containing sensitive information and data must be securely erased prior to giving the computer system to another internal or external department or for maintenance.

4. Third Party Access

(1) Access to the computer systems by other organisations shall be subjected to a similar level of security protection and controls as in these Information Technology security guidelines.

(2) In case the Data Centre uses the facilities of external service/facility provider (outsourcer) for any of their operations, the use of external service/facility providers (e.g. outsourcer) shall be evaluated in light of the possible security exposures and risks involved and all such agreements shall be approved by the information asset owner. The external service or facility provider shall also sign non-disclosure agreements with the management of the Data Centre/operational site.

(3) The external service/facility provider (e.g. outsourcer) shall provide an equivalent level of security controls as required by these Information Technology. Security Guidelines.

5. Prevention of Computer Misuse

(1) Prevention, detection, and deterrence measures shall be implemented to safeguard the security of computers and computer information from misuse. The measures taken shall be properly documented and reviewed regularly.

(2) Each organization shall provide adequate information to all persons, including management, systems developers and programmers, end-users, and third party users warning them against misuse of computers.

(3) Effective measures to deal expeditiously with breaches of security shall be established within each organisation. Such measures shall include:

(i) Prompt reporting of suspected breach;

(ii) Proper investigation and assessment of the nature of suspected breach;

(iii) Secure evidence and preserve integrity of such material as relates to the discovery of any breach;

(iv) Remedial measures.

(4) All incidents related to breaches shall be reported to the System Administrator or System Security Administrator for appropriate action to prevent future occurrence.

(5) Procedure shall be set-up to establish the nature of any alleged abuse and determine the subsequent action required to be taken to prevent its future occurrence. Such procedures shall include:

(i) The role of the System Administrator, System Security Administrator and management;

(ii) Procedure for investigation;

(iii) Areas for security review; and

(iv) Subsequent follow-up action.

6. System Integrity and Security Measures

1. Use of Security Systems or Facilities

(1) Security controls shall be installed and maintained on each computer system or computer node to prevent unauthorised users from gaining entry to the information system and to prevent unauthorised access to data.

(2) Any system software or resource of the computer system should only be accessible after being authenticated by access control system.

2. ***System Access Control***

(1) Access control software and system software security features shall be implemented to protect resources. Management approval is required to authorise issuance of user identification (ID) and resource privileges.

(2) Access to information system resources like memory, storage devices etc., sensitive utilities and data resources and programme files shall be controlled and restricted based on a "need-to-use" basis with proper segregation of duties.

(3) The access control software or operating system of the computer system shall provide features to restrict access to the system and data resources. The use of common passwords such as "administrator" or "president" or "game" etc. to protect access to the system and data resources represent a security exposure and shall be avoided. All passwords used must be resistant to dictionary attacks.

(4) Appropriate approval for the request to access system resources shall be obtained from the System Administrator. Guidelines and procedures governing access authorisations shall be developed, documented and implemented.

(5) An Access Control System manual documenting the access granted to different level of users shall be prepared to provide guidance to the System Administrator for grant of access.

(6) Each user shall be assigned a unique user ID. Adequate user education shall be provided to help users in password choice and password protection. Sharing of user IDs shall not be allowed.

(7) Stored passwords shall be encrypted using internationally proven encryption techniques to prevent unauthorised disclosure and modification.

(8) Stored passwords shall be protected by access controls from unauthorised disclosure and modification.

(9) Automatic time-out for terminal inactivity should be implemented.

(10) Audit trail of security-sensitive access and actions taken shall be logged.

(11) All forms of audit trail shall be appropriately protected against unauthorised modification or deletion.

(12) Where a second level access control is implemented through the application system, password controls similar to those implemented for the computer system shall be in place.

(13) Activities of all remote users shall be logged and monitored closely.

(14) The facility to login as another user from one user's login shall be denied. However, the system should prohibit direct login as a trusted user (e.g. root in Unix, administrator in Windows NT or Windows 2000). This means that there must be a user account configured for the trusted administrator. The system requires trusted users to change their effective username to gain access to root and to re-authenticate themselves before requesting acces to privileged functions.

(15) The startup and shutdown procedure of the security software must be automated.

(16) Sensitive Operating System files, which are more

prone to hackers must be protected against all known attacks using proven tools and techniques, That is to say no user will be able to modify them except with the permission of System Administrator.

3. Password Management

(1) Certain minimum quality standards for password shall be enforced. The quality level shall be increased progressively. The following control features shall be implemented for passwords:

(i) Minimum of eight characters without leading or trailing blanks;

(ii) Shall be different from the existing password and the two previous ones;

(iii) Shall be changed at least once every ninety days; for sensitive system, password shall be changed at least once every thirty days; and

(iv) Shall not be shared, displayed or printed.

(2) Password retries shall be limited to a maximum of three attempted logons after which the user ID shall then be revoked; for sensitive systems, the number of password retries should be limited to a maximum of two.

(3) Passwords which are easy-to-guess (e.g. user name, birth date, month, standard words etc.) should be avoided.

(4) Initial or reset passwords must be changed by the user upon first use.

(5) Passwords shall always be encrypted in storage to prevent unauthorized disclosure.

(6) All passwords used must be resistant to dictionary

attacks and all known, password cracking algorithms.

4. *Privileged User's Management*

(1) System privileges shall be granted to users only on a need-to-use basis.

(2) Login privileges for highly privileged accounts should be available only from Console and terminals situated within Console room.

(3) An audit trail of activities conducted by highly privileged users shall be maintained for two years and reviewed periodically at least every week by operator who is independent of System Administrator.

(4) Privileged user shall not be allowed to log in to the computer system from remote terminal. The usage of the computer system by the privileged user shall be allowed during a certain time period.

(5) Separate user IDs shall be allowed to the user for performing privileged and normal (non-privileged) activities.

(6) The use of user IDs for emergency use shall be recorded and approved. The passwords shall be reset after use.

5. *User's Account Management*

(1) Procedures for user account management shall be established to control access to application systems and data. The procedures shall include the following:

(i) Users shall be authorised by the computer system owner to access the computer services.

(ii) A written statement of access rights shall be given to all users.

(iii) All users shall be required to sign an undertaking to acknowledge that they understand the conditions of access.

(iv) Where access to computer services is administered by service providers, ensure that the service providers do not provide access until the authorization procedures have been completed. This includes the acknowledgement of receipt of the accounts by the users.

(v) A formal record of all registered users of the computer services shall be maintained.

(vi) Access rights of users who have been transferred, or left the organisation shall be removed immediately.

(vii) A periodic check shall be carried out for redundant user accounts and access rights that are no longer required.

(viii) Ensure that redundant user accounts are not re-issued to another user.

(2) User accounts shall be suspended under the following conditions:

(i) when an individual is on extended leave or inactive use of over thirty days. In case of protected computer system, the limit of thirty days may be reduced to fifteen days by the System Administrator.

(ii) immediately upon the termination of the services of an individual.

(iii) suspended or inactive accounts shall be deleted after a two months period. In case of protected computer systems, the limit of two months may be reduced to one month.

6. Data and Resource Protection

(1) All information assets shall be assigned an "owner" responsible for the integrity of that data/resource. Custodians shall be assigned and shall be jointly responsible for information assets by providing computer controls to assist owners.

(2) The operating system or security system of the computer system shall:

(i) Define user authority and enforce access control to data within the computer system;

(ii) Be capable of specifying, for each named individual, a list of named data objects (e.g. file, programme) or groups of named objects, and the type of access allowed.

(3) For networked or shared computer systems, system users shall be limited to a profile of data objects required to perform their needed tasks.

(4) Access controls for any data and/or resources shall be determined as part of the systems analysis and design process.

(5) Application Programmer shall not be allowed to access the production system.

7. Sensitive Systems Protection

(1) Security tokens/smart cards/bio-metric technologies such as Iris recognition, finger print verification technologies etc. shall be used to complement the usage of passwords to access the computer system.

(2) For computer system processing sensitive data, access by other organisations shall be prohibited or strictly controlled.

(3) For sensitive data, encryption of data in storage shall be considered to protect its confidentiality and integrity.

8. Data Centre Operations Security

1. Job Scheduling

(1) Procedures shall be established to ensure that all changes to the job schedules are appropriately approved. The authority to approve changes to job schedules shall be clearly assigned.

(2) As far as possible, automated job scheduling should be used. Manual job scheduling should require prior approval from the competent authority.

2. *System Operations Procedure*

(1) Procedures shall be established to ensure that only authorised and correct job stream and parameter changes are made.

(2) Procedures shall be established to maintain logs of system activities. Such logs shall be reviewed by a competent independent party for indications of dubious activities. Appropriate retention periods shall be set for such logs.

(3) Procedures shall be established to ensure that people other than well-trained computer operators are prohibited from operating the computer equipment.

(4) Procedures shall be implemented to ensure the secure storage or distribution of all outputs/ reports, in accordance with procedures defined by the owners for each system.

3. *Media Management*

(1) Responsibilities for media library management

and protection shall be clearly defined and assigned.

(2) All media containing sensitive data shall be stored in a locked room or cabinets, which must be fire resistant and free of toxic chemicals.

(3) Access to the media library (both on-site and off-site) shall be restricted to the authorized persons only. A list of personnel authorised to enter the library shall be maintained.

(4) The media containing sensitive and back up data must be stored at three different physical location in the country, which can be reached in few hours.

(5) A media management system shall be in place to account for all media stored on-site and off-site.

(6) All incoming/outgoing media transfers shall be authorised by management and users.

(7) An independent physical inventory check of all media shall be conducted at least every six months.

(8) All media shall have external volume identification. Internal labels shall be fixed, where available.

(9) Procedures shall be in place to ensure that only authorised addition/removal of media from the library is allowed.

(10) Media retention periods shall be established and approved by management in accordance with legal regulatory and user requirements.

4. Media Movement

(1) Proper records of all movements of computer

tapes/disks between on-site and off-site media library must be maintained.

(2) There shall be procedures to ensure the authorized and secure transfer to media to/from external parties and the off-site location. A means to authenticate the receipt shall be in place.

(3) Computer media that are being transported to off-site data backup locations should be stored in locked carrying cases that provide magnetic field protection and protection from impact while loading and unloading and during transportation.

9. Data Backup and Off-site Retention

(1) Back-up procedures shall be documented, scheduled and monitored.

(2) Up-to-date backups of all critical items shall be maintained to ensure the continued provision of the minimum essential level of service. These items include:

(i) Data flies

(ii) Utilities programmer

(iii) Databases

(iv) Operating system software

(v) Applications system software

(vi) Encryption keys

(vii) Pre-printed forms

(viii) Documentation (including a copy of the business continuity plans)

(3) One set of the original disks for all operating system and application software must be maintained ensure that a valid, virus-free backup exists and is available for use at any time.

(4) Backups of the system, application and data shall be performed on a regular basis. Backups should also be made for application under development and data conversion efforts.

(5) Data backup is required for all systems including personal computers, servers and distributed systems and databases.

(6) Critical system data and file server software must have full backups taken weekly.

(7) The backups must be kept in an area physically separate from the server. If critical system data on the LAN represents unique versions of the information assets, then the information backups must be rotated on a periodic basis to an off-site storage location.

(8) Critical system data and file server software must have incremental backups taken daily.

(9) Systems that are completely static may not require periodic backup, but shall be backed up after changes or updates in the information.

(10) Each LAN/system should have a primary and backup operator to ensure continuity of business operations.

(11) The business recovery plan should be prepared and tested on an annual basis.

10. Audit Trails and Verification

(1) Transactions that meet exception criteria shall be completely and accurately highlighted and reviewed by personnel independent of those that initiate the transaction.

(2) Adequate audit trails shall be captured and certain information needed to determine sensitive events

and pattern -analysis that would indicate possible fraudulent use of the system (e.g. repeated unsuccessful logons, access attempts over a series of days) shall be analyzed. This information includes such information as who, what, when, where, and any special information such as:

(i) Success or failure of the event

(ii) Use of authentication keys, where applicable

(3) Automated or manual procedures shall be used to monitor and promptly report all significant security events, such as accesses, which are out-of-pattern relative to time, volume, frequency, type of information asset, and redundancy. Other areas of analysis include:

(i) Significant computer system events (e.g. configuration updates, system crashes),

(ii) Security profile changes.

(iii) Actions taken by computer operations, system administrators, system programmers, and/or security administrators.

(4) The real time clock of the computer system shall be set accurately to ensure the accuracy of audit logs, which may be required for investigations or as evidence in legal or disciplinary cases.

(5) The real time clock of the computer or communications device shall be set to Indian Standard Time (IST). Further there shall be a procedure that checks and corrects drift in the real time clock.

(6) Computer system access records shall be kept for a minimum of two years, in either hard copy or electronic form. Records, which are of legal

nature and necessary for any legal or regulation requirement or investigation of criminal behaviour, shall be retained as per laws of the land.

(7) Computer records of applications transactions and significant events must be retained for a minimum period of two years or longer depending on specific record retention requirements.

11. Measures to Handle Computer Virus

(1) Responsibilities and duties shall be assigned to ensure that all file servers and personal computers are equipped with up-to-date virus protection and detection software.

(2) Virus detection software must be used to check storage drives both internal and external to the system on a periodic basis.

(3) All diskettes and software shall be screened and verified by virus detection software before being loaded onto the computer system. No magnetic media like tape cartridge, floppies etc. brought from outside shall be used on the data, file, PKI or computer server or personal computer on Intranet and Internet without proper screening and verification by virus detection software.

(4) A team shall be designated to deal with reported or suspected incidents of computer virus. The designated team shall ensure that latest version of anti-virus software is loaded on all data file, PKI servers and personal computers.

(5) Procedures shall be established to limit the spread of viruses to other organization information assets. Such procedures *inter alia* shall include:

(i) Communication to other business partners and users who may be at risk from an infected resource

(ii) Eradication and recovery procedures

(iii) Incident report must be documented and communicated per established procedures.

(6) An awareness and training programme shall be established to communicate virus protection practices, available controls, areas of high risk to virus infection and responsibilities.

Relocation of Hardware and Software

Whenever computers or computer peripherals are relocated (e.g. for maintenance, installation at different sites or storage), the following guidelines shall apply:

(i) All removable media will be removed from the computer system and kept at secure location.

(ii) Internal drives will be overwritten, reformatted or removed as the situation may be.

(iii) If applicable, ribbons will be removed from printers.

(iv) All paper will be removed from printers.

Hardware and Software Maintenance

Whenever, the hardware and software maintenance of the computer or computer network is being carried out, the following should be considered:

(1) Proper placement and installation of Information Technology equipment to reduce the effects of interference due to electromagnetic emanations.

(2) Maintenance of an inventory and configuration chart of hardware.

(3) Identification and use of security features implemented within hardware.

(4) Authorization, documentation, and control of change made to the hardware.

(5) Identification of support facilities including power and air conditioning.

(6) Provision of an uninterruptible power supply.

(7) Maintenance of equipment and services.

(8) Organisation must make proper arrangements for maintenance of computer hardware, software (both system and application) and firmware installed and used by them. It shall be the responsibility of the officer in charge of the operational site to ensure that contract for annual maintenance of hardware is always in place.

(9) Organisation must enter into maintenance agreements, if necessary, with the supplier of computer and communication hardware, software (both system and application) and firmware.

(10) Maintenance personnel will sign non-disclosure agreements.

(11) The identities of all hardware and software vendor maintenance staff should be verified before allowing them to carry out maintenance work.

(12) All maintenance personnel should be escorted within the operational site/computer system and network installation room by the authorized personnel of the organisation.

(13) After maintenance, any exposed security parameters such as passwords, user IDs, and accounts will be changed or reset to eliminate any potential security exposures.

(14) If the computer system, computer network or any of its devices is vulnerable to computer viruses as a result of performing maintenance, system managers or users shall scan the computer system and its devices and any media affected for viruses as a result of maintenance.

Purchase and Licensing of Hardware and Software

(1) Hardware and software products that contain or are to be used to enforce security, and intended for use or interface into any organisation system or network, must be verified to comply with these Information Technology Security Guidelines prior to the signing of any contract, purchase or lease.

(2) Software, which is capable of bypassing or modifying the security system or operating system, integrity features, must be verified to determine that they conform to these Information Technology Security Guidelines. Where such compliance is not possible, then procedures shall be in place to ensure that the implementation and operation of that software does not compromise the security of the system.

(3) There shall be procedures to identify, select, implement and control software (system and application software) acquisition and installation to ensure compliance with the Indian Copyright Act and Information Technology Security Guidelines.

(4) It is prohibited to knowingly install on any system whether test or production, any software which is not licensed for use on the specific systems or networks.

(5) No software will be installed and used on the system when appropriate licensing agreements do not exist, except during evaluation periods for which the user has documented permission to install and test the software under evaluation.

(6) Illegally acquired or unauthorized software must not be used on any computer, computer network or data communication equipment. In the event that any illegally acquired or unauthorized software is detected by the System Administrator or Network Administrator, the same must be removed immediately.

System Software

(1) All system software options and parameters shall be reviewed and approved by the management.

(2) System software shall be comprehensively tested and its security functionality validated prior to implementation.

(3) All vendor supplied default user IDs shall be deleted or password changed before allowing users to access the computer system.

(4) Versions of system software installed on the computer system and communication devices shall be regularly updated.

(5) All changes proposed in the system software must be appropriately justified and approved by an authorised party.

(6) A log of all changes to system software shall be maintained, completely documented and tested to ensure the desired results.

(7) Procedures to control changes initiated by vendors shall be in accordance with para 21 pertaining to "Change Management".

(8) There shall be no standing "Write" access to the system libraries."All "Write" access shall be logged and reviewed by the System Administrator for dubious activities.

(9) System Programmers shall not be allowed to have access to the application system's data and programme files in the production environment.

(10) Procedures to control the use of sensitive system utilities and system programmes that could-bypass intended security controls shall be in place and documented. All usage shall be logged and reviewed by the System Administrator and another person independent of System Administrator for dubious activities.

Documentation Security

(1) All documentation pertaining to application software and sensitive system software and changes made therein shall be updated to the current time, accurately and stored securely. An up-to-date inventory list of all documentation shall be maintained to ensure control and accountability.

(2) All documentation and subsequent changes shall be reviewed and approved by an independent authorised party prior to issue.

(3) Access to application software documentation and sensitive system software documentation shall be restricted to authorised personnel on a "need-to-use" basis only.

(4) Adequate backups of all documentation shall be maintained and a copy of all critical documentation and manuals shall be stored off-site.

(5) Documentation shall be classified according to the sensitivity of its contents/implications.

(6) Organisations shall adopt a clean desk policy for papers, diskettes and other documentation in order to reduce the risk of unauthorised access, loss of and damage to information outside normal working hours.

Network Communication Security

(1) All sensitive information on the network shall be protected by using appropriate techniques. The critical network devices such as routers, switches and modems should be protected from physical damage.

(2) The network configuration and inventories shall be documented and maintained.

(3) Prior authorization of the Network Administrator shall be obtained for making any changes to the network configuration. The changes made in the network configuration shall be documented. The threat and risk assessment of the network after changes in the network configuration shall be reviewed. The network operation shall be monitored for any security irregularity. A formal procedure should be in place for identifying and resolving security problems.

(4) Physical access to communications and network sites shall be controlled and restricted to authorized individuals only in accordance with para 6.4 pertaining to "Physical Access".

(5) Communication and network systems shall be controlled and restricted to authorized individuals only in accordance with para 6.2 - System Access Control.

(6) As far as possible, transmission medium within the Certifying Authority's operational site should be secured against electro magnetic transmission. In this regard, use of Optical Fibre Cable and armoured cable may be preferred as transmission media as the case may be.

(7) Network diagnostic tools, e.g., spectrum analyzer, protocol analyzer should be used on a need basis.

Firewalls

(1) Intelligent devices generally known as "Firewalls" shall be used to isolate organisation's data network with the external network. Firewall device should also be used to limit network connectivity for unauthorized use.

(2) Networks that operate at varying security levels shall be isolated from each other by appropriate firewalls. The internal network of the organization shall be physically and logically isolated from the Internet and any other external connection by a firewall.

(3) All firewalls shall be subjected to thorough test for vulnerability prior to being put to use and at least half-yearly thereafter.

(4) All web servers for access by Internet users shall be isolated from other data and host servers.

Connectivity

(1) Organisation shall establish procedure for allowing connectivity of their computer network or computer system to non-organisation computer system or networks. The permission to connect other networks and computer system shall be

approved by the Network Administrator and documented.

(2) All unused connections and network segments should be disconnected from active networks. The computer system/personal computer or outside terminal accessing an organisation's host system must adhere to the general system security and access control guidelines.

(3) The suitability of new hardware/software particularly the protocol compatibility should be assessed before connecting the same to the organisation's network.

(4) As far as possible, no Internet access should be allowed to database server/file server or server hosting sensitive data.

(5) The level of protection for communication and network resources should be commensurate with the criticality and sensitivity of the data transmitted.

Network Administrator

(1) Each organization shall designate a properly trained "Network Administrator" who will be responsible for operation, monitoring security and functioning of the network.

(2) Network Administrator shall regularly undertake the review of network and also take adequate measures to provide physical, logical and procedural safeguards for its security. Appropriate follow up of any unusual activity or pattern of access on the computer network shall be investigated promptly by the Network Administrator.

(3) System must include a mechanism for alerting the Network Administrator of possible breaches in security, e.g., unauthorized access, virus infection and hacking.

(4) Secure Network Management System should be implemented to monitor functioning of the computer network. Broadcast of network traffic should be minimized.

(5) Only authorized and legal software shall be used on the network.

(6) Shared computer systems, network devices used for business applications shall comply with the requirement established in para 6 — System Integrity and Security Measures.

Change Management

1. Change Control

(1) Procedures for tracking and managing changes in application software, system software, hardware and data in the production system shall be established. Organisational responsibilities for the change management process shall be defined and assigned.

(2) A risk and impact analysis, classification and prioritisation process shall be established.

(3) No changes to a production system shall be implemented until such changes have been formally authorised. Authorisation procedures for change control shall be defined and documented.

(4) Owners/Users shall be notified of all changes made to production system which may affect the processing of information on the said production system.

(5) Fall-back procedures in the event of a failure in the implementation of the change process shall be established and documented.

(6) Procedures to protect, control access and changes to production source code, data, execution statements and relevant system documentation shall be documented and implemented.

(7) Version changes of application software and all system software installed on the computer systems and all communication devices shall be documented. Different versions of application software and I system software must be kept in safe custody.

2. Testing of Changes to-Production System

(1) All changes in computer resource proposed in the production system shall be tesled and thc test results shall be reviewed and accepted by all concerned parties prior to implementation.

(2) All user acceptance tests in respect of changes in computer resource in production system shall be performed in a controlled environment which includes: (i) Test objectives, (ii) A documented test plan, and (iii) acceptance criteria.

3. Review of Changes

(1) Procedures shall be established for an independent review of programme changes before they are moved into a production environment to detect unauthorised or malicious codes.

(2) Procedures shall be established to schedule and review the implementation of the changes in computer resource in the production system so as to ensure proper functioning.

(3) All emergency changes/fixes in computer resource in the production system shall be reviewed and approved.

(4) Periodic management reports on the status of the changes implemented in the computer resource in the production system shall be submitted for management review.

Problem Management and Reporting

(1) Procedures for identifying, reporting and resolving problems, such as non-functioning of Certifying Authority's system; breaches in Information Technology security; and hacking, shall be established and communicated to all personnel concerned. It shall include emergency procedures. Periodic reports shall be submitted for management review.

(2) A help desk shall be set up to assist users in the resolution of problems.

(3) A system for recording, tracking and reporting the status of reported problems shall be established to ensure that they are promptly managed and resolved with minimal impact on the user of the computing resources.

Emergency Preparedness

(1) Emergency response procedures for all activities connected with computer operation shall be developed and documented. These procedures should be reviewed periodically.

(2) Emergency drills should be held periodically to ensure that the documented emergency procedures are effective.

Contingency Recovery: Equipment and Services

(1) Commitment shall be obtained in writing from computer equipment and supplies vendors to replace critical equipment and supplies within a specified period of time following a destruction of the computing facility.

(2) The business continuity plan shall be developed which *inter alia* include the procedures for emergency ordering of the equipment and availability of the services.

(3) The need for backup hardware and other peripherals should be evaluated in accordance to business needs.

Security Incident Reporting and Response

(1) All security related incidents must be reported to a central coordinator, appointed by the management to coordinate and handle security related incidents. This central coordinator shall be the single point of contact at the organisation.

(2) All incidents reported, actions taken, follow-up actions, and other related in formation shall be documented.

(3) Procedures shall be defined for dealing with all security related incidents, including malicious software, break-ins from networks, software bugs which compromised the security of the system.

Disaster Recovery/Management

(1) Disaster recovery plan shall be developed, properly documented, tested and maintained to ensure that in the event of a failure of the information system or destruction of the facility, essential level of service will be provided. The

disaster recovery framework should include:

(a) emergency procedures, describing the immediate action to be taken in case of a major incident

(b) fall back procedure, describing the actions to be taken to relocate essential activities or support services to a backup site

(c) restoration procedures, describing the action to be taken to return to normal operation at the original site

(2) The documentation should include:

(a) definition of a disaster;

(b) condition for activating the plan;

(c) stages of a crisis;

(d) who will make decisions in the crisis;

(e) role of individuals for each component of the plan;

(f) composition of the recovery team; and

(g) decision making process for return to normal operation.

(3) Specific disaster management plan for critical applications shall be developed, documented, tested and maintained on a regular basis.

(4) Responsibilities and reporting structure shall be clearly defined which will take effect immediately on the declaration of a disaster.

(5) Each component/aspect of the plan should have a person and a backup assigned to its execution.

(6) Periodic training of personnel and users associated with computer system and network should be conducted defining their roles and responsibilities in the event of a disaster.

(7) Test plan shall be developed, documented and maintained. Periodic tests shall be carried out to test the effectiveness of the procedures in the plan. The results of the tests shall be documented for management review.

(8) Disaster recovery plan should be updated regularly to ensure its continuing effectiveness.

SCHEDULE-III

[See rule 19(2)]

Security Guidelines for Certifying Authorities

Introduction

This document prescribes security guidelines for the management and operation of Certifying Authorities (CAs), and is aimed at protecting the integrity, confidentiality and availability of their services, data and systems. These guidelines apply to Certifying Authories that perform all the functions associated with generation, issue and management of Digital Signature Certificate such as:

(1) Verification of registration, suspension and revocation request;

(2) Generation, issuance, suspension and revocation of Digital Signature Certificates; and

(3) Publication and archival of Digital Signature Certificates, suspension and revocation of information.

Security Management

The Certifying Authority shall define Information Technology security policies for its operation on the lines defined in Schedule-II and Schedule-Ill. The policy shall be communicated to all personnel and widely published throughout the organisation to ensure that the personnel follow the policies.

Physical Controls—Site Location, Construction and Physical Access

(1) The site location, design, construction and physical security of the operational site of Certifying Authority shall be in accordance with para 4 of the Information Technology Security Guidelines given at Schedule-II.

(2) Physical access to the operational site housing computer servers, PKI server, communications and network devices shall be controlled and restricted to the authorized individuals only in accordance with para 4.4 of the Information Technology Security Guidelines given at Schedule-II.

(3) A Certifying Authority must:

(i) ensure that the operational site housing PKI servers, communications and networks is protected with fire suppression system in accordance with para 4.2 of the Information Technology Security Guidelines given at Schedule-II.

(ii) ensure that power and air-conditioning facilities are installed in accordance with para 1 of the Information Technology Security Guidelines given at Schedule-H.

(iii) ensure that all removable media and papers containing sensitive or plain text information are listed, documented and stored in a container properly identified.

(iv) ensure unescorted access to Certifying Authority's server is limited to those personnel identified on an access list.

(v) ensure that the exact location of Digital

Signature Certification System shall not be publicly identified.

(vi) ensure that access security system is installed to control and audit access to the Digital Signature Certification System.

(vii) ensure that dual control over the inventory and access cards/keys are in place.

(viii) ensure that up-to-date list of personnel who possess the access cards/keys is maintained at the Certifying Authority's operational site. Loss of access cards/keys shall be reported immediately to the Security Administrator; who shall take appropriate actions to prevent unauthorised access.

(ix) ensure personnel not on the access list are properly escorted and supervised.

(x) ensure a site access log is maintained at the Certifying Authority's operational site and inspected periodically.

(4) Multi-tiered access mechanism must be installed at the Certifying Authority's operational site. The facility should have clearly laid out security zones within its facility with well-defined access rights to each security zone. Each security zone must be separated from the other by floor to ceiling concrete reinforced walls. Alarm and intrusion detection system must be installed at every stage with adequate power backup capable of continuing operation even in the event of loss of main power. Electrical/Electronic circuits to external security alarm monitoring service (if used) must be supervised. No single person must have complete access to PKI Server, root keys or any computer system or network device

on his/her own.

(5) Entrance to the main building where the Certifying Authority's facilities such as Data Centre, PKI Server and Network devices are housed and entrance to each security zone must be video recorded round the clock. The recording should be carefully scrutinized and maintained for at least one year.

(6) A Certifying Authority site must be manually or electronically monitored for unauthorised intrusion at all times in accordance with the Information Technology Security Guidelines given at Schedule-II.

(7) Computer System/PKI Server performing Digital Signature Certification function shall be located in a dedicated room or partition to facilitate enforcement of physical access control. The entry and exit of the said room or partition shall be automatically locked with time stamps and shall be reviewed daily by the Security Administrator.

(8) Access to infrastructure components essential to operation of Certifying Authority such as power control panels, communication infrastructure, Digital Signature Certification system, cabling, etc., shall be restricted to authorised personnel.

(9) By-pass or deactivation of normal physical security arrangements shall be authorised and documented by security personnel.

(10) Intrusion detection systems shall be used to monitor and record physical access to the Digital Signature Certification system during and after office hours.

(11) Computer System or PKI Server performing the Digital Signature Certification functions shall be dedicated to those functions and should not be used for any other purposes.

(12) System software shall be verified for integrity in accordance with para 15 of the Information Technology Security Guidelines given at Schedule-II.

Media Storage

A Certifying Authority must ensure that storage media used by his system are protected from environment threats such as temperature, humidity and magnetic and are transported and managed in accordance with para 8.3 and para 8.4 of the Information Technology Security Guidelines given at Schedule-II.

Waste Disposal

All media used for storage of information pertaining to all functions associated with generation, production, issue and management of Digital Signature Certificate shall be scrutinized before being destroyed or released for disposal.

Off-site Backup

A Certifying Authority must ensure that facility used for off-site backup, if any, shall be within the country and shall have the same level of security as the primary Certifying Authority site.

Change and Configuration Management

(1) The components of the Certifying Authority infrastructure (e.g. cryptographic algorithm and its key parameters, operating system, system software, computer system, PKI server, firewalls,

physical security, system security etc.) shall be reviewed every year for new technology risks and appropriate action plan shall be developed to manage the disks identified for each component.

(2) The application software, system software and hardware, which are procured from questionable sources, shall not be installed and used for any function associated with generation and management of Digital Signature Certificate.

(3) Software updates and patches shall be reviewed for security implications before being implemented on Certifying Authority's system.

(4) Software updates and patches to rectify security vulnerability in critical systems used for Certifying Authority's operation shall be promptly reviewed and implemented.

(5) Information on the software updates and patches and their implementation on Certifying Authority's system shall be clearly and properly documented.

Network and Communications Security

(1) Certifying Authority's systems shall be protected to ensure network access control to critical systems and services from other systems in accordance with para 17 para 18, para 19 and para 20 of the Information Technology Security Guidelines given at Schedule-II.

(2) Network connections from the Certifying Authority's system to external networks shall be restricted to only those connections which are essential to facilitate Certifying Authority's functional processes and services. Such network

connections to the external network shall be properly secured and monitored regularly.

(3) Network connections should be initiated by the systems performing the functions of generation and management of Digital Signature Certificate to connect those systems performing the registration and repository functions but not vice versa. If this is not possible, compensating controls (e.g. use of proxy servers) shall be implemented to protect the systems performing the function of generation and management of Digital Signature Certificate from potential attacks.

(4) Systems performing the Digital Signature Certification function should be isolated to minimise their exposure to attempts to compromise the confidentiality, integrity and availability of the certification function.

(5) Communication between the Certifying Authority systems connected on a network shall be secure to ensure confidentiality and integrity of the information. For example, communications between the Certifying Authority's systems connected on a network should be encrypted and digitally signed.

(6) Intrusion detection tools should be deployed to monitor critical networks and perimeter networks and alert administrators of network intrusions and penetration attempts in a timely manner.

System Security Audit Procedures

1. Types of Event Recorded

(1) The Certifying Authority shall maintain record of all events relating to the security of his system.

The records should be maintained in audit log file and shall include such events as:

(i) System start-up and shutdown;

(ii) Certifying Authority's application start-up and shutdown;

(iii) Attempts to create, remove, set passwords or change the system privileges of the PKI Master Officer, PKI Officer, or PKI Administrator;

(iv) Changes to keys of the Certifying Authority or any of his other details;

(v) Changes to Digital Signature Certificate creation policies, e.g. validity period;

(vi) Login and logoff attempts;

(vii) Unauthorised attempts at network access to the Certifying Authority's system;

(viii) Unauthorised attempts to access system files;

(ix) Generation of own keys;

(x) Creation and revocation of Digital Signature Certificates;

(xi) Attempts to initialize remove, enable, and disable subscribers, and update and recover their keys;

(xii) Failed read-and-write operations on the Digital Signature Certificate and Certificate Revocation List (CRL) directory.

(2) Monitoring and Audit Logs

(i) A Certifying Authority should consider the use of automated security management and monitoring tools providing an integrated view of the security situation at any point in time. Records of the following application transactions shall be maintained:

(a) Registration;

(b) Certification;

(c) Publication;

(d) Suspension; and

(e) Revocation.

(ii) Records and log files shall be reviewed regularly for the following activities:

(a) Misuse;

(b) Errors;

(c) Security violations;

(d) Execution of privileged functions;

(e) Change in access control lists;

(f) Change in system configuration.

(3) All logs, whether maintained through electronic or manual means, should contain the date and time of the event, and the identity of the subscriber/subordinate/entity which caused the event.

(4) A Certifying Authority should also collect and consolidate, either electronically or manually, security information which may not be generated by his system, such as:

(i) Physical access logs;

(ii) System configuration changes and maintenance;

(iii) Personnel changes;

(iv) Discrepancy and compromise reports;

(v) Records of the destruction of media containing key material, activation data, or personal subscriber information.

(5) To facilitate decision-making, all agreements and correspondence relating to services provided by Certifying Authority should be collected and consolidated, either electronically or manually, at a single location.

2. Frequency of Audit Log Monitoring

The Certifying Authority must ensure that its audit logs are reviewed by its personnel at least once every two weeks and all significant events are detailed in an audit log summary. Such reviews should involve verifying that the log has not been tampered with, and then briefly inspecting all log entries, with a more thorough investigation of any alerts or irregularities in the logs. Action taken following these reviews must be documented.

3. Retention Period for Audit Log

The Certifying Authority must retain its audit logs onsite for at least twelve months and subsequently retain them in the manner described in para 10 of the Information Technology Security Guidelines as given in Schedule-II.

4 Protection of Audit Log

The electronic audit log system must include mechanisms to protect the log files from unauthorized viewing, modification, and deletion.

Manual audit information must be protected from unauthorised viewing, modification and destruction.

5. Audit Log Backup Procedures

Audit logs and audit summaries must be backed up or copied if in manual form.

6. Vulnerability Assessments

Events in the audit process are logged, in part, to monitor system vulnerabilities. The Certifying Authority must ensure that a vulnerability assessment is performed, reviewed and revised, if necessary, following an examination of these monitored events.

Records Archival

(1) Digital Signature Certificates stored and generated by the Certifying Authority must be retained for at least seven year after the date of its expiration. This requirement does not include the backup of private signature keys.

(2) Audit information as detailed in para 9, subscriber agreements, verification, identification and authentication information in respect of subscriber shall be retained for at least seven years.

(3) A second copy of all information retained or backed up must be stored at three locations within the country including the Certifying Authority site and must be protected either by physical security alone, or a combination of physical and cryptographic protection. These secondary sites must provide adequate protection from environmental threats such as temperature, humidity and magnetism. The secondary site should be reachable in few hours.

(4) All information pertaining to Certifying Authority's operation, Subscriber's application, verification, identification, authentication and Subscriber agreement shall be stored within the country. This information shall be taken out of the country only with the permission of Controller and where a properly constitutional warrant or such other legally enforceable document is produced.

(5) The Certifying Authority should verify the

integrity of the backups at least once every six months.

(6) Information stored off-site must be periodically verified for data integrity.

Compromise and Disaster Recovery

1. Computing Resources, Software and/or Data are Corrupted

The Certifying Authority must establish business continuity procedures that outline the steps to be taken in the event of the corruption or loss of computing and networking resources, nominated website, repository, software and/or data. Where a repository is not under the control of the Certifying Authority, the Certifying Authority must ensure that any agreement with the repository provides for business continuity procedures.

2. Secure Facility after a Natural or Other Type of Disaster

The Certifying Authority must establish a disaster recovery plan outlining the steps to be taken to re-establish a secure facility in the event of a natural or other type of disaster. Where a repository is not under the control of the Certifying Authority, the Certifying Authority must ensure that any agreement with the repository provides that a disaster recovery plan be established and documented by the repository.

3. Incident Management Plan

An incident management plan shall be developed and approved by the management. The plan shall include the following areas:

(i) Certifying Authority's certification key compromise;

(ii) Hacking of systems and network;

(iii) Breach of physical security;
(iv) Infrastructure availability;
(v) Fraudulent registration and generation of Digital Signature Certificates; and
(vi) Digital Signature Certificate suspension and revocation information.

An incident response action plan shall be established to ensure the readiness of the Certifying Authority to respond to incidents. The plan should include the following areas:

(i) Compromise control;
(ii) Notification to user community; (if applicable)
(iii) Revocation of affected Digital Signature Certificates; (if applicable)
(iv) Responsibilities of personnel handling incidents;
(v) Investigation of service disruption;
(vi) Service restoration procedure;
(vii) Monitoring and audit trail analysis; and
(viii) Media and public relations.

Number of Persons Required Per Task

The Certifying Authority must ensure that no single individual may gain access to the Digital Signature Certificate server and the computer server maintaining all information associated with generation, issue and management of Digital Signature Certificate and private keys of the Certifying Authority. Minimum two individuals, preferably using a split-knowledge technique, such as twin passwords, must perform any operation associated with generation, issue and management of Digital Signature Certificate and application of private key of the Certifying Authority.

Identification and Authentication for Each Role

All Certifying Authority personnel must have their identity and authorization verified before they are:

(i) included in the access list for the Certifying Authority's site;

(ii) included in the access list for physical access to the Certifying Authority's system;

(iii) given a certificate for the performance of their Certifying Authority role;

(iv) given an account on the PKI system.

Each of these certificates and accounts (with the exception of Certifying Authority's signing certificates) must:

(i) be directly attributable to an individual

(ii) not be shared;

(iii) be restricted to actions authorized for that role; and

(iv) procedural controls.

Certifying Authority's operations must be secured using techniques of authentication and encryption, when accessed across-a shared network.

Personnel Security Controls

The Certifying Authority must ensure that all personnel performing duties with respect to its operation must:

(i) be appointed in writing;

(ii) be bound by contract or statute to the terms and conditions of the position they are to fill;

(iii) have received comprehensive training with respect to the duties they are to perform;

(iv) be bound by statute or contract not to disclose sensitive Certifying Authority's security related information or subscriber information;

(v) not be assigned duties that may cause a conflict of interest with their Certifying Authority's duties: and

(vi) be aware and trained in the relevant aspects of the Information Technology Security Policy and Security Guidelines framed for carrying out Certifying Authority's operation.

Training Requirements

A Certifying Authority shall ensure that all personnel performing duties with respect to its operation, must receive comprehensive training in:

(i) relevant aspects of the Information Technology Security Policy and Security Guidelines framed by the Certifying Authority;

(ii) all PKI software versions in use on the Certifying Authority's system;

(iii) all PKI duties they are expected to perform; and

(iv) disaster recovery and business continuity procedures.

Retraining Frequency and Requirements

The requirements of para 15 must be kept current to accommodate changes in the Certifying Authority's system. Refresher training must be conducted as and when required, and the Certifying Authority must review these requirements at least once a year.

Documentation Supplied to Personnel

A Certifying Authority must make available to his personnel the Digital Signature Certificate policies it supports, its Certification Practice Statement, Information Technology Security Policy and any specific statutes, policies or contracts relevant to their position.

Key Management

1. Generation

(1) The subscribers key pair shall be generated by the subscriber or on a key generation system in the presence of the subscriber.

(2) The key generation process shall generate statistically random key values that are resistant to known attacks.

2. Distribution of Keys

Keys shall be transferred from the key generation system to the storage device (if the keys are not stored on the key generation system) using a secure mechanism that ensures confidentiality and integrity.

3. Storage

(1) Certifying Authority's keys shall be stored in tamper-resistant devices and can only be activated under split-control by parties who are not involved in the set-up and maintenance of the systems and operations of the Certifying Authority. The key of the Certifying Authority may be stored in a tamper-resistant cryptographic module or split into sub-keys stored in tamper-resistant devices under the custody of the key custodians.

(2) The Certifying Authority's key custodians shall ensure that the Certifying Authority's key component or the activation code is always under his sole custody. Change of key custodians shall be approved by the Certifying Authority's management and documented.

4. Usage

(1) A system and software integrity check shall be performed prior to Certifying Authority's key loading.

(2) Custody of and access to the Certifying Authority's keys shall be under split control. In particular, Certifying Authority's key loading shall be performed under split control.

5. Certifying Authority's Public Key Delivery to Users

The Certifying Authority's, public verification key must be delivered to the prospective Digital Signature Certificate holder in an on-line transaction in accordance with PKIX-3 Certificate Management Protocol, or via an equally secure manner.

Private Key Protection and Backup

(1) The Certifying Authority must protect its private, keys from disclosure.

(2) The Certifying Authority must back-up its private keys. Backed-up keys must be stored in encrypted form and protected at a level no lower than those followed for storing the primary version of the key.

(3) The Certifying Authority's private key backups should be stored in a secure storage facility, away from where the original key is stored.

Method of Destroying Private Key

Upon termination of use of a private key, all copies of the private key in computer memory and shared disk space must be securely destroyed by over-writing. Private key destruction procedures must be described in the Certification Practice Statement or other publicly available document.

Usage Periods for the Public and Private Keys

Key Change

(1) Certifying Authority and Subscriber keys shall be changed periodically.

(2) Key change shall be processed as per Key Generation guidelines,

(3) The Certifying Authority shall provide reasonable notice to the Subscriber's relying parties of any change to a new key pair used by the Certifying Authority to sign Digital Signature Certificates.

(4) The Certifying Authority shall define its key change process that ensures reliability of the process by showing how the generation of key interlocks—such as signing a hash of the new key with the old key.

All keys must have validity periods of no more than five years.

Suggested validity period:

(a) Certifying Authority's root keys and associated certificates—five years;

(b) Certifying Authority's private signing key—two years;

(c) Subscriber Digital Signature Certificate key—three years;

(d) Subscriber private key - three years.

Use of particular key lengths should be determined in accordance with departmental Threat-Risk Assessments.

2. Destruction

Upon termination of use of a Certifying Authority signature private key, all components of the private key and all its backup copies shall be securely destroyed.

3. Key Compromise

(1) A procedure shall be pre-established to handle cases where a compromise of the Certifying Authority's Digital Signature private key has occurred. In such case, the Certifying Authority shall immediately revoke all affected Subscriber Digital Signature Certificates.

(2) The Certifying Authority should immediately revoke the affected keys and Digital Signature Certificates in the case of Subscriber private key compromise.

(3) The Certifying Authority's public keys shall be archived permanently to facilitate audit or investigation requirements.

(4) Archives of Certifying Authority's public keys shall be protected from unauthorised modification.

Confidentiality of Subscriber's Information

(1) Procedures and security controls to protect the privacy and confidentiality of the subscribers' data under the Certifying Authority's custody shall be implemented. Confidential information provided by the subscriber must not be disclosed to a third party without the subscribers' consent, unless the information is required to be disclosed under the law or a court order.

(2) Data on the usage of the Digital Signature Certificates by the subscribers and other transactional data relating to the subscribers' activities generated by the Certifying Authority in the course of its operation shall be protected to ensure the subscribers' privacy.

(3) A secure communication channel between the

Certifying Authority and its subscribers shall be established to ensure the authenticity, integrity and confidentiality of the exchanges (e.g. transmission of Digital Signature Certificate, password, private key) during the Digital Signature Certificate issuance process.

SCHEDULE-IV

[See Rule 23]

Form for Application for issue of Digital Signature Certificate

For Individual/Hindu Undivided Family Applicant

1. Full Name* [Name of the Karta in case of Hindu Undivided Family]

   Last Name/Surname ________________

   First Name ________________

   Middle Name

2. Have you ever been known by any other name? If Yes,

   Last Name/Surname ________________

   First Name ________________

   Middle Name ________________

3. Address

*Residential Address**

Flat/Door/Block No. ________________

Name of Premises/Building/Village________________

Road/Street/Lane/Post Office________________

Area/Locality/Taluka/Sub-Division________________

Town/City/District ________________

State/Union Territory __________ Pin: __________

Telephone No. ________________

Fax ________________

Mobile Phone No. ________________

*Office Adaress **

Name of Office ________________

Flat/Door/Block No. ____________________
Name of Premises/Building/Village____________________
Road/Street/Lane/Post Office____________________
Area/Locality/Taluka/Sub-Division____________________
Town/City/District ____________________
State/Union Territory ____________ Pin: ________
Telephone No. ____________________
Fax ____________________

4. Address for Communication* Tick ✓ as applicable A ☐ or B ☐
5. Father's Name*
    Last Name/Surname ____________________
    First Name ____________________
    Middle Name ____________________
6. Sex * (For individual Applicant only) Tick ✓ as applicable: Male / Female
7. Date of Birth (dd/mm/yyyy)* __/___/_____
8. Nationality * ____________________
9. In case of foreign national, visa details____________________
10. Credit Card Details
    Credit Card Type ____________________
    Credit Card No. ____________________
    Issued By ____________________
11. E-mail Address ____________________
12. Web URL address ____________________
13. Passport Details #
    Passport No. ____________________
    Passport issuing authority ____________________
    Passport expiry date ____________________
14. Voter's Identity Card No. # ____________________
15. Income Tax PAN no. # ____________________
16. ISP Details
    ISP Name* ____________________
    ISP's Website Address, if any____________________
    Your User Name at ISP, if any____________________
17. Personal Web page URL, if any____________________

For Company/Firm/Body of Individuals/Association of Persons/Local Authority

18. Registration Number*
19. Date of Incorporation/Agreement/Partnership* __/___/____
20. Particulars of Business, if any:*

 Head Office ____________________

 Name of Office ____________________

 Flat/Door/Block No. ____________________

 Name of Premises/Building/Village____________________

 Road/Street/Lane/Post Office ____________________

 Area/Locality/Taluka/Sub-Division____________________

 Town/City/District ____________Pin: ________

 State/Union Territory ____________________

 Telephone No. ____________________

 Fax ____________________

 Web page URL, if any ____________________

 No. of Branches ____________________

 Nature of Business ____________________

21. Income Tax PAN No.* ____________________
22. Turnover in the last financial year Rs. ____________________
23. Names, Addresses etc., of Partners/Members/Directors (For Information about more persons, please, add separate sheet(s) in the format given below)*

 Details of Partners/Members/Directors

 No. of Partners/Members/Directors____________

 Full Name

 Last Name/Surname ____________________

 First Name ____________________

 Middle Name ____________________

 Address

 Flat/Door/Block No. ____________________

 Name of Premises/Building/Village____________________

 Road/Street/Lane/Post Office ____________________

 Area/Locality/Taluka/Sub-Division____________________

 Town/City/District ____________________

State/Union Territory __________ Pin __________

Telephone No. __________

Fax No. __________

Mobile Phone No. __________

Nationality __________

in case of foreign national, Visa details __________

Passport Details #

Passport No. __________

Passport issuing authority __________

Passport expiry date __________

Voter's Identity Card No. # __________

Income Tax PAN no. # __________

E-mail Address __________

Personal Web page URL if any __________

For Government Organisations/Agencies

24. Particulars of Organisation/Agency: *

Name of Organisation __________

Administrative Ministry/Department __________

Under State/Central Government __________

Flat/Door/Block No. __________

Name of Premises/Building/Village __________

Road/Street/Lane/Post Office __________

Area/Locality/Taluka/Sub-Division __________

Town/City/District __________

State/Union Territory __________ Pin: __________

Telephone No. __________

Fax No. __________

Name of the Head of Organisation __________

Designation __________

E-mail Address __________

25. Bank Details

Bank Name * __________

Branch * __________

Bank Account No. * __________

Type of Bank Account * __________

26. Type of Digital Signature Certificate required * ______________________
27. Any other detail ______________________

Date Signature of the Applicant

Instructions:

1. Columns marked with * are mandatory as applicable.
2. For the columns marked with #. details for at least one is mandatory.
3. Column No. 1 to 17 are to be filled up by individual applicants.
4. Column No. 18 to 23 ard to be filled up if applicant is a Company/Firm/Body of Individuals/Association of Persons/Local Authority.
5. Column No. 24 is to be filled up if applicant is a Government organization.
6. Column No. 25 & 26 are to be filled up by all applicants.

SCHEDULE-V

Glossary

ACCEPT (A DIGITAL SIGNATURE CERTIFICATE): To demonstrate approval of a Digital Signature Certificate by a Digital Signature Certificate applicant while knowing or having notice of its informational contents.

ACCESS: Gaining entry into, instructing or communicating with the logical, arithmetical, or memory function resources of a computer, computer system or computer network.

ACCESS CONTROL: The process of limiting access to the resources of a computer system only to authorized users, programs or otlwcomputer systems.

ACCREDIATION: A formal declaration by the Controller that a particular information system, professional or other employee or contractor, or organization is approved to perform certain duties and to operate in a specific security mode, using a prescribed set of safeguards.

AUTHORITY REVOCATION LIST (ARL): A list of revoked Certifying Authority certificates. An ARL is a CRL for Certifying Authority cross-certificates.

ADDRESSEE: A person who is intended by the originator to receive the electronic record but does not include any intermediary.

AFFILIATED CERTIFICATE: A certificate issued to an affiliated individual. *(See also* AFFILIATED INDIVIDUAL)

AFFIRM / AFFIRMATION: To state or indicate by conduct that data is correct or information is true.

AFFIXING DIGITAL SIGNATURE: With its grammatical variations and cognate expressions means adoption of any methodology or procedure by a person for the purpose of authenticating an electronic record by means of digital signature;

ALIAS: A pseudonym.

APPLICANT ***(See*** **CA APPLICANT; CERTIFICATE APPLICANT)**

APPLICATION SOFTWARE: A software that is specific to the solution of an application problem, it is the software ceded by or for an end user that performs a service or relates to the user's work.

APPLICATION SYSTEM: A family of products designed to offer solutions for commercial data processing, office, and communications environments, as well as to provide simple, consistent programmer and end user interfaces for businesses of all sizes.

ARCHIVE: To store records and associated journals for a given period of time for security, backup, or auditing purposes.

ASSURANCES: Statements or conduct intended to convey a general intention, supported by a good-faith effort, to provide and maintain a specified service. "Assurances" does not necessarily imply a guarantee that the services will be performed fully and satisfactorily. Assurances are distinct from insurance, promises, guarantees, and warranties, unless otherwise expressly indicated.

ASYMMETRIC CRYPTO SYSTEM: A system of a secure key pair consisting of a private key for creating a digital signature and a public key to verify the digital signature.

AUDIT: A procedure used to validate that controls are in place and adequate for their purposes. Includes recording and analyzing activities to detect intrusions or abuses into an information system. Inadequacies found by an audit are reported to appropriate management personnel.

AUDIT TRAIL: A chronological record of system activities providing documentary evidence of processing that, enables management staff to reconstruct, review, and examine the sequence of states and activities surrounding or leading to each event in the path of a transaction from its inception to output of final results.

AUTHENTICATED RECORD: A signed document with appropriate assurances of authentication or a message with a digital signature verified by a relying party. However, for suspension and revocation notification purposes, the digital signature contained in such notification message must have been created by the private key corresponding to the public key contained in the Digital Signature Certificate.

AUTHENTICATION: A process used to confirm the identity of a person or to prove the integrity of specific information. Message authentication involves determining its source and verifying that it has not been modified or replaced in transit. (*See also* VERIFY (a DIGITAL SIGNATURE))

AUTHORIZATION: The granting of rights, including the ability to access specific information or resources.

AVAILABILITY: The extent to which information or processes are reasonably accessible and usable, upon demand, by an authorized entity, allowing authorized access to resources and timely performance of time-critical operations.

BACKUP: The process of copying critical information, data and software for the purpose of recovering essential processing back to the time the backup was taken.

BINDING: An affirmation by a Certifying Authority of the relationship between a named entity and its public key.

CERTIFICATE: A Digital Signature Certificate issued by Certifying Authority.

CERTIFICATE CHAIN: An ordered list of certificates containing an end-user subscriber certificate and Certifying Authority certificates (See VALID CERTIFICATE). .

CERTIFICATE EXPIRATION: The time and date specified in the Digital Signature Certificate when the operational period ends, without regard to any earlier suspension or revocation.

CERTIFICATE EXTENSION: An extension field to a Digital Signature Certificate which may convey additional information about the public key being certified, the certified subscriber, the Digital Signature Certificate issuer, and/or the certification process. Standard extensions are defined in Amendment I to ISO/IEC 9594-8: 1995 (X.509). Custom extensions can also be defined by communities of interest.

CERTIFICATE ISSUANCE: The actions performed by a Certifying Authority in creating a Digital Signature Certificate and notifying the Digital Signature Certificate applicant (anticipated to become a subscriber) listed in the Digital Signature Certificate of its contents.

CERTIFICATE MANAGEMENT (MANAGEMENT OF DIGITAL SIGNATURE CERTIFICATE): Certificate management includes, but is not limited to, storage, distribution, dissemination, accounting, publication, compromise, recovery, revocation, suspension and administration of Digital Signature Certificates. A Certifying Authority undertakes Digital Signature Certificate management functions by serving as a registration authority for subscriber Digital Signature Certificates. A Certifying Authority designates issued and accepted Digital Signature Certificates as valid by publication.

CERTIFICATE POLICY: A specialized form of administrative policy tuned to electronic transactions performed during Digital Signature Certificate management. A Certificate policy addresses all aspects associated with the generation, production, distribution, accounting, compromise recover and administration of digital certificates. Indirectly, a certificate policy can also govern the transactions conducted using a communications system protected by a certificate-based security system. By controlling critical certificate extensions, such policies and associated enforcement technology can support provision of the security services required by particular applications.

CERTIFICATE REVOCATION (See REVOKE A CERTIFICATE)

CERTIFICATE REVOCATION LIST (CRL): A periodically (or exigently) issued list, digitally signed by a Certifying Authority, of identified Digital Signature Certificates that have been suspended or revoked prior to their expiration dates. The list generally indicates the CRL issuer's name, the date of issue, the date of the next scheduled CRL issue, the suspended or revoked Digital Signature Certificates' serial numbers, and the specific times and reasons for suspension and revocation.

CERTIFICATE SERIAL NUMBER: A value that unambiguously identifies a Digital Signature Certificate generated by a Certifying Authority.

CERTIFICATE SIGNING REQUEST (CSR): A machine-readable form of a Digital Signature Certificate application.

CERTIFICATE SUSPENSION (*See* SUSPEND A CERTIFICATE)

CERTIFICATION / CERTIFY: The process of issuing a Digital Signature Certificate by a Certifying Authority.

CERTIFYING AUTHORITY (CA): A person who has been granted a licence to issue a Digital Signature Certificate under Section 24 of information Technology Act, 2000.

CERTIFYING AUTHORITY SOFTWARE: The cryptographic software required to manage the keys of end entities.

CERTIFYING AUTHORITY SYSTEM: All the hardware and software system (e.g. Computer, PKI servers, network devices etc.) used by the certifying Authority for generation, production, issue and management of Digital Signature certificate.

CERTIFICATION PRACTICE STATEMENT (CPS): A statement issued by a Certifying Authority to specify the practices that the Certifying Authority employs in issuing Digital Signature Certificates.

CERTIFIER *(See* **ISSUING AUTHORITY)**

CHALLENGE PHRASE: A set of numbers and/or letters that are chosen by a Digital Signature certificate applicant, communicated to the Certifying Authority with a Digital Signature Certificate application, and used by the Certifying Authority to authenticate the subscriber for various purposes as required by the Certification Practice Statement. A challenge phrase is also used by a secret share holder to authenticate himself, herself, or itself to a secret share issuer.

CERTIFICATE CLASS: A Digital Signature Certificate of a specified level of trust.

CLIENT APPLICATION: An application that runs on a personal computer or workstation and relies on a server to perform some operation.

COMMON KEY: Some systems of cryptographic hardware require arming through a secret-sharing process and require that the last of these shares remain physically attached to the hardware in order for it to stay armed. In this case, "common key",refers to this last share. It is not assumed to be secret as it is not continually in an individual's possession.

COMMUNICATION/NETWORK SYSTEM: A set of related, remotely connected devices and communications facilities including more than one computer system with the capability to transmit data among them through the communications facilities (covering ISDN, lease lines, dial-up, LAN, WAN, etc.).

COMPROMISE: A violation (or suspected violation) of a security policy, in which an unauthorized disclosure of, or loss of control over, sensitive information may have occurred. *(Cf.,* DATA INTEGRITY)

COMPUTER: Any electronic, magnetic, optical or other high-speed data processing device or system which performs logical, arithmetic, and memory functions by manipulations of electronic, magnetic or optical impulses, and includes all input, output, processing, storage, computer software, or communication facilities which are connected or related to the computer in a computer system or computer network.

COMPUTER CENTRE (See DATA CENTRE)

COMPUTER DATA BASE: Means a representation of information, knowledge, facts, concepts or instructions in text, image, audio, video that are being prepared or have been prepared in a formalised manner or have been produced by a computer, computer system or computer network and are intended for use in a computer, computer system or computer network.

COMPUTER NETWORK: Interconnection of one or more computers through—

(i) the use of satellite, microwave, terrestrial line or other communication media; and

(ii) terminals or a complex consisting of two or more interconnected computers whether or not the interconnection is continuously maintained.

COMPUTER PERIPHERAL: Means equipment that works in conjunction with a computer but is not a part of the main computer itself, such as printer, magnetic tape reader, etc.

COMPUTER RESOURCE: Means computer, computer system, computer network, data, computer database or software.

COMPUTER SYSTEM: A device or collection of devices, including input and output support devices and excluding calculators which are not programmable and capable of being used in conjunction with external files, which contain computer programmes, electronic instructions, input data and output data, that performs logic, arithmetic, data storage and retrieval, communication control and other functions.

COMPUTER VIRUS (*See* VIRUS)

CONFIDENTIALITY: The condition in which sensitive data is kept secret and disclosed only to authorized parties.

CONFIRM: To ascertain through appropriate inquiry and investigation. (*See also* **AUTHENTICATION; VERIFY A DIGITAL SIGNATURE)**

CONFIRMATION OF DIGITAL SIGNATURE CERTIFICATE CHAIN: The process of validating a Digital Signature Certificate chain and subsequently validating an end-user subscriber Digital Signature Certificate.

CONTINGENCY PLANS: The establishment of emergency response, (backup operation, and post-disaster recovery processes maintained by an information processing facility or for an information system.

Establish the strategy for recovering from unplanned disruption of information processing operations. The strategy includes the identification and priority of what must be done, who performs the required action, and what tools must be used.

A document, developed in conjunction with application owners and maintained at the primary and backup computer installation, which describes procedures and identifies the personnel necessary to respond to abnormal situations such as disasters. Contingency plans help managers ensure that computer application owners continue to process (with or without computers) mission-critical applications in the event that computer support is interrupted.

CONTROLS: Measures taken to ensure the integrity and quality of a process.

CORRESPOND: To belong to the same key pair. (*See also* PUBLIC KEY; PRIVATE KEY)

CRITICAL INFORMATION: Data determined by the data owner as mission critical or essential to business purposes.

CROSS-CERTIFICATE: A Certificate used to establish a trust relationship between two Certifying Authorities.

CRYPTOGRAPHIC ALGORITHM: A clearly specified mathematical process for computation; a set of rules that produce a prescribed result.

CRYPTOGRAPHY: .(*See also* **PUBLIC KEY CRYPTOGRAPHY)**

(i) The mathematical science used to secure the confidentiality and authentication of data by replacing it with a transformed version that can be reconverted to reveal the original data only by someone holding the proper cryptographic algorithm and key.

(ii) A discipline that embodies the principles, means, and methods for transforming data in order to hide its information content, prevent its undetected modification, and/or prevent its unauthorized uses.

DAMAGE: Means to destroy, alter, delete, add, modify or rearrange any computer resource by any means.

DATA: Means a representation of information, knowledge, facts, concepts or instructions which are being prepared or have been prepared in a formalised manner, and is intended to be processed, is being processed or has been processed in a computer system or computer network, and may be in any form (including computer printouts magnetic or optical storage media, punched cards, punched tapes) or stored internally in the memory of the computer.

DATA BASE: (*See* **COMPUTER DATABASE)**

DATA CENTRE (as also **COMPUTER CENTRE):** The facility covering the computer room, media library, network area, server area, programming and administration areas, other storage and support areas used to carry out of the computer processing functions. Usually refers to the computer room and media library.

DATA CONFIDENTIALITY *(See* **CONFIDENTIALITY)**

DATA INTEGRITY: A condition in which data has not been altered or destroyed in an unauthorized manner. *(See also* THREAT; COMPROMISE)

DATA SECURITY: The practice of protecting data from accidental or malicious modification, destruction, or disclosure.

DEMO CERTIFICATE: A Digital Signature Certificate issued by a Certifying Authority to be used exclusively for demonstration and presentation purposes and not for any secure or confidential communications. Demo Digital Signature Certificates may be used by authorized persons only.

DIGITAL CERTIFICATE APPLICANT: A person that requests the issuance of a public key Digital Signature Certificate by a Certifying Authority. *(See also* CA APPLICANT; SUBSCRIBER)

DIGITAL CERTIFICATE APPLICATION: A request from a Digital Signature Certificate applicant (or authorized agent) to a Certifying Authority for the issuance of a Digital Signature Certificate. *(See also* CERTIFICATE APPLICANT; CERTIFICATE SIGNING REQUEST)

DIGITAL SIGNATURE: Means authentication of any electronic record by a subscriber by means of an electronic method or procedure in accordance with the provisions of Section 3 of the Information Technology .Act, 2000.

DIGITAL SIGNATURE CERTIFICATE: Means a Digital Signature Certificate issued under sub-section *(4)* of Section 35 of the Information Technology Act, 2000.

DISTINGUISHED NAME: A set of data that identifies a real-world entity, such as a person in a computer-based context.

DOCUMENT: A record consisting of information inscribed on a tangible medium such as paper rather than computer-based information. (*See also* MESSAGE; RECORD)

ELECTRONIC FORM: With reference to information means any information generated, sent, received or stored in media, magnetic, optical, computer memory, micro-film, computer generated micro fiche or similar device.

ELECTRONIC MAIL ("E-MAIL"): Messages"sent received or forwarded in digital form via a computer-based communication mechanism.

ELECTRONIC RECORD: Means data, record or data generated, image or sound stored, received or sent in an electronic form or microfilm or computer generated micro-fiche.

ENCRYPTION: The process of transforming plaintext data into an unintelligible form (cipher text) such that the original data either cannot be recovered (one-way encryption) or cannot be recovered without using an inverse decryption process (two-way encryption).

EXTENSIONS: Extension fields in X.509 v3 certificates. (See X.509)

FIREWALL/DOUBLE FIREWALL: One of several types of intelligent devices (such as routers or gateways) used to isolate networks. Firewalls make it difficult for attackers to jump from network to network. A double firewall is two firewalls connected together. Double firewalls are used to minimise risk if one firewall gets compromised or provide address translation functions.

FILE TRANSFER PROTOCOL (FTP): The application protocol that offers file system access from the Internet suite of protocols.

FUNCTION: In relation to a computer, includes logic, control, arithmetical process, deletion, storage and retrieval and communication or telecommunication from or within a computer.

GATEWAY: Hardware or software that is used to translate protocols between two or more systems.

GENERATE A KEY PAIR: A trustworthy process of creating private keys during Digital Signature Certificate application whose corresponding public keys are submitted to the applicable Certifying Authority during Digital Signature Certificate application in a manner that demonstrates the applicant's capacity to use the private key.

HARD COPY: A copy of computer output that is printed on paper in a visually readable form; e.g. printed reports, listing, and documents.

HASH (HASH FUNCTION): An algorithm that maps or translates one set of bits into another (generally smaller) set in such a way that:

(i) A message yields the same result every time the algorithm is executed using the same message as input.

(ii) It is computationally infeasible for a message to be derived or reconstituted from the result produced by the algorithm.

(iii) It is computationally infeasible to find two different messages that produce the same hash result using the same algorithm.

HIGH-SECURITY ZONE: An area to which access is controlled through an entry point and limited to authorized, appropriately screened personnel and properly escorted visitors. High-Security Zones should be accessible only from Security Zones, and are separated from Security Zones and Operations Zones by a perimeter. High-Security Zones are monitored 24 hours a day a week by security staff, other personnel or electronic means.

IDENTIFICATION / IDENTITY: The process of confirming the identity of a person. Identification is facilitated in public key cryptography by means of certificates.

IDENTITY: A unique piece of information that marks or signifies a particular entity within a domain Such information is only unique within a particular domain.

INFORMATION: Includes data, text, images, sound, voice, codes, computer programmes, software and databases or micro-film or computer generated micro fiche.

INFORMATION ASSETS: Means all information resources utilized in the course of any organisation's business and includes all information, application software (developed or purchased), and technology (hardware, system software and networks).

INTERMEDIARY: With respect to any particular electronic message means any person who on behalf of another person receives, stores or transmits that message or provides any service with respect to that message.

INFORMATION TECHNOLOGY SECURITY: All aspects related to defining, achieving, and maintaining confidentiality, integrity, availability, accountability, authenticity, and reliability.

INFORMATION TECHNOLOGY SECURITY POLICY: Rules, directives and practices that govern how information assets, including sensitive information, are managed, protected and distributed within an organization and its Information Technology systems.

KEY: A sequence of symbols that controls the operation of a cryptographic transformation (e.g. encipherment, decipherment, cryptographic check function computation, signature generation, or signature verification).

KEY GENERATION: The trustworthy process of creating a private key/public key pair.

KEY MANAGEMENT: The administration and use of the generation, registration, certification, deregistration, distribution, installation, storage, archiving, revocation, derivation and destruction of keying material in accordance with a security policy.

KEY PAIR: In an asymmetric crypto system, means a private key and, its mathematically related public key, which are so related that the public key can verify a digital signature created by the private key.

LICENCE: Means a licence granted to a Certifying Authority.

LOCAL AREA NETWORK (LAN): A geographically small network of computers and supporting components used by a group or department to share related software and hardware resources.

LOW-SENSITIVE: Applies to information that, it compromised, could reasonably be expected to cause injury outside the national interest, for example, disclosure of an exact salary figure.

MANAGEMENT OF DIGITAL SIGNATURE CERTIFICATE *(See* **CERTIFICATE MANAGEMENT)**

MEDIA: The material or configuration on which data is recorded. Examples include magnetic tapes and disks.

MESSAGE: A digital representation of information; a computer-based record. A subset of RECORD. *(See also* RECORD)

NAME: A set of identifying attributes purported to describe an entity of a certain type.

NETWORK: A set of related, remotely connected devices and communications facilities including more than one computer system with the capability to transmit data among them through the communications facilities.

NETWORK ADMINISTRATOR: The personal a computer network installation who designs, controls, and manages the use of the computer network.

NODE: In a network, a point at which one or more functional units connect channels or data circuits.

NOMINATED WEBSITE: A website designated by the Certifying Authority for display of information such as fee schedule, Certification Practice Statement, Certificate Policy etc.

NONREPUDIATION: Provides proof of the origin or delivery of data in order to protect the sender against a false denial by the recipient that the data has been received or to protect the recipient against false denial by the sender that the data has been sent. Note: Only a trier of fact (someone with the authority to resolve disputes) can make an ultimate determination of non-repudiation. By way of illustration, a digital signature verified pursuant to this Certification Practice Statement can provide proof in support of a determination of non-repudiation by a trier of fact, but does not by itself constitute non-repudiation.

NOTARY: A natural person authorized by an executive governmental agency to perform notarial services such as taking acknowledgments, administering oaths or affirmations, witnessing or attesting signatures, and noting protests of negotiable instruments.

ON-LINE: Communications that provide a real-time connection.

OPERATIONS ZONE: An area where access is limited to personnel who work there and to properly escorted visitors. Operations Zones should be monitored at least periodically, based on a threat risk assessment (TRA), and should preferably be accessible from a Reception Zone.

OPERATIONAL CERTIFICATE: A Digital Signature Certificate which is within its operational period at the present date and time or at a different specified date and time, depending on the context.

OPERATIONAL MANAGEMENT: Refers to all business/service unit management (i.e. the user management) as well as Information Technology management.

OPERATIONAL PERIOD: The period starting with the date and time a Digital Signature Certificate is issued (or on a later date and time certain if stated in the Digital Signature Certificate) and ending with the dale and time on which the Digital Signature Certificate expires or is earlier suspended or revoked.

ORGANIZATION: An entity with which a user is affiliated. An organization may also be a user.

ORIGINATOR: A person who sends, generates, stores or transmits any electronic message or causes any electronic message to be sent, generated, stored or transmitted to any other person but does not include an intermediary.

PASSWORD (PASS PHRASE; PIN NUMBER): Confidential authentication information usually composed of a string of characters used to provide access to a computer resource.

PARTICULARLY SENSITIVE: Applies to information that, if compromised, could reasonably be expected to cause serious injury outside the national interest, for example loss of reputation or competitive advantage.

PC CARD ***(See also*** **SMART CARD):** A hardware token compliant with standards promulgated by the Personal Computer Memory Card International Association (PCMCIA) providing expansion capabilities to computers, including the facilitation of information security.

PERSON: Means any company or association or individual or body of individuals, whether incorporated or not.

PERSONAL PRESENCE: The act of appearing (physically rather than virtually or figuratively) before a Certifying Authority or its designee and proving one's identity as a prerequisite to Digital Signature Certificate issuance under certain circumstances.

PKI (PUBLIC KEY INFRASTRUCTURE) / PKI SERVER: A set of policies, processes, server platforms, software and workstations used for the purpose of administering Digital Signature Certificates and public-private key pairs, including the ability to generate, issue, maintain, and revoke public key certificates.

PKI HIERARCHY: A set of Certifying Authorities whose functions are organized according to the principle of delegation of authority and related to each other as subordinate and superior Certifying Authority.

PLEDGE (*See* SOFTWARE PUBLISHER'S PLEDGE)

POLICY: A brief document that states the high-level organization position, states the scope, and establishes who is responsible for compliance with the policy and the corresponding standards. Following is an abbreviated example of what a policy may contain

- Introduction
- Definitions
- Policy Statement identifying the need for "something" (e.g. data security)
- Scope
- People playing a role and their responsibilities
- Statement of Enforcement, including responsibility

PRIVATE KEY: The key of a key pair used to create a digital signature.

PROCEDURE: A set of steps performed to ensure that a guideline is met.

PROGRAM: A detailed and explicit set of instructions for accomplishing some purpose, the set being expressed in some language suitable for input 10 a computer, or in machine language.

PROXY SERVER: A server that sits between a client application such as a web browser and a real server. It intercepts all requests to the real server to see if it can fulfill the request itself. If not, it forwards the request to the real server.

PUBLIC ACCESS ZONE: Generally surrounds or forms part of a government facility. Examples include the grounds surrounding a building, and public corridors and elevator lobbies in multiple-occupancy buildings. Boundary designators such as signs and direct or remote surveillance may be used to discourage unauthorized activity.

PUBLIC KEY: The key of a key pair used to verify a digital signature and listed in the Digital Signature Certificate.

PUBLIC KEY CERTIFICATE (*See* CERTIFICATE)

PUBLIC KEY CRYPTOGRAPHY *(See* CRYPTOGRAPHY): A type of cryptography that uses a key pair of mathematically related cryptographic keys. The public key can de made available to anyone who wishes to use it and can encrypt information or verify a digital signature; the private key is kept secret by its holder and can decrypt information or generate a digital signature.

PUBLIC KEY INFRASTRUCTURE (PKI): The architecture, organization, techniques, practices, and procedures that collectively support the implementation and operation of a certificate-based public key cryptographic system. It includes a set of policies, processes, server platforms, software and workstations, used for the purpose of administering Digital Signature Certificates and keys.

PUBLIC/PRIVATE KEY PAIR *(See* PUBLIC KEY; PRIVATE KEY; KEY PAIR)

RECIPIENT (of a DIGITAL SIGNATURE) A person who receives a digital signature and who is in a position to rely on it, whether or not such reliance occurs. *(See also* RELYING PARTY)

RECORD: Information that is inscribed on a tangible medium (a document) or stored in an electronic or other medium and retrievable in perceivable form. The term "record" is a superset of the two terms "document" and "message". *(See also* DOCUMENT; MESSAGE)

RE-ENROLLMENT *(See also* RENEWAL)

RELY/RELIANCE (on a CERTIFICATE and DIGITAL SIGNATURE): To accept a digital signature and act in a manner that could be detrimental to oneself were the digital signature to be ineffective. *(See also* RELYING PARTY; RECIPIENT)

RELYING PARTY: A recipient who acts in reliance on a certificate and digital signature. *(See also* RECIPIENT; RELY or RELIANCE (on a CERTIFICATE and DIGITAL SIGNATURE))

RENEWAL: The process of obtaining a new Digital Signature Certificate of the same class and type for the same subject once an existing Digital Signature Certificate has expired.

REPOSITORY: A database of Digital Signature Certificates and other relevant information accessible on-line.

REPUDIATION (See also NONREPUDIATION): The denial or attempted denial by an entity involved in a communication of having participated in all or part of the communication.

REVOKE A CERTIFICATE: The process of permanently ending the operational period of a Digital Signature Certificate from a specified time forward.

RISK: The potential of damage to a system or associated assets that exists as a result of the combination of security threat and vulnerability.

RISK ANALYSIS: The process of identitying security risks, determining their magnitude, and identifying areas needing safeguards.

RISK ASSESSMENT: An analysis of system assets and vulnerabilities to establish an expected loss from certain events based on estimated probabilities of the occurrence of those events.

RISK MANAGEMENT: The total process of identifying, controlling, and eliminating or minimizing uncertain events that may affect Information Technology system resources.

RSA: A public key cryptographic system invented by Rivest, Shamir & Adelman.

SECRET SHARE: A portion of a cryptographic secret split among a number of physical tokens.

SECRET SHARE HOLDER: An authorized holder of a physical token containing a secret share.

SECURE CHANNEL: A cryptographically enhanced communications path that protects messages against perceived security threats.

SECURE SYSTEM: Means computer hardware, software, and procedure that —

(a) are reasonably secure from unauthorised access and misuse;
(b) provide a reasonable level of reliability and correct operation;
(c) are reasonably suited to performing the intended functions; and
(d) adhere to generally accepted security procedures.

SECURITY PROCEDURE: Means the security procedure prescribed under Section 16 of the Information Technology Act, 2000.

SECURITY: The quality or state of being protected from unauthorized access or uncontrolled losses or effects. Absolute security is impossible to achieve in practice and the quality of a given security system is relative. Within a state-model security system, security is a specific "state" to be preserved under various operations.

SECURITY POLICY: A document which articulates requirements and good practices regarding the protections maintained by a trustworthy system. .

SECURITY SERVICES: Services provided by a set of security frameworks and performed by means of certain security mechanisms. Such services include, but are not limited to, access control, data confidentiality, and data integrity.

SECURITY ZONE: An area to which access is limited to authorised personnel and to authorised and properly escorted visitors. Security Zones should preferably be accessible from an Operations Zone, and through a specific entry point. A Security Zone need not be separated from an Operations Zone by a secure perimeter. A Security Zone should be monitored 24 hours a day and 7 days a week by security staff, other personnel or electronic means.

SELF-SIGNED PUBLIC KEY: A data structure that is constructed the same as a Digital Signature Certificate but that is signed by its subject. Unlike a Digital Signature Certificate, a self-signed public key cannot be used in a trustworthy manner to authenticate a public key to other parties.

SERIAL NUMBER *(See* CERTIFICATE SERIAL NUMBER)

SERVER: A computer system that responds to requests from client systems.

SIGN: To create a digital signature for a message, or to affix a signature to a document, depending upon the context.

SIGNATURE *(See* DIGITAL SIGNATURE)

SIGNER: A person who creates a digital signature for a message, or a signature for a document.

SMART CARD: A hardware token that incorporates one or more integrated circuit (IC) chips to implement cryptographic functions and that possesses some inherent resistance to tampering.

S/MIME: A specification for E-mail security exploiting a cryptographic message syntax in an Internet MIME environment

SUBJECT (OF A CERTIFICATE): The holder of a private key corresponding to a public key. The term "subject" can refer to both the equipment or device that holds a private key and to the individual person, if any, who controls that equipment or device. A subject is assigned an unambiguous name which is bound to the public key contained in the subject's Digital Signature Certificate.

SUBJECT NAME: The unambiguous value in the subject name field of a Digital Signature Certificate, which is bound to ike public key.

SUBSCRIBER: A person in whose name the Digital Signature Certificate is issued.

SUBSCRIBER AGREEMENT: The agreement executed between a subscriber and a Certifying Authority for the provision of designated public certification services in accordance with this Certification Practice Statement.

SUBSCRIBER INFORMATION: Information supplied to a certification authority as part of a Digital Signature Certificate application. (*See also* CERTIFICATE APPLICATION)

SUSPEND A CERTIFICATE: A temporary "hold" placed on the effectiveness of the operational period of a Digital Signature Certificate without permanently revoking the Digital Signature Certificate. A Digital Signature Certificate suspension is invoked by, *e.g.*, a CRL entry with a reason code. (*See also* REVOKE A CERTIFICATE)

SYSTEM ADMINISTRATOR: The person at a computer installation who designs, controls, and manages the use of the computer system.

SYSTEM SECURITY: A system function that restricts the use of objects to certain users.

SYSTEM SOFTWARE: Application-independent software that supports the running of application software. It is a software that is part of or made available with a computer system and that determines how application programs are run; for example, an operating system.

TEST CERTIFICATE: A Digital Signature Certificate issued by a Certifying Authority for the limited purpose of internal technical testing. Test certificates may be used by authorized persons only.

THREAT: A circumstance or event with the potential to cause harm to a system, including the destruction, unauthorized disclosure, or modification of data and/or denial of service.

TIME-OUT: A security feature that logs off a user if any entry is not made at the terminal within a specified period of time.

TIME STAMP: A notation that indicates (at least) the correct date and time of an action, and identity of the person or device that sent or received the time stamp.

TOKEN: A hardware security token containing a user's private key(s), public key certificate, and, optionally, a cache of other certificates, including all certificates in the user's certification chain.

TRANSACTION: A computer-based transfer of business information, which consists of specific processes to facilitate communication over global networks.

TRUST: Generally, the assumption that an entity will behave substantially as expected. Trust may apply only for a specific function. The key role of this term in an authentication framework is to describe the relationship between an authenticating entity and a Certifying Authority. An authenticating entity must be certain that ii can trust the Certifying Authority to create only valid and reliable Digital Signature Certificates, and users of those Digital Signature Certificates rely upon the authenticating entity's determination of trust.

TRUSTED POSITION: A role that includes access to or control over cryptographic operations that may materially affect the issuance, use, suspension, or revocation of Digital Signature Certificates, including operations that restrict access to a repository.

TRUSTED THIRD PARTY: In general, an independent, unbiased third party that contributes to the ultimate security and trustworthiness of computer-based information transfers. A trusted third party does not connote the existence of a trustor-trustee or other fiduciary relationship. *(Cf.,* TRUST)

TRUSTWORTHY SYSTEM: Computer hardware, software, and procedures that are reasonably secure from intrusion and misuse; provide a reasonable level of availability, reliability, and correct operation; are reasonably suited to performing their intended functions; and enforce the applicable security policy. A trustworthy system is not necessarily a "trusted system" as recognized in classified government nomenclature.

TYPE (OF CERTIFICATE): The defining properties of a Digital Signature Certificate, which limit its intended purpose to a class of application uniquely, associated with that type.

UNAMBIGUOUS NAME *(See* **DISTINGUISHED NAME)**

UNIFORM RESOURCE LOCATOR (URL): A standardized device for identifying and locating records and other resources located on the World Wide Web.

USER: An authorized entity that uses a certificate as applicant, subscriber, recipient or relying party, but not including the Certifying Authority issuing the Digital Signature Certificate. (*See also* CERTIFICATE APPLICANT; ENTITY; PERSON; SUBSCRIBER)

VALID CERTIFICATE: A Digital Signature Certificate issued by a Certifying Authority and accepted by the subscriber listed in it.

VALIDATE A CERTIFICATE (i.e., of an **END-USER SUBSCRIBER CERTIFICATE):** The process performed by a recipient or relying party to confirm that an end-user subscriber Digital Signature Certificate is valid and was operational at the date and time a pertinent digital signature was created.

VALIDATION (OF CERTIFICATE APPLICATION): The process performed by the Certifying Authority or its agent following submission of a Digital Signature Certificate application as a prerequisite to approval of the application and the issuance of a Digital Signature Certificate. (*See also* AUTHENTICATION; SOFTWARE VALIDATION)

VALIDATION (OF SOFTWARE) (*See* SOFTWARE VALIDATION)

VERIFY (A DIGITAL SIGNATURE): In relation to a digital signature, electronic record or public key, with its grammatical variations and cognate expressions means to determine whether —

(a) the initial electronic record was affixed with the digital signature by the use of private key corresponding to the public key of the subscriber,

(b) the initial electronic record is retained intact or has been altered since such electronic record was so affixed with the digital signature.

VIRUS: Means any computer instruction, information, data or programme that destroys, damages, degrades or adversely affects the performance of a computer resource or attaches itself to another computer resource and operates when a programme, data or instruction is executed or some other event takes place in that computer resource.

VULNERABILITY: A weakness that could be exploited to cause damage to the system or the assets it contains.

WEB BROWSER: A software application used to locate and display web pages.

WORLD WIDE WEB (WWW): A hypertext-based, distributed information system in which users may create, edit, or browse hypertext documents. A graphical document publishing and retrieval medium; a collection of linked documents that reside on the Internet.

WRITING: Information in a record that is accessible and usable for subsequent reference.

X.509: The ITU-T (International Telecommunications Union-T) standard for Digital Signature Certificates. X.509 v3 refers to certificates containing or capable of containing extensions.

ACRONYMS

ARL	Authority Revocation List
CA	Certification Authority
CP	Certificate Policy
CPS	Certification Practice Statement
CRL	Certificate Revocation List
CSR	Certificate Signing Request
DN	Distinguished Name
e-mail	Electronic mail
FTP	File Transfer Protocol
ISDN	Integrated Service Digital Network
ITU	International Telecommunications Union
LAN	Local Area Network
PIN	Personal Identification Number
PKI	Public Key Infrastructure
PKIX	Public Key Infrastructure X.509
URL	Uniform Resource Locator
WAN	Wide Area Network

2 TELECOM REGULATORY AUTHORITY OF INDIA

New Delhi

March 9, 1999/ Phalguna 18, 1920

In exercise of the powers conferred upon it under sub-section (2) of Section 11 of the Telecom Regulatory Authority of India Act, 1997 to notify, by an Order in the Official Gazette, tariffs at which Telecommunication Services within India and outside India shall be provided, the Telecom Regulatory Authority of India hereby makes the following Order.

THE TELECOMMUNICATION TARIFF ORDER 1999

SECTION 1

Title, Extent and Commencement

1. Short title, extent and commencement:

(i) This Order shall be called "The Telecommunication Tariff Order 1999.

(ii) The Order shall cover tariffs for all Telecommunication Services throughout the territory of India as also those originating in India and terminating outside India.

(iii) The Order shall come into force on the date of its notification in the Official Gazette.

SECTION II
Definitions

2. Definitions

In this Order, unless the context otherwise requires :

(a) *"Act"* means the Telecom Regulatory Authority Act of India, 1997

(b) *"Authority"* means the Telecom Regulatory Authority of India.

(c) *"Basic Telecommunication Services"* mean services derived from Public Switched Telephone Network (PSTN).

(d) *"Ceiling (s)"* mean(s) the upper limit(s) for tariff for telecommunication services as specified by the Authority from time to time.

(e) *"Domestic Long Distance Telecommunication Service"* means the telecommunication services required to connect one local area of a public telecommunication network to another within the territorial limits of India so as to allow for transmission of voice and non-voice signals across different geographical areas.

(f) *"Floor"* means the lower limit of a tariff for a telecommunication service as specified by the Authority from time to time below which such tariffs may not be offered.

(g) *"Forbearance"* denotes that the Authority has not, for the time being, notified any tariff for a particular telecommunication service and the service provider is free to fix any tariff for such service.

(h) *"International Long Distance Telecommunication Service"* means telecommunication services required to connect a local area of a public telecommunication network within India to a local area of a public telecommunication network in another country so as to allow for the transmission of voice and non-voice signals.

(i) *"International Subscriber Dialing"* means direct interconnection between an end user in India with another end user in another country by means of direct dialing through public networks.

(j) *"Leased Circuits"* mean telecommunication facilities leased to subscribers or service providers to provide for technology transparent transmission capacity between network termination points which the user can control as part of the leased circuit provision and which may also include systems allowing flexible use of leased circuit bandwidth.

(k) *"Non-discrimination"* means that service providers shall not, in the matter of application of tariffs, discriminate between subscribers of the same class and such classification of subscribers shall not be arbitrary.

(l) *"Reporting Requirement"* means the obligation of a service provider to report to the Authority at least **five** working days before implementing any new tariff for telecommunication services under this Order and any changes thereafter.

(m) *"Special Services"* mean those support and other ancillary services like phonogram, directory enquiry, manual trunk service, assistance, emergency services such as police, fire and ambulance provided by service providers through special interfaces located at the edge of the PSTN.

(n) *"Standard package"* means a package of tariffs

which *inter-alia* comprises rental call charges, free calls, deposits and other charges as may be determined by the Authority for specific telecommunication services from time to time.

(o) *"Subscriber"* means an end user of telecommunication services.

(p) *"Subscriber Trunk Dialing"* means direct interconnection between two end users within India by means of direct dialing through public networks.

(q) *"Supplementary Services"* mean services which are provided specific to a subscriber's directory number and controlled either by the subscriber or by the service provider such as automatic alarm call service, call waiting, call diversion on busy or no reply, and any other such service.

(r) *"Tariff(s)"* mean(s) rates and related conditions at which telecommunication services within India and outside India may be provided including rates and related conditions at which messages shall be transmitted to any country outside India, deposits, installation fees, rentals, free calls, usage charges and any other related fees or service charge.

(s) Words and expressions used in this Order and not defined but defined in the Act shall have the same meanings respectively assigned to them in the Act.

SECTION III

Tariffs for Telecommunication Services

3. Tariffs

Tariffs for various telecommunication services and their

dates of implementation shall be as set out in Schedules I to IX.

4. Forbearance

Where the Authority has, for the time being, forborne from fixing tariff for any telecommunication service or part thereof, a service provider shall be at liberty to fix any tariff for such telecommunication services :

Provided that the service provider shall comply with the reporting requirements in respect of such tariff.

5. Deposits

Unless otherwise provided for, no service provider shall seek or obtain from any subscriber in any form any amount as deposit for any telecommunication service in excess of one year's rental chargeable from the subscriber for the particular telecommunication service as specified in the relevant standard package.

6. Flexibility and Packages

(i) The service provider shall offer the standard package(s) to all subscribers.

(ii) Where a tariff has been specified as a ceiling, no tariff shall be fixed in excess of such ceiling.

(iii) Where a tariff has been specified as a floor, no tariff shall be fixed below such floor.

(iv) In all other cases, a service provider may, in addition to the standard package, offer alternative combinations of tariff to different classes of subscribers in a non-discriminatory manner.

7. Reporting Requirement

(i) All service providers shall comply with the Reporting Requirement in respect of tariffs specified for the first time under this Order and also all subsequent changes.

(ii) No service provider shall alter any tariff of any telecommunication service or any part thereof without complying with the Reporting Requirement.

(iii) Unless the Authority intervenes within the mandatory notice period of **five** working days, the service provider may implement the proposed tariff.

8. Review of Tariffs

(i) The Authority may, from time to time, review and modify a tariff for any telecommunication service or a part thereof.

(ii) The Authority may also at any time, on reference from any affected party, and for good and sufficient reasons, review and modify any tariff.

SECTION IV

Transparency and Consumer Protection

9. Publication of Tariffs

(i) Tariffs to be charged by service providers from subscribers for telecommunication services along with the conditions thereof shall be published in such manner as the Authority may from time to time direct.

(ii) Information of tariff packages that a service provider may choose to offer to subscribers shall be accompanied by a comparison of the financial implications to subscribers under each package vis-a-vis the specified standard package(s).

10. Non-discrimination

No service provider shall, in any manner, discriminate between subscribers of the same class and such classification of subscribers shall not be arbitrary.

11. Terms and Conditions of Service

Service providers shall clearly indicate the terms and conditions of the provision of telecommunication services to subscribers which shall not in any manner be inconsistent with the provisions of this Order. Such terms and conditions shall *inter-alia* include the following :

(a) Terms and conditions under which such services may be obtained, utilised and terminated;

(b) Terms and conditions relating to the use of service, billing, repair, fault rectification and the like;

(c) Choice of tariff packages available to a subscriber and the procedure available for revising the choice along with the conditions thereof.

SECTION V

12. Explanatory Memorandum

This Order contains at Annex A, an explanatory memorandum to provide clarity and transparency to the tariffs specified in this Order.

SECTION VI

Residuary Clauses

13. Over-riding Effect

In respect of matters covered by this Order the provisions thereof shall have over-riding effect over Rules framed under the Indian Telegraph Act, 1885, as also the terms and conditions of the licence of a service provider and any tariffs or conditions as may have been set by the service providers for provision of telecommunication services to subscribers.

14. Interpretation

In case of dispute regarding interpretation of any of the provisions of this Order, the decision of the Authority shall be final and binding.

ANNEXURE

IN THE SUPREME COURT OF INDIA CIVIL APPELLATE JURISDICTION

Civil Appeal No. 325 (MCM) of 1970

Sh. Narayana Iyer .... Appellant

Vs

The Union of India .... Respondents

JUDGEMENT

This appeal is by certificate from the judgement dated 28th March, 1969 of the High Court of Madras. The question in this appeal is whether the appellant in a writ petition can challenge the telephone rates and charges and obtain any relief in that behalf.

The appellant is a retired Distt. Manager (Telephones), Madras. He filed a writ petition in the High Court for a writ of prohibition, directing the General Manager (Telephones), Madras to forbear from enforcing the revised Telephone Tariff as per the Indian Telegraph Amendment Rules, 1966. Under the rules, the rental and call charges were increased by *58* per cent and Trunk Call charges by about 30 to 35 per cent. The petitioner alleged that the telephone system is a public utility service and not a Revenue earning establishment and the charges can be only in the nature of a fee which must be commensurate with the best of rendering the service. The petitioner further alleged that the loss incurred by the Government in another establishment service is not a legitimate ground for raising telephone rates.

The Trial Court held that Telephone Tariff was unjust and unreasonable. The Trial Court allowed the writ petition.

The High Court on appeal held that the High Court could not interfere with the tariff. The High Court said that the principle upon which public utility rates regulation has developed in the United States is not applicable here in our country.

It should be said at the outset that there was some discussion in the judgement on Article 19 but counsel for the appellant properly abandoned any reference to Article 19. The appellant's contentions are three. First, the expression "rates" in Section 7(2) of the Indian Telegraph Act means rates which are to be determined should be fair, just and reasonable from the point of view of both the consumer and the producer. Second, the Court has jurisdiction to determine whether the rates fixed by the Government are reasonable. Third, the rates are increased expressely for the purpose of off-setting the losses in the Post and Telegraph Services. If a proper allocation is made according to proper commercial accounting it will be found that there is a wrongful deduction of crores of rupees as revenue expense and unlawful debit. These errors in the accounting have resulted in reducing the profits earned by the Telephones.

There are three principal reasons why the writ petition is incompetent and not maintainable and the appeal should fail.

First, when any subscriber to a telephone enters into a contract with the State, the subscriber has the option to enter into a contract or not. If he does so, he has to pay the rates which are charged by the State for installation. A subscriber cannot say that the rates are not fair. No one is compelling one to subscribe.

Second, Telephone tariff is subordinate legislation and a legislative process. Under Indian Telegraph Act, Section 7 empowers the Central Govt. to make rules *inter alia* for rates. These rules are laid before each House of Parliament. The Rules take affect when they are passed by the Parliament.

Third, the question of rates if first gone into by the Tariff enquiry committee. The Committee is headed by non-officials. The Tariff rates are placed before the House in the shape of Budget proposals. The Parliament goes into all the Budget proposals. The rates are sanctioned by the Parliament. The rates, therefore, become a legislative policy as well as a legislative process.

The Courts have no jurisdiction under Article 226 to go into reasonableness of rates. These rates are decided as policy matter in fiscal planning. There is legislative prescription of rates. Rates are a matter for legislative judgement and not for judicial determination.

The appeal is dismissed. There will be no order as to costs.

THE TELECOM REGULATORY AUTHORITY OF INDIA ACT, 1997

(No. 24 of 1997) [28th March, 1997]

An Act to provide for the establishment of the Telecom Regulatory

Authority of India to regulate the telecommunication services, and for matters connected therewith or incidental thereto.

Be it enacted by Parliament in the Forty-eighth Year of the Republic of India as follows :-

I. PRELIMINARY

1. Short title, extent and commencement

(1) This Act may be called the Telecom Regulatory Authority of India Act, 1997.

(2) It extends to the whole of India.

(3) It shall be deemed to have come into force on the 25th day of January, 1997.

2. Definitions

(1) In this Act, unless the context otherwise requires.—

(a) *"appointed day"* means the date with effect from which the Authority is established under sub-section (7) of Section 3;

(b) *"Authority"* means the Telecom Regulatory Authority of India established under sub-section (1) of Section 3;

(c) *"Chairperson"* means the Chairperson of the Authority appointed under sub-section *(3)* of Section 3;

(d) *"Fund"* means the Fund constituted under sub-section (1) of Section 22;

(e) *"licensee"* means any person licensed under sub-section (7) of Section 4 of the Indian Telegraph Act, 1885 for providing specified public telecommunication services;

(f) *"member"* means a member of the Authority appointed under sub-section (3) of Section 3 and includes the Chairperson and the Vice-Chairperson;

(g) *"notification"* means a notification published in the Official Gazette;

(h) *"prescribed"* means prescribed by rules made under this Act;

(i) *"regulations"* means regulations made by the Authority under this Act;

(j) *"service provider"* means the Government and includes a licensee;

(k) *"telecommunication service"* means service of any description (including electronic mail, voice mail, data services, audiotex services, videotex services, radio paging and cellular mobile telephone services) which is made available to users by means of any transmission or reception of signs, signals, writing, images and sounds or intelligence of any nature, by wire, radio, visual or other electromagnetic means but shall not include broadcasting services.

(2) Words and expressions used and not defined in this Act but defined in the Indian Telegraph Act, 1885 or the Indian Wireless Telegraphy Act, 1933, shall have the meanings respectively assigned to them in those Acts.

(3) Any reference in this Act to a law which is not in force in the State of Jammu and Kashmir shall in relation to that State be construed as a reference to the corresponding law, if any, in that State.

II. TELECOM REGULATORY AUTHORITY OF INDIA

3. Establishment and Incorporation of Authority

(1) With effect from such date as the Central Government

may, by notification appoint, there shall be established, for the purposes of this Act, an Authority to be called the Telecom Regulatory Authority of India.

(2) The Authority shall be a body corporate by the name aforesaid, having perpetual succession and a common seal, with power, subject to the provisions of this Act, to acquire, hold and dispose of property, both movable and immovable, and to contract, and shall, by the said name, sue or be sued.

(3) The Authority shall consist of a Chairperson, and not less than two, but not exceeding six members, to be appointed by the Central Government.

(4) The head office of the Authority shall be at New Delhi.

4. Qualifications for Appointment of Chairperson and Other Members

(1) The Chairperson shall be a person who is or has been a Judge of the Supreme Court or who is or has been the Chief Justice of a High Court.

(2) A member shall be a person who has special knowledge of, and professional experience in, telecommunication, industry, finance, accountancy, law, management and consumer affairs :

Provided that a person who is or has been in the service of Government shall not be appointed as a member unless such person has held the post of Secretary or Additional Secretary, or the post of Additional Secretary and Secretary to the Government of India or any equivalent post in the Central Government or the State Government for a period of three years.

5. Term of Office, Conditions of Service, Etc., of Chairperson and Other Members

(1) Before appointing any person as the Chairperson or member, the Central Government shall satisfy itself that the person does not have any such financial or other interest as is likely to affect prejudicially his functions as such member.

(2) The Chairperson shall hold office for a term of five years from the date on which he enters upon his office.

(3) *A* member shall hold office for a term of five years from the date on which he enters upon his office or until he attains the age of sixty-five years, whichever is earlier.

(4) The employee of the Government on his selection as member shall have to retire from sei-vice before joining as a member.

(5) The salary and allowances payable to and the other terms and conditions of service of the Chairperson and other members shall be such as may be prescribed.

(6) The salary, allowances and other conditions of service of the Chairperson or of a member shall not be varied to his disadvantage after appointment.

(7) Notwithstanding anything contained in sub-section (2) or sub-section (3), a member may—

(a) relinquish his office by giving in writing to the Central Government notice of not less than three months; or

(b) be removed from his office in accordance with the provisions of Section 7.

(8) The Chairperson or any other member ceasing to hold office as such, shall—

(a) be ineligible for further employment under the Central Government or any State Government; or

(b) not accept any commercial employment, for a period of two years from the date he ceases to hold such office.

(9) A vacancy caused to the office of the Chairperson or any other member shall be filled up within a period of three months from the date on which such vacancy occurs.

Explanation :— For the purposes of this section, "commercial employment" means employment in any capacity under, or agency of, a person engaged in trading, commercial, industrial or financial business in any field and includes also a director of a company or partner of a firm and it also includes setting up practice either independently or as partner of a firm or as an adviser or a consultant.

6. Powers of Chairperson and Vice-Chairperson

(1) The Chairperson shall have powers of general superintendence and directions in the conduct of the affairs of the Authority and he shall, in addition to presiding over the meetings of the Authority, exercise and discharge such powers and functions of the Authority and shall discharge such other powers and functions as may be prescribed.

(2) The Central Government may appoint one of the members to be a Vice-Chairperson of the Authority who shall exercise and discharge such powers and functions of the Chairperson as may be prescribed or as may be delegated to him by the Authority.

7. Removal and suspension of member from office in certain circumstances

(1) The Central Government may remove from office any member, who,—

(a) has been adjudged an insolvent; or

(b) has been convicted of an offence which, in the opinion of the Central Government, involves moral turpitude; or

(c) has become physically or mentally incapable of acting as a member; or

(d) has acquired such financial or other interest as is likely to affect prejudicially his functions as a member; or

(e) has so abused his position as to render his continuance in office prejudicial to the public interest.

(2) Notwithstanding anything contained in sub-section (7), no member shall be removed from his office on the ground specified in clause *(d)* or clause *(e)* of that sub-section unless the Supreme Court on a reference being made to it in this behalf by the Central Government, has, on an enquiry, held by it in accordance with such procedure as prescribed in this behalf, reported that the member ought on such ground or grounds to be removed.

(3) The Central Government may suspend from office a member in respect of whom a reference has been made to the Supreme Court under sub-section (2) until the Central Government has passed an order on receipt of the report of the Supreme Court on such reference.

8. Meetings

(7) The Authority shall meet at such times and places, and shall observe such rules of procedure in regard to the transaction of business at its meetings (including quorum at such meetings) as may be provided by regulations.

(2) The Chairperson or, if for any reason, he is unable to attend a meeting of the Authority, Vice-Chairperson

and in his absence, any other member chosen by the members present from amongst themselves at the meeting shall preside at the meeting.

(3) All questions which come up before any meeting of the Authority shall be decided by a majority vote of the members present and voting, and in the event of an equality of votes, the Chairperson or in his absence, the person presiding, shall have a second or casting vote.

(4) The Authority may make regulations for the transaction of business at its meetings.

9. Vacancies, Etc., Not to Invalidate Proceedings of Authority

No act or proceeding of the Authority shall be invalid merely by reason of—

(a) any vacancy in, or any defect in the constitution of, the Authority; or

(b) any defect in the appointment of a person acting as a member of the Authority; or

(c) any irregularity in the procedure of the Authority not affecting the merits of the case.

10. Officers and Other Employees of Authority

(1) The Authority may appoint officers and such other employees as it considers necessary for the efficient discharge of its functions under this act.

(2) The salary and allowances payable to and the other conditions of service of the officers and other employees of the Authority appointed under sub-section (1) shall be such as may be determined by regulations.

III. POWERS AND FUNCTIONS OF THIS AUTHORITY

11. Functions of the Authority

(1) Notwithstanding anything contained in the Indian Telegraph Act, 1885, the functions of the Authority shall be to—

(a) recommend the need and timing for introduction of new service provider;

(b) recommend the terms and conditions of licence to a service provider;

(c) ensure technical compatibility and effective inter-connection between different service providers;

(d) regulate arrangement amongst service providers of sharing their revenue derived from providing telecommunication services;

(e) ensure compliance of terms and conditions of licence;

(f) recommend revocation of licence for non-compliance of terms and conditions of licence;

(g) lay down and ensure the time period for providing local and long distance circuits of telecommunication between different service providers;

(h) facilitate competition and promote efficiency in the operation of telecommunication services so as to facilitate growth in such services;

(i) protect the interest of the consumers of telecommunication service;

(j) monitor the quality of service and conduct the periodical survey of such service provided by the service providers;

(k) inspect the equipment used in the network and recommend the type of equipment to be used by the service providers;

(l) maintain register of interconnect agreements and of all such other matters as may be provided in the regulations;

(m) keep register maintained under clause (l) open for inspection to any member of public on payment of such fee and compliance of such other requirements as may be provided in the regulations;

(n) settle disputes between service providers;

(o) render advice to the Central Government in the matters relating to the development of telecommunication technology and any other matter relatable to telecommunication industry in general;

(p) levy fees and other charges at such rates and in respect of such services as may be determined by regulations;

(q) ensure effective compliance of universal service obligations;

(r) perform such other functions including such administrative and financial functions as may be entrusted to it by the Central Government or as may be necessary to carry out the provisions of this Act.

(2) Notwithstanding anything contained in the Indian Telegraph Act, 1885, the Authority may, from time to time, by order, notify in the Official Gazette the rates at which the telecommunication services within India and outside India shall be provided under this Act including the rates at which messages shall be transmitted to any country outside India :

Provided that the Authority may notify different rates for different persons or class of persons for similar telecommunication services and where different rates are fixed as aforesaid the Authority shall record the reasons therefor.

(3) While discharging its functions under sub-section *(J)*, the Authority shall not act against the interest of the sovereignty and integrity of India, the security of the State, friendly relations with foreign States, public order, decency or morality.

(4) The Authority shall ensure transparency while exercising its powers and discharging its functions.

12. Powers of Authority to call for information, conduct investigations, etc.

(1) Where the Authority considers it expedient so to do, it may, by order in writing, —

(a) call upon any service provider at any time to furnish in writing such information or explanation relating to its affairs as the Authority may require; or

(b) appoint one or more persons to make an inquiry in relation to the affairs of any service provider; and

(c) direct any of its officers or employees to inspect the books of account or other documents of any service provider.

(2) Where any inquiry in relation to the affairs of a service provider has been undertaken under sub-section (1). —

(a) every officer of the Government Department, if such service provider is a department of the Government;

(b) every director, manager, secretary or other officer, if such service provider is a company; or

(c) every partner, manager, secretary or other officer, if such service provider is a firm; or

(d) every other person or body of persons who has had dealings in the course of business with any of the persons mentioned in clauses *(b)* and (c), shall be bound to produce before the Authority making the inquiry, all such books of account or other documents in his custody or power relating to, or havings bearing on the subject-matter of such inquiry and also to furnish to the Authority with any such statement or information relating thereto, as the case may be, required of him, within such time as may be specified.

(3) Every service provider shall maintain such books of account or other documents as may be prescribed.

(4) The Authority shall have the power to issue such directions to service providers as it may consider necessary for proper functioning by sei-vice providers.

13. Power of Authority to Issue Directions

The Authority may, for the discharge of its functions under sub-section *(1)* of Section 11, issue such directions from time to time to the service providers, as it may consider necessary.

IV. SETTLEMENT OF DISPUTES

14. Authority to Settle Disputes

(1) If a dispute arises, in respect of matters referred to in sub-section (2), among service providers or between service providers and a group of consumers, such disputes shall be adjudicated by a bench constituted by the Chairperson and such bench shall consist of two members:

Provided that if the members of the bench differ on any point or points they shall state the point or points on which they differ and refer the same to a third member for hearing on such point or points and such point or points shall be decided according to the opinion of that member.

(2) The bench constituted under sub-section (1) shall exercise, on and from the appointed day all such jurisdiction, powers and authority as were exercisable immediately before that date by any Civil Court on any matter relating to —

(i) technical compatibility and inter-connections between service providers;

(II) revenue sharing arrangements between different service providers;

(iii) quality of telecommunication services and interest of consumers;

Provided that nothing in this sub-section shall apply in respect of matters relating to —

(a) the monopolistic trade practice, restrictive trade practice and unfair trade practice which are subject to the jurisdiction of the Monopolies and Restrictive Trade Practices Commission established under sub-section (1) of Section 5 of the Monopolies ; Restrictive Trade Practices Act, 1969;

(b) the complaint of an individual consumer maintainable before a Consumer Disputes Redressal Forum or a Consumer Disputes Redressal Commission or the National Consumer Redressal Commission established under Section 9 of the Consumer Protection Act, 1986;

(c) dispute between telegraph authority and any

other person referred to in sub-section (1) of Section 7B of the Indian Telegraph Act, 1885.

15. Filing of Application to Authority and Procedure for Passing Order by it

(1) An aggrieved person may make an application in respect of matters referred to in sub-section (2) of Section 14 within such period as may be prescribed.

Explanation :—For the purposes of this sub-section, the expression "aggrieved person" means—

(i) any service provider who has a dispute in respect of matters referred to in clauses (*i*) and (*ii*) of sub-section (2) of Section 14;

(ii) where any loss or damage is caused to a group of consumers, any member representing such group of consumers.

(2) On receipt of an application made under sub-section *(l)*, the Authority may, after giving the parties an opportunity of being heard, pass such orders as it thinks fit preferably within a period of six months from the date of filing of such application and shall record reasons in writing if final order cannot be passed within the said period.

(3) While arriving at a decision, the Authority shall record in writing the reasons for such decision.

(4) Every decision of the Authority shall be published in the annual report of the Authority.

(5) The orders and directions of the Authority shall be binding on the service providers, Government and all other persons concerned.

16. Procedure and Powers of Authority

(1) The Authority shall be guided by the principles of natural justice.

(2) The Authority shall have, for the purpose of discharging their functions under this Chapter, the same powers as are vested in a civil court under the Code of Civil Procedure, 1908 in respect of the following matters, namely:—

(a) summoning and enforcing the attendance of any person and examining him on oath;

(b) requiring the discovery and production of documents;

(c) receiving evidence on affidavits;

(d) issuing commissions for the examination of witnesses or documents;

(e) reviewing its decisions;

(f) dismissing an application for default or deciding it *ex parte;*

(g) setting aside any order of dismissal of any application for default or any order passed by it *ex parte:*

(h) any other matter which may be prescribed.

(3) Every proceeding before the Authority shall be deemed to be a judicial proceeding within the meaning of Sections 193 and 228, and for the purpose of Section 196 of the Indian Penal Code and the Authority shall be deemed to be a Civil Court for all the purposes of Section 195 and Chapter XXVI of the Code of Criminal Procedure, 1973.

17. Right to Legal Representation

The applicant may either appear in person or authorise one or more legal practitioners or any of its officers to present his or its case before the Authority.

18. Appeal to High Court

Any person aggrieved by any decision or order of the Authority may file an appeal to the High Court within thirty days from the date of communication of the decision or order of the Authority to him :

Provided that the High Court may, if it is satisfied that the appellant was prevented by sufficient cause from filing the appeal within the said period, allow it to be filed within a further period not exceeding sixty days.

19. Orders Passed by Authority or High Court to be Executable as a Decree

Every order made by the Authority under this Act or the order made by the High Court in any appeal against any order of the Authority shall, on a certificate issued by any officer of the Authority or the Registrar of the High Court, as the case may be, be deemed to be decree of the Civil Court and shall be executable in the same manner as a decree of that Court.

20. Penalty for wilful failure to comply with orders of Authority or High Court

If any person wilfully fails to comply with the orders of the Authority or any order of the High Court, as the case may be, he shall be punishable with fine which may extend to one lakh rupees and in case of a second or subsequent offence with fine which may extend to two lakh rupees and in the case of continuing contravention with additional fine which may extend to two lakh rupees for every day during which the default continues.

V. FINANCE, ACCOUNTS AND AUDIT

21. Grants by Central Government

The Central Government may, after due appropriation made by Parliament by law in this behalf, make to the Authority grants of such sums of money as are required to pay salaries and allowances payable to the Chairperson and the members and the administrative expenses including the salaries, allowances and pension payable to or in respect of officers and other employees of the Authority:

22. Fund

(1) There shall be constituted a Fund to be called the Telecom Regulatory Authority of India General Fund and there shall be credited thereto—

(a) all grants fees and charges received by the Authority under this Act; and

(b) all sums received by the Authority from such other sources as may be decided upon by the Central Government.

(2) The Fund shall be applied for meeting—

(a) the salaries and allowances payable to the Chairperson and members and the administrative expenses including the salaries, allowances and pension payable to or in respect of officers and other employees of the Authority; and

(b) the expenses on objects and for purposes authorised by this Act.

23. Accounts and audit

(1) The Authority shall maintain proper accounts and other relevant records and prepare an annual statement of accounts in such form as may be prescribed by the Central Government in consultation with the Comptroller and Auditor-General of India.

(2) The accounts of the Authority shall be audited by the Comptroller and Auditor-General of India at such intervals as may be specified by him and any expenditure incurred in connection with such auditor shall be payable by the Authority to the Comptroller and Auditor-General of India.

(3) The Comptroller and Auditor-General of India and any other person appointed by him in connection with the audit of the accounts of the Authority shall have the same rights and privileges and authority in connection with such audit as the Comptroller and Auditor-General generally has, in connection with the audit of the Government accounts and, in particular, shall have the right to demand the production of books, accounts, connected vouchers and other documents and papers and to inspect any of the offices of the Authority.

(4) The accounts of the Authority as certified by the Comptroller and Auditor-General of India or any other person appointed by him in this behalf together with the audit report thereon shall be forwarded annually to the Central Government and that Government shall cause the same to be laid before each House of Parliament.

24. Furnishing of Returns, Etc., to Central Government

(1) The Authority shall furnish to the Central Government at such time and in such form and manner as may be prescribed or as the Central Government may direct, such returns and statements and such particulars in regard to any proposed or existing programme for the promotion and development of the telecommunication services, as the Central Government may from time to time, require.

(2) The Authority shall prepare once every year in such form and at such time as may be prescribed, an annual report giving a summary of its activities during the previous year and copies of the report shall be forwarded to the Central Government.

(3) A copy of the report received under sub-section *(2)* shall be laid, as soon as may be after it is received, before each House of Parliament.

VI. MISCELLANEOUS

25. Power of Central Government to Issue Directions

(1) The Central Government may, from time to time, issue to the Authority such directions as it may think necessary in the interest of the sovereignty and integrity of India, the security of the State, friendly relations with foreign States, public order, decency or morality.

(2) Without prejudice to the foregoing provisions, the Authority shall, in exercise of its powers or the performance of its functions, be bound by such directions on questions of policy as the Central Government may give in writing to it from time to time :

Provided that the Authority shall, as far as practicable, be given an opportunity to express its views before any direction is given under this sub-section.

(3) The decision of the Central Government whether a question is one of policy or not shall be final.

26. Members, Officers and Employees of Authority to be Public Servants

All members, officers and other employees of the Authority shall be deemed, when acting or purporting to act in pursuance of any of the provisions of this Act to be public servants within the meaning of Section 21 of the Indian Penal Code.

27. Bar of Jurisdiction

No civil court shall have jurisdiction in respect of any matter which the Authority is empowered by or under this Act to determine.

28. Protection of Action Taken in Good Faith

No suit, prosecution or other legal proceedings shall

lie against the Central Government or the Authority or any officer of the Central Government or any member, officer or other employees of the Authority for anything which is in good faith done or intended to be done under this Act or the rules or regulations made thereunder.

29. Penalty for Contravention of Directions of Authority

If a person violates directions of the Authority, such person shall be punishable with fine which may extend to one lakh rupees and in case of second or subsequent offence with fine which may extend to two lakh rupees and in the case of continuing contravention with additional fine which may extend to two lakh rupees for every day during which the default continues.

30. Offences by Companies

(1) Where an offence under this Act has been committed by a company, every person who at the time, the offence was committed was in charge of, and was responsible to, the company for the conduct of the business of the company, as well as the company, shall be deemed to be guilty of the offence and shall be liable to be proceeded against and punished accordingly :

Provided that nothing contained in this sub-section shall render any such person liable to any punishment provided in this Act if he proves that the offence was committed without his knowledge or that he has exercised all due diligence to prevent the commission of such offence.

(2) Notwithstanding anything contained in sub-section (1), where an offence under this Act has been committed by a company and it is proved that the offence has been committed with the consent or connivance of, or is attributable to, any neglect on the part of any director, manager, secretary or other officer of the company, such

director, manager, secretary or other officer shall also be deemed to be guilty of the offence and shall be liable to be proceeded against and punished accordingly.

Explanation :— For the purposes of this section—

(a) *"company"* means any body corporate and includes a firm or other association of individuals; and

(b) *"director"*, in relation to a firm, means a partner in the firm.

31. Offences by Government Departments

(1) Where an offence under this Act has been committed by any Department of Government, the Head of the Department shall be deemed to be guilty of the offence and shall be liable to be proceeded against and punished accordingly unless he proves that the offence was committed without his knowledge or that he exercised all due diligence to prevent the commission of such offence.

(2) Notwithstanding anything contained in sub-section *(1)*, where an offence under this Act has been committed by a Department of Government and it is proved that the offence has been committed with the consent or connivance of, or is attributable to any neglect on the part of, any officer, other than the Head of the Department, such officer shall also be deemed to be guilty of that offence and shall be liable to be proceeded against and punished accordingly.

32. Exemption from tax on wealth and income

Notwithstanding anything contained in the Wealth-tax Act, 1957, the Income-tax Act, 1961, or any other enactment for the time being in force relating to tax on wealth, income, profits or gains, the Authority shall not be liable to pay wealth-tax, income-tax or any other tax in respect of their wealth, income, profits or gains derived.

33. Delegation

The Authority may, by general or special order in writing, delegate to any member, officer of the Authority or any other person subject to such conditions, if any, as may be specified in the order, such of its powers and functions under this Act (except the power to settle dispute under and to make regulation under Section 36) as it may deem necessary.

34. Cognizance of Offences

(1) No court shall take cognizance of any offence punishable under this Act or the rules or regulations made thereunder, save on a complaint made by the Authority.

(2) No court inferior to that of a Chief Metropolitan Magistrate or a Chief Judicial Magistrate of first class shall try any offence punishable under this Act.

35. Power to make rules

(1) The Central Government may, by notification, make rules for carrying out the purposes on this Act.

(2) In particular, and without prejudice to the generality of the foregoing power, such rules may provide for all or any of the following matters, namely :—

(a) the salary and allowances payable to and the other conditions of service of the Chairperson and members under sub-section (5) of Section 5;

(b) the powers and functions of the Chairperson under sub-section (1) of Section 6;

(c) the procedure of conducting an inquiry made under sub-section (2) of Section 7;

(d) the category of books of account or other documents which are required to be maintained under sub-section (3) of Section 12;

(e) the period within which an application is to be made under sub-section (1) of Section 15;

(f) the manner in which the accounts of the Authority shall be maintained under sub-section (7) of Section 23;

(g) the time within which and the form and manner in which returns and report are to be made to the Central Government under sub-sections (1) and *(2)* of Section 24;

(h) any other matter which is to be, or may be, prescribed, or in respect of which provision is to be made, by rules.

36. Power to Make Regulations

(1) The Authority may, by notification, make regulations consistent with this Act and the rules made thereunder to carry out the purposes of this Act.

(2) In particular, and without prejudice to the generality of the foregoing power, such regulations may provide for all or any of the following matters, namely :—

(a) the times and places of meetings of the Authority and the procedure to be followed at such meetings under sub-section (1) of Section 8, including quorum necessary for the transaction of business;

(b) the transaction of business at the meetings of the Authority under sub-section (4) of Section 8;

(c) the salaries and allowances payable to and the other conditions of service of officers and other employees of the Authority under sub-section (2) of Section 10;

(d) matters in respect of which register is to be maintained by the Authority under clause (l) of sub-section (1) of Section 11;

(e) levy of fee and lay down such other requirements on fulfillment of which a copy of register may be obtained under clause (m) of sub-section (1) of Section 11;

(f) levy of fees and other charges under clause (p) of sub-section (1) of Section 11

37. Rules and Regulations to be Laid Before the Parliament

Every rule and every regulation made under this Act shall be laid, as soon as may be after it is made, before each House of Parliament, while it is in session, for a total period of thirty days which may be comprised in one session or in two or more successive sessions, and if, before the expiry of the session immediately following the session or the successive sessions aforesaid, both Houses agree in making any modification in the rule or regulation or both Houses agree that the rule or regulation should not be made, the rule or regulation shall thereafter have effect only in such modified form or be of no effect, as the case may be; so, however, that any such modification or annulment shall be without prejudice to the validity of anything previously done under that rule or regulation.

38. Application of Certain Laws

The provisions of this Act shall be in addition to the provisions of the Indian Telegraph Act, 1885 and the Indian Wireless Telegraphy Act, 1933 and, in particular, nothing in this Act shall affect any jurisdiction, powers and functions required to be exercised or performed by the Telegraph Authority in relation to any area falling within the jurisdiction of such Authority.

39. Power to Remove Difficulties

(1) If any difficulty arises in giving effect to the provisions of this Act, the Central Government may, by order, published

in the Official Gazette, make such provisions not inconsistent with the provisions of this Act as may appear to be necessary for removing the difficulty:

Provided that no order shall be made under this section after the expiry of two years from the date of commencement of this Act.

(2) Every order made under this section shall be laid, as soon as may be after it is made, before each House of Parliament.

40. Repeal and Saving

(1) The Telecom Regulatory Authority of India Ordinance, 1997 is hereby repealed.

(2) Notwithstanding such repeal, anything done or any action taken under the said Ordinance shall be deemed to have been done or taken under the corresponding provisions of this Act.

3 THE INDIAN TELEGRAPH ACT, 1885

ACT NO. 13 OF 1885

An Act to Amend the Law Relating to Telegraphs in India

[22nd July, 1885]

Whereas it is expedient to amend the law relating to telegraphs in India; It is hereby enacted as follows:—

PART I

Preliminary

1. Short Title, Local Extent and Commencement

(1) This Act may be called the Indian Telegraph Act, 1885.

[(2) It extends to whole of India***.]

(3) It shall come into force on the first day of October, 1885.

2. [*Repeal and savings.*]

Rep. by the Repealing Act, 1938(1 *of* 1938), *Section* 2 *and Sch.*

3. Definitions

In this Act, unless there is something repugnant in the subject or context,—

[(1) "telegraph" means any appliance, instrument, material or apparatus used or capable of use for transmission or reception of signs, signals, writing, images, and sounds or intelligence of any nature by wire, visual or other electro-magnetic emissions, Radio waves or Hertzian waves, galvanic, electric or magnetic means;

Explanation.—"Radio waves" or "Hertzian waves" means electromagnetic waves of frequencies lower than 3,000 giga-cyclcs per second propagated in space without artificial guide.]

(2) "telegraph officer" means any person employed either permanently or temporarily in connection with a telegraph established, maintained or worked by [the Central Government] or by a person licensed under this act;

(3) "message" means any communication sent by telegraph, or given to a telegraph officer to be sent by telegraph or to be delivered;

(4) "telegraph line" means a wire or wires used for the purpose of a telegraph, with any casing, coating, tube or pipe enclosing the same, and any appliances and apparatus connected therewith for the purpose or fixing or insulating the same;

(5) "post" means a post, pole, standard, stay, strut or other above-ground contrivance for carrying, suspending or supporting a telegraph line;

(6) "telegraph authority" means the Director General of [Posts and Telegraphs], and includes any officer empowered by him to perform all or any of the functions of the telegraph authority under this Act;

(7) "local authority" means any municipal committee, district board, body of port commissioners or other authority,

legally entitled to, or entrusted by [the Central or any State Government] with, the control or management of any municipal or local fund.

PART II

PRIVILEGES AND POWERS OF THE GOVERNMENT

4. Exclusive Privilege in Respect of Telegraphs, and Power to Grant Licenses

[(1)] Within [India], the Central Government shall have the exclusive privilege of establishing, maintaining and working telegraphs :

Provided that the Central Government may grant a license, on such conditions and in consideration of such payments as it thinks fit, to any person to establish, maintain or work a telegraph within any part of [India] :

[Provided further that the Central Government may, by rules made under this Act and published in the Official Gazette, permit, subject to such restrictions and conditions as it thinks fit, the establishment, maintenance and working—

(a) of wireless telegraphs on ships within Indian territorial waters [and on aircraft within or above [India], or Indian territorial waters], and

(b) of telegraphs other than wireless telegraphs within any part of [India]].

[(2) The Central Government may, by notification in the Official Gazette, delegate to the telegraph authority all or any of its powers under the first proviso to sub-section (1).

The exercise by the telegraph authority of any power so delegated shall be subject to such restrictions and conditions as the Central Government may, by the notification, think fit to impose.]

[5. Power for Government to Take Possession of Licensed Telegraphs and to Order Interception of Messages

(1) On the occurrence of any public emergency, or in the interest of the public safety, the Central Government or a State Government, or any officer specially authorized in this behalf by the Central or a State Government, may, if satisfied that it is necessary or expedient so to do, take temporary possession (for so long as the public emergency exists or the interest of the public safety requires the taking of such action) of any telegraph established, maintained or worked by any person licensed under this Act.

(2) On the occurrence of any public emergency, or in the interest of the public safety, the Central Government or a State Government or any officer specially authorised in this behalf by the Central Government or a State Government may, if satisfied that it is necessary or expedient so to do in the interests of the sovereignty and integrity of India, the security of the State, friendly relations with foreign States or public order or for preventing incitement to the commission of an offence, for reasons to be recorded in writing, by order, direct that any message or class of messages to or from any person or class of persons, or relating to any particular subject, brought for transmission by or transmitted or received by any telegraph, shall not be transmitted, or shall be intercepted or detained, or shall be disclosed to the Government making the order or an officer thereof mentioned in the order :

Provided that press messages intended to be published in India of correspondents accredited to the Central Government or a State Government shall not be intercepted or detained, unless their transmission has been prohibited under this sub-section.]

6. Power to Establish Telegraph on Land of Railway Company

Any Railway Company, on being required so to do by the Central Government, shall permit the Government to establish and maintain a telegraph upon any part of the land of the Company, and shall give every reasonable facility for working the same.

[6- A. Power to notify rates for transmission of messages to countries outside India .

(1) The Central Government may, from time to time, by order, notify the rates at which and the other conditions and restrictions subject to which messages shall be transmitted to any country outside India.

(2) In notifying the rates under sub-section (1), the Central Government shall have due regard to all or any of the following factors, namely :

(a) the rates for the time being in force for transmission of messages, in countries outside India;

(b) the foreign exchange rates for the time being in force;

(c) the rates for the time being in force for transmission of messages within India;

(d) such other relevant factors as the Central Government may think fit in the circumstances in the case.]

7. Power to Make Rules for the Conduct of Telegraphs

(1) The Central Government may, from time to time, by notification in the Official Gazette, make rules consistent

with this Act for the conduct of all or any telegraphs established, maintained or worked by the Government or by the persons licensed under this Act.

(2) Rules under this section may provide for all or any of the following among other matters, that is to say : —

(a) the rates at which, and the other conditions and restrictions subject to which, messages shall be transmitted [within India];

(b) the precautions to be taken for preventing the improper interception or disclosure of messages;

(c) the period for which, and the conditions subject to which, telegrams and other documents belonging to, or being in the custody of, telegraph offices shall be preserved;

(d) the fees to be charged for searching for telegrams or other documents in the custody of any telegraph officer.

[(e) the conditions and restrictions subject to which any telegraph line, appliance or apparatus for telegraphic communication shall be established, maintained, worked, repaired, transferred, shifted, withdrawn or disconnected;]

[(ee) the charges in respect of any application for providing any telegraph line, appliance or apparatus;]

(f) the charges in respect of—

(i) the establishment, maintenance, working, repair, transfer, or shifting of any telegraph line, appliance or apparatus;

(ii) the services of operators operating such line, appliances or apparatus;

(g) the matters in connection with the transition from a system whereunder rights and obligations relating to the establishment, maintenance, working, repair, transfer or shifting of any telegraph line, appliance or apparatus for telegraphic communication attach by virtue of any agreement to a system whereunder such rights and obligations attach by virtue of rules made under this section;

(h) the time at which, the manner in which, the conditions under which and the persons by whom the rates, charges and fees mentioned in this sub-section shall be paid and the furnishing of security for the payment of such rates, charges and fees;

(i) the payment of compensation to the Central Government for any loss incurred in connection with the provision of any telegraph line, appliance or apparatus for the benefit of any person—

(i) where the line, appliance or apparatus is, after it has been connected for use, given up by that person before the expiration of the period fixed by these rules, or

(ii) where the work done for the purpose of providing the line, appliance or apparatus is, before it is connected for use, rendered abortive by some act or omission on the part of that person;

(j) the principles according to which and the authority by whom the compensation referred to in clause (1) shall be assessed;

[(jj) the qualifications to be possessed and the examinations, if any, to be passed by the persons employed for the establishment, maintenance or working of any telegraph and the fees to be charged for admission to such examination;] and

(k) any other matter for which provision is necessary for the proper and efficient conduct of all or any telegraphs under this Act.]

(3) When making rules for the conduct of any telegraph established, maintained or worked by any person licensed under this Act, the Central Government may by the rules prescribe fines for any breach of the same :

Provided that the fines so prescribed shall not exceed the following limits, namely:—

(i) when the person licensed under this Act is punishable for the breach, one thousand rupees, and in the case of a continuing breach a further fine of two hundred rupees for every day after the first during the whole or any part of which the breach continues;

(ii) when a servant of the person so licensed, or any other person, is punishable for the breach, one-fourth of the amounts specified in clause (*i*).

[(4) Nothing in this section or in any rules made hereunder shall be construed as—

(a) precluding the Central Government from entering into an agreement with a person for the establishment, maintenance and working by that Government on terms and conditions specified in the agreement, of any telegraph line, appliance or apparatus for the purpose of affording means of telegraphic communication, where having regard to the number of the lines, appliance or apparatus required by that person for telegraphic communication, it is necessary or expedient to enter into such agreement with him, or

(b) subjecting the Central Government to any obligation to provide any telegraph line, appliance or apparatus for the purpose of affording means of telegraphic communication.

[(5) Every rule made under this section shall be laid as soon as may be after it is made before each House of Parliament while it is in session for a total period of thirty days [which may be comprised in one session or in two or more successive sessions, and if, before the expiry of the session immediately following the session or the successive sessions aforesaid,] both Houses agree in making any modification in the rule or both Houses agree that the rule should not be made, the rule shall thereafter have effect only in such modified form or be of no effect, as the case may be; so however, that any such modification or annulment shall be without prejudice to the validity of anything previously done under that rule.]]

[7-A. Saving of Existing Agreements

Nothing in Section 7 shall authorise the making of any rules determining any agreement entered into by the Central Government with any person before the commencement of the Indian Telegraph (Amendment) Act, 1957, relating to the establishment, maintenance or working of any telegraph line, appliance or apparatus for telegraphic communication; and all rights and obligations thereunder relating to such establishment, maintenance or working shall be determined in accordance with the terms and conditions of such agreement.

7-B. Arbitration of Disputes

(1) Except as otherwise expressly provided in this Act, if any dispute concerning any telegraph line, appliance or apparatus arises between the telegraph authority and the

person for whose benefit the line, appliance or apparatus is, or has been, provided, the dispute shall be determined by arbitration, and shall, for the purposes of such determination, be referred to an arbitrator appointed by the Central Government either specially for the determination of that dispute or generally for the determination of disputes under this section.

(2) The award of the arbitrator appointed under sub-section (1) shall be conclusive between the parties to the dispute and shall not be questioned in any court.]

8. Revocation of Licenses

The Central Government may, at any time, revoke any license granted under Section 4, on the breach of any of the conditions therein contained, or in default of payment of any consideration payable thereunder.

9. Government not Responsible for Loss or Damage

The [Government] shall not be responsible for any loss or damage which may occur in consequence of any telegraph officer failing in his duty with respect to the receipt, transmission or delivery of any message; and no such officer shall be responsible for any such loss or damage, unless he causes the same negligently, maliciously or fraudulently.

PART III

POWER TO PLACE TELEGRAPH LINES AND POSTS

10. Power for Telegraph Authority to Place and Maintain Telegraph Lines and Posts

The telegraph authority may, from time to time, place and maintain a telegraph line under, over, along or across, and posts in or upon, any immoveable property :

Provided that—

(a) the telegraph authority shall not exercise the powers conferred by this section except for the purposes of a telegraph established or maintained by the [Central Government], or to be so established or maintained;

(b) the [Central Government] shall not acquire any right other than that of user only in the property under, over, along, across, in or upon which the telegraph authority places any telegraph line or post; and

(c) except as hereinafter provided, the telegraph authority shall not exercise those powers in respect of any property vested in or under the control or management of any local authority, without the permission of that authority; and

(d) in the exercise of the powers conferred by this section, the telegraph authority shall do as little damage as possible, and, when it has exercised those powers in respect of any property other than that referred to in clause (c); shall pay full compensation to all persons interested for any damage sustained by them by reason of the exercise of those powers.

11. Power to Enter on Property in Order to Repair or Remove Telegraph Lines or Posts

The telegraph authority may, at any time, for the purpose of examining, repairing, altering or removing any telegraph line or post, enter on the property under, over, along, across, in or upon which the line or post has been placed.

Provisions applicable to property vested in or under the control or management of local authorities

12. Power for Local Authority to Give Permission Under Section 10, Clause (c) Subject to Conditions

Any permission given by a local authority under Section 10, clause *(c)*, may be given subject to such reasonable conditions as that authority thinks fit to impose, as to the payment of any expenses to which the authority will necessarily be put in consequence of the exercise of the powers conferred by that section, or as to the time or mode of execution of any work, or as to any other thing connected with or relative to any work undertaken by the telegraph authority under those powers.

13. Power for Local Authority to Require Removal or Alteration of Telegraph Line or Post

When, under the foregoing provisions of this Act, a telegraph line or post has been placed by the telegraph authority under, over, along, across, in or upon any property vested in or under the control or that its position should be altered, the local authority may require regard to circumstances which have arisen since the telegraph line or post was so placed, considers it expedient that it should be removed or that its position should be altered, the local authority may-require the telegraph authority to remove it or alter its position, as the case may be.

14. Power to Alter Position of Gas or Water Pipes or Drains

The telegraph authority may, for the purpose of exercising the powers conferred upon it by this Act in respect of any property vested in or under the control or management of a local authority, alter the position thereunder of any pipe (not being a main) for the supply of gas or water, or of any drain (not being a main drain) :

Provided that—

(a) when the telegraph authority desires to alter the position of any such pipe or drain it shall give reasonable notice of its intention to do so, specifying the time at which it will begin to do so, to the local authority, and, when the pipe or drain is not under the control of the local authority, to the person under whose control the pipe or drain is;

(b) a local authority or person receiving notice under clause (a) may send a person to superintend the work, and the telegraph authority shall execute the work to the reasonable satisfaction of the person so sent.

15. Disputes Between Telegraph Authority and Local Authority

(1) If any dispute arises between the telegraph authority and a local authority in consequence of the local authority refusing the permission referred to in Section 10, clause (c), or prescribing any condition under Section 12, or in consequence of the telegraph authority omitting to comply with a requisition made under Section 13, or otherwise in respect of the exercise of the powers conferred by this Act, it shall be determined by such officer as the [Central Government] may appoint either generally or specially in this behalf.

(2) An appeal from the determination of the officer so appointed shall lie to the [Central Government]; and the order of the [Central Government] shall be final.

Provisions Applicable to Other Property

16. Exercise of powers conferred by Section 10, and disputes as to compensation, in case of property other than that of a local authority

(1) If the exercise of the powers mentioned in Section

10 in respect of property referred to in clause *(d)* of that section is resisted or obstructed, the District Magistrate may, in his discretion, order that the telegraph authority shall be permitted to exercise them.

(2) If, after the making of an order under sub-section (1), any person resists the exercise of those powers, or, having control over the property, does not give all facilities for their being exercised, he shall be deemed to have committed an offence under Section 188 of the Indian Penal Code (45 of 1860).

(3) If any dispute arises concerning the sufficiency of the compensation to be paid under Section 10, clause *(d)*, it shall, on application for that purpose by either of the disputing parties to the District Judge within whose jurisdiction the property is situate, be determined by him.

(4) If any dispute arises as to the persons entitled to receive compensation, or as to the proportions in which the persons interested are entitled to share in it, the telegraph authority may pay into the Court of the District Judge such amount as he deems sufficient or, where all the disputing parties have in writing admitted the amount tendered to be sufficient or the amount has been determined under sub-section (3), that amount; and the District Judge, after giving notice to the parties and hearing such of them as desire to be heard, shall determine the persons entitled to receive the compensation or, as the case may be, the proportions in which the persons interested are entitled to share in it.

(5) Every determination of a dispute by a District Judge under sub-section (3) or sub-section (4) shall be final:

Provided that nothing in this sub-section shall affect

the right of any person to recover by suit the whole or any part of any compensation paid by the telegraph authority, from the person who has received the same.

17. Removal or Alteration of Telegraph Line or Post on Property Other than that of a Local Authority

(1) When, under the foregoing provisions of this Act, a telegraph line or post has been placed by the telegraph authority under, over, along, across, in or upon any property, not being property vested in or under the control or management of a local authority, and any person entitled to do so desires to deal with that property in such a manner as to render it necessary or convenient that the telegraph line or post should be removed to another part thereof or to a higher or lower level or altered in from, he may require the telegraph authority to remove or alter the line or post accordingly :

Provided that, if compensation has been paid under Section 10, clause *(d)*, he shall, when making the requisition, tender to the telegraph authority the amount requisite to defray the expense of the removal or alterations, or half of the amount paid as compensation, whichever may be the smaller sum.

(2) If the telegraph authority omits to comply with the requisition, the person making it may apply to the District Magistrate within whose jurisdiction the property is situate to order the removal or alteration.

(3) A District Magistrate receiving an application under sub-section (2) may, in his discretion, reject the same or make an order, absolutely or subject to conditions, for the removal of the telegraph line or post to any other part of the property or to a higher or lower level or for the alteration of its form; and the order so made shall be final.

PROVISIONS APPLICABLE TO ALL PROPERTY

18. Removal of Trees Interrupting Telegraphic Communication

(1) If any tree standing or lying near a telegraph line interrupts, or is likely to interrupt telegraphic communication, a Magistrate of the first or second class may, on the application of the telegraph authority, cause the tree to be removed or dealt with in such other way as he deens fit.

(2) When disposing of an application under sub-section (1), the Magistrate shall, in the case of any tree in existence before the telegraph line was placed, award to the persons interested the tree such compensation as he thinks reasonable, and the award shall be final.

19. Telegraph Lines and Posts Placed Before the Passing of this Act

Every telegraph line or post placed before the passing of this Act under, over, along, across, in or upon any property, for the purposes of a telegraph established or maintained by the [Central Government], shall be deemed to have been placed in exercise of the powers conferred by, and after observance of all the requirements of, this Act.

[19-A. Person exercising legal right likely to damage telegraph or interfere with telegraphic communication to give notice

(1) Any person desiring to deal in the legal exercise of a right with any property in such a manner as is likely to cause damage to a telegraph line or post which has been duly placed in accordance with the provisions of this Act or to interrupt or interfere with telegraphic communication, shall give not less than one month's notice in writing of

the intended exercise of such right to the telegraph authority, or to any telegraph officer whom the telegraph authority may empower in this behalf.

(2) If any such person without having complied with the provisions of sub-section (1) deals with any property in such a manner as is likely to cause damage to any telegraph line or post, or to interrupt or interfere with telegraphic communication, a Magistrate of the first or second class may, on the application of the telegraph authority, order such person to abstain from dealing with such property in such manner for a period not exceeding one month from the date of his order and forthwith to take such action with regard to such property as may be in the opinion of the Magistrate necessary to remedy or prevent such damage, interruption or interference during such period.

(3) A person dealing with any property in the manner referred to in sub-section (1) with the *bona fide* intention of averting imminent danger of personal injury to himself or any other human being shall be deemed to have complied with the provisions of the said sub-section if he gives such notice of the intended exercise of the right as is in the circumstances possible, or where no such previous notice can be given without incurring the imminent danger referred to above, if he forthwith gives notice of the actual exercise of such right to the authority or officer specified in the said sub-section.

19-B. Power to Confer Upon Licensee Powers of Telegraph Authority Under This Part

The Central Government may, by notification in the Official Gazette, confer upon any licensee under Section 4, in respect of the extent of his license and subject to any conditions and restrictions which the Central Government may think fit to impose and to the provisions of this Part, all or any of the powers which the telegraph authority possesses under this part with regard to a telegraph established or maintained by the Government or to be so established or maintained:

Provided that the notice prescribed in Section 19-A shall always be given to the telegraph authority or officer empowered to receive notice under Section 19-A (1).]

PART IV

PENALTIES

[20. Establishing, Maintaining or Working Unauthorised Telegraph

(1) If any person establishes, maintains or works a telegraph within [India] in contravention of the provisions of Section 4 or otherwise than as permitted by rules made under that section, he shall be punished, if the telegraph is a wireless telegraph, with imprisonment, which may extend to three years, or with fine, or with both, and, in any other case, with a fine which may extend to one thousand rupees.

(2) Notwithstanding anything contained in the Code of Criminal Procedure, 1898 *(5* of 1898), offences under this section in respect of a wireless telegraph shall, for the purposes of the said Code, be bailable and non-cognizable.

(3) When any person is convicted of an offence punishable under this section, the Court before which he is convicted may direct that the telegraph in respect of which the offence has been committed, or any part of such telegraph, be forfeited to Government.]

[20-A. Breach of Condition of License

If the holder of a license granted under Section 4 contravenes any condition contained in his license, he shall be punished with fine which may extend to one thousand rupees, and with a further fine which may extend to five hundred rupees for every week during which the breach of the condition continues.]

21. Using Unauthorized Telegraphs

If any person, knowing or having reason to believe that a telegraph has been established or is maintained or worked, in contravention of this Act, transmits or receives any message by such telegraph, or performs any service incidental thereto, or delivers any message for transmission by such telegraph or accepts delivery of any message sent thereby, he shall be punished with fine which may extend to fifty rupees.

22. Opposing Establishment of Telegraphs on Railway Land

If a Railway Company, or an officer of a Railway Company, neglects or refuses to comply with the provisions of Section 6, it or he shall be punished with fine which may extend to one thousand rupees for every day during which the neglect or refusal continues.

23. Intrusion into Signal Room, Trespass in Telegraph Office or Obstruction

If any person —

(a) without permission of competent authority, enters the signal-room of a telegraph office of the Government, or of a person licensed under this Act, or

(b) enters a fenced enclosure round such a telegraph office in contravention of any rule or notice not to do so, or

(c) refuses to quit such room or enclosure on being requested to do so by any officer or servant employed therein, or

(d) wilfully obstructs or impedes any such officer or servant in the performance of his duty,

he shall be punished with fine which may extend to five hundred rupees.

24. Unlawfully Attempting to Learn Contents of Messages

If any person does any of the acts mentioned in Section 23 with the intention of unlawfully learning the contents of any message, or of committing any offence punishable under this Act, he may (in addition to the fine with which he is punishable under Section 23) be punished with imprisonment for a term which may extend to one year.

25. Intentionally Damaging or Tampering with Telegraphs

If any person, intending—

(a) to prevent or obstruct the transmission or delivery of any message, or

(b) to intercept or to acquaint himself with the contents of any message, or

(c) to commit mischief, damages, removes, tampers with or touches any battery, machinery, telegraph line, post or other thing whatever, being part of or used in or about any telegraph or in the working thereof,

he shall be punished with imprisonment for a term which may extend to three years, or with fine, or with both.

[25-A. Injury to or Interference with a Telegraph Line or Post

If, in any case not provided for by Section 25, any person deals with any property and thereby wilfully or negligently damages any telegraph line or post duly placed on such property in accordance with the provisions of this Act, he shall be liable to pay the telegraph authority such expenses (if any) as may be incurred in making good such damage, and shall also, if the telegraphic communication is by reason of the damage so caused interrupted, be punishable with a fine which may extend to one thousand rupees :

Provided that the provisions of this section shall not apply where such damage or interruption is caused by a person dealing with any property in the legal exercise of a right if he has complied with the provisions of Section 19-A-(1).]

26. Telegraph Officer or Other Official Making Away with or Altering, or Unlawfully Intercepting or Disclosing Messages, or Divulging Perport of Signals

If any telegraph officer, or any person, not being a telegraph officer but having official duties connected with any office which is used as a telegraph office,—

(a) wilfully secretes makes away with or alters any message which he has received for transmission or delivery, or

(b) wilfully, and otherwise than in obedience to an order of the Central Government or of a State Government, or of an officer specially authorized [by the Central or a State Government] to make the order, omits to transmit, or intercepts or detains, any message or any part thereof, or otherwise than in pursuance of his official duty or in obedience to the direction of a competent Court, discloses the contents or any part of the contents of any message, to any person not entitled to receive the same, or

(c) divulges the purport of any telegraphic signal to any person not entitled to become acquainted with the same,

he shall be punished with imprisonment for a term which may extend to three years, or with fine, or with both.

27. Telegraph Officer Fraudulently Sending Messages Without Payment

If any telegraph officer transmits by telegraph any message on which the charge prescribed by the [Central Government] or by a person licensed under this Act, as the case may be, has not been paid, intending thereby to defraud the [Central Government] or that person, he shall be punished with imprisonment for a term which may extend to three years, or with fine, or with both.

28. Misconduct

If any telegraph officer, or any person not being a telegraph officer but having official duties connected with any office which is used as a telegraph office, is guilty of any act of drunkenness, carelessness or other misconduct whereby the correct transmission or the delivery of any message is impeded or delayed, or if any telegraph officer loiters or delays in the transmission or delivery of any message, he shall be punished with imprisonment for a term which may extend to three months, or with fine which may extend to one hundred rupees, or with both.

29. Sending Fabricated Message

[* * *]

[29-A. Penalty

If any person, without due authority,—

(a) makes or issues any document of a nature reasonably calculated to cause it to be believed that the document has been issued by, or under the authority of, the Director-General of [Posts and Telegraphs], or

(b) makes on any document any mark in imitation of, or similar to, or purporting to be, any stamp or mark of any telegraph office under the Director-General of [Posts and Telegraphs], or a mark of a nature reasonably calculated to cause it to be believed that the document so marked has been issued by, or under the authority of, the Director-General of [Posts and Telegraphs],

he shall be punished with fine which may extend to fifty rupees.]

30. Retaining a Message Delivered by Mistake

If any person fraudulently retains, or wilfully secretes, makes away with or detains a message which ought to have been delivered to some other person, or, being required by a telegraph officer to deliver up any such message, neglects or refuses to do so, he shall be punished with imprisonment for a term which may extend to two years, or with fine, or with both.

31. Bribery

A telegraph officer shall be deemed a public servant within the meaning of Sections 161, 162, 163, 164 and 165 of the Indian Penal Code (45 of 1860); and in the definition of "legal remuneration" contained in the said Section 161, the word "Government" shall, for the purposes of this Act, be deemed to include a person licensed under this Act.

32. Attempts to Commit Offences

Whoever attempts to commit any offence punishable under "this Act shall be punished with the punishment herein provided for the offence.

PART V

SUPPLEMENTAL PROVISION

33. Power to Employ Additional Police in Places Where Mischief to Telegraphs is Repeatedly Committed

(1) Whenever it appears to the State Government that any act causing or likely to cause wrongful damage to any telegraph is repeatedly and maliciously committed in any place, and that the employment of an additional police-force in that place is thereby rendered necessary, the State Government may send such additional police-force as it thinks fit to the place, and employ the same therein so long as, in the opinion of that Government, the necessity of doing so continues.

(2) The inhabitants of the place shall be charged with the cost of the additional police-force, and the District Magistrate shall, subject to the orders of the State Government, assess the proportion in which the cost shall be paid by the inhabitants according to his judgment of their respective means.

(3) All moneys payable under sub-section (2) shall be recoverable either under the warrant of a Magistrate by distress and sale of the moveable property of the defaulter within the local limits of his jurisdiction, or by suit in any competent Court.

(4) The State Government may, by order in writing, define the limits of any place for the purposes of this section.

34. Application of Act to Presidency-Towns

(1) This Act, in its application to the Presidency-towns, shall be read as if for the words "District Magistrate" in Section 16, sub-section (1), and Section 17, sub-sections (2) and (3), for the words "Magistrate of the first or second

class" in Section 18, sub-section (1), [and Section 19-A, sub-section (2)] and for the word "Magistrate" in Section 18, sub-section (2), there had been enacted the words "Commissioner of Police", and for the words "District Judge" in Section 16, sub-sections (3), (4) and (5), the words "Chief Judge of the Court of Small Causes".

(3) The fee in respect of an application to the Chief Judge of a Presidency Court of Small Causes under sub-section (3) of Section 16 shall be the same as would be payable under the Court-fees Act, 1870 (7 of 1870), in respect of such an application to a District Judge beyond the limits of a Presidency-town, and fees for summonses and other processes in proceedings before the Chief Judge under sub-section (3) or sub-section (4) of that section shall be payable according to the scale set forth in the Fourth Schedule to the Presidency Small Cause Courts Act, 1882 (15 of 1882.)]

35. *[Reference to Certain Laws of Part B States]*

Rep. by the Part B States (Laws) Act. 1951 (3 of 1951). S. 3 and Sch.

4 THE RESERVE BANK OF INDIA ACT, 1934

[ACT 2 OF 1934]

An Act to Constitute a Reserve Bank of India

[6th March, 1934]

Whereas it is expedient to constitute a Reserve Bank of India to regulate the issue of Bank notes and the keeping of reserves with a view to securing monetary stability in India and generally to operate the currency any credit system of the country to its advantage;

And whereas in the present disorganisation of the monetary systems of the world it is not possible to determine what will be suitable as a permanent basis for the Indian monetary system;

But whereas it is expedient to make temporary provision on the basis of the existing monetary system, and to leave the question of the monetary standard best suited to India to be considered when the international monetary position has become sufficiently clear and stable to make it possible to frame permanent measures;

It is hereby enacted as follows:

I. PRELIMINARY

1. Short Title, Extent and Commencement

(1) This Act may be called the Reserve Bank of India Act, 1934.

(2) It extends to the whole of India.

(3) This section shall come into force at once, and the remaining provisions of this Act shall come into force on such date or dates as the Central Government may, by notification in the Gazette of India, appoint.

2. Definitions

In this Act, unless there is anything repugment in the subject or context,—

(a) [* * *]

(ai) [* * *]

(aii) "the Bank" means the Reserve Bank of India constituted by this Act;

(aiii) "Bank for International Settlements", means the body corporate established with the said name under the law of Switzerland in pursuance of an agreement dated the 20th January, 1930, signed at the Hague;

(b) "the Central Board" means the Central Board of Directors of the Bank;

(bi) [* * *]

(bii) [* * *]

(biii) [* * *]

(biv) [* * *]

(bv) [* * *]

(bvi) "Deposit Insurance Corporation" means the Deposit Insurance Corporation established

under Section 3 of the Deposit Insurance Corporation Act, 1961 (47 of 1961);

(bvii) "Development Bank" means the Industrial Development Bank of India established under the Industrial Development Bank of India Act, 1964 (18 of 1964);

(bviii) [* * *]

[*(bviiia)* "Exim Bank" means the Export-Import Bank of India established under the Export-Import Bank of India Act, 1981;]

(bix) "foreign currency" and "foreign exchange" have the meanings respectively assigned to them in the Foreign Exchange Regulation Act, 1973 (46 of 1973);

(c) "Industrial Finance Corporation" means the Industrial Finance Corporation of India established under the Industrial Finance Corporation Act, 1948 (15 of 1948);

(ca) "International Development Association" means the "Association" referred to in the International Development Association (Status, Immunities and Privileges) Act I960 (32 of 1960);

(cb) "International Finance Corporation" means the "Corporation" referred to in the International Finance Corporation (Status, Immunities and Privileges) Act, 1958 (42 of 1958);

(cc) "International Monetary Fund" and "International Bank for Reconstruction and Development" mean respectively the "International Fund" and the "International Bank", referred to in the International Monetary Fund and Bank Act, 1945;

[(ccc) "National Bank" means the National Bank for Agriculture and Rural Development established under Section 3 of the National Bank for Agriculture and Rural Development Act, 1981;]

[(cccc) "National Housing Bank" means the National Housing Bank established under Section.3 of the National Housing Bank Act, 1987;]

(cf) to (civ) [* * *]

[(cv) "Reconstruction Bank" means the Industrial Reconstruction Bank of India established under Section 3 of the Industrial Reconstruction Bank of India Act, 1984;]

(d) "rupee coin" means rupees which are legal tender in India under the provisions of the Indian Coinage Act, 1906 (3 of 1906);

(e) "scheduled bank" means a bank included in the Second Schedule;

[(el) "Small Industries Bank" means the Small Industries Development Bank of India established under Section 3 of the Small Industries Development Bank of India Act, 1989;]

(ed) "Sponsor Bank" means a Sponsor Bank as defined in the Regional Rural Banks Act, 1976;

(eb) "State Bank" means the State Bank of India constituted under the State Bank of India Act, 1955 (23 of 1955);

(f) [***]

(fi) "State Financial Corporation" means any State Financial Corporation established under the State Financial Corporations Act, 1951 (63 of 1951);

(*g*) "Unit Trust" means the Unit Trust of India established under Section 3 of the Unit Trust of India Act, 1963 (52 of 1963);

[(*h*) "agricultural operations", "central co-operative bank", "co-operative society", "crops", "marketing of crops", "pisciculture", "regional rural bank" and "State co-operative bank" shall have the meanings respectively assigned to them in the National Bank for Agriculture and Rural Development Act, 1981;

(*i*) "co-operative bank", "co-operative credit society", "director", "primary agricultural credit society", "primary co-operative bank" and "primary credit society" shall have the meanings respectively assigned to them in Part V of the Banking Regulation Act, 1949 (10 of 1949).]

II. INCORPORATION, CAPITAL, MANAGEMENT, AND BUSINESS

3. Establishment and Incorporation of Reserve Bank

(1) A bank to be called the Reserve Bank of India shall be constituted for the purposes of taking over the management of the currency from the Central Government and of carrying on the business of banking in accordance with the provisions of this Act.

(2) The Bank shall be a body corporate by the name of the Reserve Bank of India, having perpetual succession and a common seal, and shall by the said name sue and be sued.

4. Capital of the Bank

The capital of the Bank shall be five crores of rupees.

5. [*Increase and reduction of share capital.*]

Rep. by Act 62 of 1948. S. 7 and Sch. (w. e.f. 1-1-1949)].

6. Offices, Branches and Agencies

The Bank shall as soon as may be, establish offices in Bombay, Calcutta, Delhi and Madras and may establish branches or agencies in any other place in India or, with the previous sanction of the Central Government elsewhere.

7. Management

(1) The Central Government may from time to time give such directions to the Bank as it may, after consultation with the Governor of the Bank, consider necessary in the public interest.

(2) Subject to any such directions, the general superintendence and direction of the affairs and business of the Bank shall be entrusted to a Central Board of Directors which may exercise all powers and do all acts and things which may be exercised or done by the Bank.

(3) Save as otherwise provided in regulations made by the Central Board, the Governor and in his absence the Deputy Governor nominated by him in his behalf, shall also have powers of general superintendence and direction of the affairs and the business of the Bank, and may exercise all powers and do all acts and things which may be exercised or done by the Bank.

8. Composition of the Central Board, and Term of Office of Directors

(1) The Central Board shall consist of the following Directors, namely:—

(a) a Governor and not more than four Deputy Governors to be appointed by the Central Government;

(b) four Directors to be nominated by the Central Government, one from each of the four Local Boards as constituted by Section 9;

(c) ten Directors to be nominated by the Central Government; and

(d) one Government official to be nominated by the Central Government.

(2) The Governor and Deputy Governors shall devote their whole time to the affairs of the Bank, and shall receive such salaries and allowances as may be determined by the Central Board, with the approval of the Central Government:

Provided that the Central Board may, if in its opinion it is necessary in the public interest so to do, permit the Governor or a Deputy Governor to undertake, at the request of the Central Government or any State Government, such part-time honorary work, whether related to the purposes of this Act or not, as is not likely to interfere with his duties as Governor or Deputy Governor, as the case may be:

[Provided further that the Central Government may, in consultation with the Bank, appoint a Deputy Governor as the Chairman of the National Bank, on such terms and conditions as that Government may specify.]

(3) A Deputy Governor and the Director nominated under clause *(d)* of sub-section (1) may attend any meeting of the Central Board and take part in its deliberations but shall not be entitled to vote:

Provided that when the Governor is, for any reason, unable to attend any such meeting, a Deputy Governor authorised by him in this behalf in writing may vote for him at that meeting.

(4) The Governor and a Deputy Governor shall hold office for such term not exceeding five years as the Central Government may fix when appointing them, and shall be eligible for re-appointment.

A Director nominated under clause *(c)* of sub-section (1) shall hold office for a period of four years and thereafter until his successor shall have been nominated.

A Director nominated under clause *(d)* of sub-section (1) shall hold office during the pleasure of the Central Government.

(5) No act or proceeding of the Board shall be questioned on the ground merely of the existence of any vacancy in, or any defect in the constitution of, the Board.

[* * * * * *]

(7) A retiring Director shall be eligible for re-nomination.

9. Local Boards, Their Constitution, and Functions

(1) A Local Board shall be constituted for each of the four areas specified in the First Schedule and shall consist of five members to be appointed by the Central Government to represent, as far as possible, territorial and economic interests and the interests of co-operative and indigenous banks.

(2) The members of the Local Board shall elect from amongst themselves one person to be the chairman of the Board.

(3) Every member of a Local Board shall hold office for a term of four years and thereafter until his successor shall have been appointed and shall be eligible for re-appointment.

(4) A Local Board shall advise the Central Board on such matters as may be generally or specifically referred to

it and shall perform such duties as the Central Board may delegate to it.

10. Disqualifications of Directors and Members of Local Boards

(1) No person may be a Director or a member of a Local Board who—

(a) is a salaried Government official, or

(b) is, or at any time has been, adjudicated an insolvent, or has suspended payment or has compounded with his creditors, or

(c) is found lunatic or becomes of unsound mind, or

(d) is an officer or employee of any bank, or

(e) is a Director of banking company within the meaning of clause (c) of Section 5 of the Banking Regulation Act,1949 (10 of 1949), or of a co-operative bank.

(2) No two persons who are partners of the same mercantile firm, or are Directors of the same private company, or one of whom is the general agent of or holds a power of procuration from the other, or from a mercantile firm of which the other is a partner, may be Directors or members of the same Local Board at the same time.

(3) Nothing in clause *(a)*, clause *(d)* or clause *(e)* of sub-section (1) shall apply to the Governor, or to a Deputy Governor or to the Director nominated under clause *(d)* of sub-section (1) of Section 8.

11. Removal from and Vacation of Office

(1) The Central Government may remove from office the Governor, or a Deputy Governor or any other Director or any member of Local Board:

[* * * * *]

(2) A Director nominated under clause *(b)* or clause *(c)* of sub-section (1) of Section 8 shall cease to hold office if without leave from the Central Board he absents himself from three consecutive meetings of the Board convened under sub-section (1) of Section 13.

(3) The Central Government shall remove from office any Director, and the Central Board shall remove from office any member of a Local Board, if such Director or member becomes subject to any of the disqualifications specified in sub-section (1) or sub-section (2) of Section 10.

(4) A Director or member of Local Board removed or ceasing to hold office under the foregoing sub-sections shall not be eligible for re-appointment either as Director or as member of a Local Board until the expiry of the term for which his appointment was made.

(5) The nomination as Director or member of a Local Board of any person who is a member of Parliament or the Legislature of any State shall be void, unless within two months of the date of his nomination he ceases to be such member, and if any Director or member of a Local Board is elected or nominated as a member of Parliament or any such Legislature, he shall cease to be a Director or member of the Local Board as from the date of such election or nomination, as the case may be.

(6) A Director may resign his office to the Central Government, and a member of a Local Board may resign his office to the Central Board, and on the acceptance of the resignation the office shall become vacant.

12. Casual vacancies and absences

(1) If the Governor or a Deputy Governor by infirmity or otherwise is rendered incapable of executing his duties or is absent on leave or otherwise in circumstances not

involving the vacation of his appointment, the Central Government may, after consideration of the recommendations made by the Central Board in this behalf, appoint another person to officiate for him, and such person may, notwithstanding anything contained in clause *(d)* of sub-section (1) of Section 10, be an officer of the Bank.

[* * * * * *]

(3) Where any casual vacancy in the office of any member of a Local Board occurs, the Central Board may nominate thereto any person recommended by the other members of the Local Board.

(4) Where any casual vacancy occurs in the office of a Director other than the vacancies provided for in sub-section (1), the vacancy shall be filled by the Central Government.

(5) A person nominated under this section to fill a casual vacancy shall hold office for the unexpired portion of the term of his predecessor.

13. Meetings of the Central Board

(1) Meetings of the Central Board shall be convened by the Governor at least six times in each year and at least once in each quarter.

(2) Any four Directors may require the Governor to convene a meeting of the Central Board at any time and the Governor shall forthwith convene a meeting accordingly.

(3) The Governor or if for any reason, he is unable to attend, the Deputy Governor authorised by the Governor under the proviso to sub-section (3) of Section 8 to vote for him, shall preside at meetings of the Central Board, and, in the event of an equality of votes, shall have a second or casting vote.

14. [*General meetings.*]

15. [*First constitution of the Central Board.*]

16. [*First constitution of Local Boards.*]

17. Business Which the Bank May Transact

The Bank shall be authorised to carry on and transact the several kinds of business hereinafter specified, namely:—

(1) the accepting of money on deposit without interest from and the collection of money for, the Central Government, the State Governments, local authorities, banks and any other persons;

(2) (a) the purchase, sale and rediscount of bills of exchange and promissory notes, drawn on and payable in India and arising out of *bona fide* commercial or trade transactions bearing two or more good signatures, one of which shall be that of a scheduled bank or a State co-operative bank or any financial institution, which is predominantly engaged in the acceptance or discounting of bills of exchange and promissory notes and which is approved by the Bank in this behalf and maturing,—

(i) in the case of bills of exchange and promissory notes arising out of any such transaction relating to the export of goods from India, within one hundred and eighty days, and

(ii) in any other case, within ninety days,

from the date of such purchase or rediscount exclusive of days of grace;

(b) the purchase, sale and rediscount of bills of exchange and promissory notes, drawn and payable in India and bearing two or more good signatures, one of which shall be that of a scheduled bank or a State co-operative bank or any financial institution, which is predominantly engaged in the acceptance or discounting of bills of exchange and promissory notes and which is approved by the Bank in this behalf and drawn or issued for the purpose of financing agricultural operations or the marketing of crops, and maturing within fifteen months from the date of such purchase or rediscount, exclusive of days of grace;

[******]

(bb) the purchase, sale and rediscount of bills of exchange and promissory notes drawn and payable in India and bearing two or more good signatures, one of which shall be that of a State co-operative bank or a state financial corporation or any financial institution, which is predominantly engaged in the acceptance or discounting of bills of exchange and promissory notes and which is approved by the Bank in this behalf, and drawn or issued for the purpose of financing the production or marketing activities of cottage and small scale industries approved by the Bank and maturing within twelve months from the date of such purchase or rediscount, exclusive of days of grace, provided that the payment of the principal and interest of such bills of exchange or promissory notes is fully guaranteed by the State Government;

(c) the purchase, sale and rediscount of bills of exchange and promissory notes drawn and payable in India and bearing the signature of a scheduled bank, and issued or drawn for the purpose of holding or trading in securities of the Central Government or a State Government, and maturing within ninety days from the date of such purchase or rediscount, exclusive of days of grace;

(3) (a) the purchase from and sale to scheduled banks of foreign exchange;

(b) the purchase, sale and rediscount of bills of exchange (including treasury bills) drawn in or on any place in any country outside India which is a member of the International Monetary Fund and maturing,—

(i) in the case of bills of exchange arising out of and *bona fide* transaction relating to the export of goods from India, within one hundred and eighty days, and

(ii) in any other case, within ninety days,

from the date of such purchase or rediscount:

Provided that no such purchase, sale or rediscount shall be made in India except with a scheduled bank or a State, co-operative bank;

[******]

(3-A) the making to any scheduled bank or State co-operative bank, of loans and advances, against promissory notes of such bank, repayable on demand or on the expiry of fixed periods not exceeding one hundred and eighty days:

Provided that the borrowing bank furnishes a declaration in writing, to the effect that—

(i) it holds bills of exchange arising out of any transaction relating to the export of goods from

India of a value not less than the amount of such loans or advances,—

(a) drawn in India and on any place in any country outside India which is a member of the International Monetary Fund or in any other country notified in this behalf by the Bank in the Gazette of India, and

(b) maturing not later than one hundred and eighty days from the date of the loan or advance, and it will, so long as any part of such loans and advances remains unpaid, continue to hold such bills of exchange of a value not less than the amount of such loans or advances outstanding for the time being; or

(ii) it has granted a pre-shipment loan or advance to an exporter or any other person in India in order to enable him to export goods from India, the amount of the loan or advance drawn and outstanding at any time being not less than the outstanding amount of the loan or advance obtained by the borrowing bank from the Bank;

(3-B) the making to any scheduled bank or State co-operative bank or loans and advances repayable on demand or on the expiry of fixed periods not exceeding one hundred and eighty days against promissory notes of such bank:

Provided that the borrowing bank furnishes a declaration in writing to the effect that it has made loans and advances for *bona fide* commercial or trade transactions or for financing agricultural operations or the marketing of crops or for other agricultural purposes as set out in the declaration and the said declaration includes such other particulars as may be required by the Bank;

(4) the making to local authorities, scheduled banks, State co-operative banks and State Financial Corporations of loans and advances, repayable on demand or on the expiry of fixed periods not exceeding ninety days, against the security of—

(a) stocks, funds and securities (other than immovable property) in which a trustee is authorized to invest trust money by any Act of Parliament of the United Kingdom or by any law for the time being in force in India;

(b) gold or silver or documents of title to the same;

(c) such bills of exchange and promissory notes as are eligible for purchase or rediscount by the Bank or as are fully guaranteed as to the repayment of the principal and payment of interest by a State Government;

(d) promissory notes of any scheduled bank or State co-operative bank, supported by documents of title to goods such documents having been transferred, assigned, or pledged to any such bank as security for a loan or advance made for *bona fide* commercial or trade transactions, or for the purpose of financing agricultural operations or the marketing of crops:

Provided that loans and advances made against the security of bills of exchange and promissory notes arising out of any transaction relating to the export of goods from India shall be repayable on demand or on the expiry of fixed periods not exceeding one hundred and eighty days;

(4-A) the making to any State Financial Corporation of loans and advances repayable on the expiry of fixed, periods not exceeding eighteen months from the date of such loan or advance, against securities of the Central Government or of any State Government, of any maturity, or against bonds and debentures issued by that Corporation and guaranteed by the State Government concerned and maturing within a period not exceeding eighteen months from the date of such loan or advance:

Provided that the previous approval of the State Government shall be obtained for the borrowing by the State Financial Corporation and the amount of loans and advances granted to that Corporation under this clause shall not, at any time, exceed in the aggregate [twice] the paid-up share capital thereof;

[(4-AA) the making of annual contributions to the National Rural Credit (Long Term Operations) Fund and the National Rural Credit (Stabilisation) Fund established under Sections 42 and 43, respectively, of the National Bank for Agriculture and Rural Development Act, 1981;]

(4-B) the making to the Industrial Finance Corporation of India of loans and advances, —

(a) repayable on demand or on the expiry of fixed periods not exceeding ninety days from the date of such loan or advance, against securities of the Central Government or of any State Government; or

(b) repayable on the expiry of fixed periods not exceeding eighteen months from the date of such loan or advance, against securities of the Central Government of any maturity or against bonds and debentures issued by the said Corporation and guaranteed by the Central Government and maturing within a period not exceeding eighteen months from the date of such loan or advance:

[* * *]

(4-BB) the making to any financial institution notified by the Central Government in this behalf, of loans and advances, —

(a) repayable on demand or on the expiry of fixed periods not exceeding ninety days from the date of such loan or advance, against the securities of the Central Government or of any Slate Government; or

(b) repayable on the expiry of fixed periods not exceeding eighteen months from the date of such loan or advance, against securities of the Central Government or of any State Government, of any maturity, or against bonds and debentures issued by that financial institution and guaranteed by the Central Government or any State Government, end maturing within a period not exceeding eighteen months from the date of such loan or advance:

Provided that the amount of loans and advances granted to a financial institution under sub-clausc *(b)* shall not at any time, exceed in the aggregate sixty per cent of the paid-up share capital thereof:

(4-BBB) the making to the Unit Trust of loans and advances—:

(i) repayable on demand or on the expiry of a fixed period not exceeding ninety days from the date of such loan or advance against the security of stocks, funds and securities (other than immovable property) in which a trustee is authorised to invest trust money by any law for the time being in force in India;

(ii) repayable on demand or within a period of eighteen months from the date of such loan or advance against the security of the bonds of the Unit Trust issued with the approval of and guaranteed by the Central Government;

(iii) for the purpose of any scheme other than the first unit scheme under the Unit Trust of India Act, 1963 (52 of 1963) on such terms and conditions and against the security of such other property of the Unit Trust as may be specified in this behalf by the Bank;

(4-C) the making to a Warehousing Corporation established under the Agricultural Produce (Development and Warehousing) Corporations Act, 1956 (28 of 1956) of loans and advances,—

(a) repayable on demand or on the expiry of fixed periods not exceeding ninety days, from the date of such loan or advance, against securities of the Central Government or of any State Government, or

(b) repayable on the expiry of fixed periods not exceeding eighteen months from the date of such loan or advance, against securities of the Central Government or of any State Government, of any maturity, or against bonds and debentures issued by the Corporation to which the loan or advance is made, and guaranteed by the Central or a State Government, and maturing within a period not exceeding eighteen months from the date of such loan or advance:

Provided that the amount of loans and advances granted under clause *(b)* shall not at any time exceed, in the aggregate, three crores of rupees in the case of the Central Warehousing Corporation and fifty lakhs of rupees in the case of a State Warehousing Corporation;

(4-D) the making to the Deposit Insurance Corporation of loans and advances; and generally assisting the Corporation in such manner and on such terms as may be determined by the Central Board;

[(4-DD) the making to the National Housing Bank of loans and advances and generally assisting the National Housing Bank in such manner and on such terms as may be determined by the Central Board;]

[(4-E) the making to the National Bank of loans and advances repayable on demand or on the expiry of fixed period not exceeding eighteen months from the date of making of the loan or advance, either—

- (i) against the security of stocks, funds and securities (other than immovable property) in which a trustee is authorised to invest trust money by any law for the time being in force in India; or
- (ii) on such other terms and conditions as the Bank may specify;]

(4-F) contributing to the initial capital of the Unit Trust;

(4-G) the making of loans and advances to, and the purchasing of bonds and debentures of, the Development Bank [or the Exim Bank] [or the Reconstruction Bank] [or the Small Industries Bank] out of the National Industrial Credit (Long Term Operations) Fund established under Section 46-C;

[(4-GG) the making of loans and advances to, and the purchasing of bonds and debentures of, the National Housing Bank out of the National Housing Credit (Long Term Operations) Fund established under Section 46-D;]

(4-H) the making to the Development Bank [or the Small Industries Bank] of loans and advances —

(a) repayable on demand or on the expiry of fixed periods not exceeding ninety days, from the date of such Joan or advance against the security of stocks, funds and securities (other than immovable property) in which a trustee is authorised to invest trust money by any law for the time being in force in India; or

(b) against the security of bills of exchange or promissory notes, arising out of *bona fide* commercial or trade transactions bearing two or more good signatures and maturing within five years from the date of such loan or advance;

(4-1) thc making to scheduled banks, the Development Bank, [the Exim Bank,] [[the Reconstruction Bank or the Small Industries Bank]] the Industrial Finance Corporation and any other financial institution as may, on the recommendation of the Bank, be approved in this behalf by the Central Government of loans and advances repayable on demand or otherwise and against such security and on such other terms and conditions as may be approved in this behalf by the Central Board for the purpose of enabling such banks, or financial institution, as the case may be, to purchase foreign exchange from the Bank for the purpose of financing the import of capital goods or for such other purposes as may be approved by the Central Government;

[(4-J) the making to the Exim Bank of loans and advances—

(a) repayable on demand or on the expiry of a fixed period not exceeding ninety days, from the date of such loan or advance against the security of stocks, funds and securities (other than immovable property) in which a trustee is authorised to invest trust money by any law for the time being in force in India; or

(b) against the security of bills of exchange or promissory notes, arising out of bona fide commercial or trade transactions bearing two or more good signatures and maturing within five years from the date of such loan or advance;]

[(4-K) the making to the Reconstruction Bank of loans and advances—

(a) repayable on demand or on the expiry of a fixed period not exceeding ninety days, from the date of such loan or advance against the security of stocks, funds and securities (other than immovable property) in which a trustee is authorised to invest trust money by any law for the time being in force in India; or

(b) against the security of bills of exchange or promissory notes, arising out of *bona fide* commercial or trade transactions bearing two or more good signatures and maturing within five years from the date of such loan or advance;]

(5) the making to the Central Government and State Governments of advances repayable in each case not later than three months from the date of the making of the advance;

(6) the issue of demand drafts, telegraphic transfers and other kinds of remittances made payable at its own offices or agencies, the purchase of telegraphic transfers, and the making issue and circulation of bank post bills;

[* * * * *]

(8) the purchase and sale of securities of the Central Government or a State Government of any maturity or of such securities of a local authority as may be specified in this behalf by the Central Government on the recommendation of the Central Board:

Provided that securities fully guaranteed as to principal and interest by any such Government or authority shall be deemed for the purposes of this clause to be securities of such Government or authority;

[* * * * *]

(8-A) The purchase and sale of shares in, or the capital of the [National Bank] the Deposit Insurance Corporation, the Development Bank, the State Bank or any other bank or financial institution notified by the Central Government in this behalf;

[(8-AA) the promoting, establishing, supporting or aiding in the promotion, establishment and support of any financial institution, whether as its subsidiary or otherwise;]

(8-B) the keeping of deposits with the State Bank for such specific purposes as may be approved by the Central Government in this behalf;

(9) the custody of monies, securities and other articles of value, and the collection of the proceeds, whether principal, interest or dividends, of any such securities;

(10) the sale and realisation of all property, whether movable or immovable which may in any way come into the possession of the Bank in satisfaction, or part satisfaction, of any of its claims;

(11) the acting as agent for the Central Government or

any State Government or any local authority or the Industrial Finance Corporation of India or any other body corporate which is established or constituted by or under any other law or the Government of any such country outside India or any such person or authority as may be approved in this behalf by the Central Government in the transaction or any of the following kinds of business, namely:—

(a) the purchase and sale of gold or silver or foreign exchange;

(b) the purchase, sale, transfer and custody of bills of exchange, securities or shares in any company;

(c) the collection of the proceeds, whether principal, interest or dividends, of any securities or shares;

(d) the remittance of such proceeds, at the risk of the principal, by bills of exchange payable either in India or elsewhere;

(e) the management of public debt;

(f) the issue and management of bonds and debentures;

(11-A) the acting as agent for the Central Government,—

[(a) *in guaranteeing the due performance by any small scale industrial concern, approved by the Central Government, of its obligations to any bank or other financial institution in respect of loans and advances made, or other credit facilities provided, to it by such bank or other financial institution and the making as such agent of payments in connection with such guarantee, and]*

(b) in administering any scheme for subsidising the rate of interest or other charges in relation to any loans or advances made, or other credit facilities provided, by banks or other financial institutions for the purpose of financing or facilitating any export from India and the making as such agent of payments on behalf of the Central Government;

(12) the purchase and sale of gold or silver coins and gold and silver bullion and foreign exchange and the opening of a gold account with the principal currency authority of any foreign country or the Bank for International Settlements or any international or regional bank or financial institution formed by such principal currency authority or authorities or by the Government of any foreign country;

(12-A) the purchase and sale of securities issued by the Government of any country outside India or by any institution or body corporate established outside India and expressed to be payable in a foreign currency or any international or composite currency unit, being in the case of purchase by the Bank securities maturing within a period of ten years from the date of purchase:

Provided that in the case of securities of an institution or body corporate, the repayment of principal and payment of interest in respect of such securities shall be guaranteed by the Government of the country concerned;

(12-B) the making of loans and advances in foreign currencies to scheduled banks, the Development Bank, [the Exim Bank,] [[the Reconstruction Bank or the Small Industries Bank]] the Industrial Finance Corporation, any State Financial Corporation and any other financial institution as may, on the recommendation of the Bank, be approved by the Central Government and on such terms and conditions as may be specified by the Central Board in this behalf, against promissory notes of such bank or financial institution, as the case may be:

Provided that the borrowing bank or financial institution,

as the case may be, furnishes a declaration in writing to the effect that—

(a) it has made loans and advances in foreign currencies for financing international trade or for the import of capital goods or for such other purposes as may be approved by the Central Government; and

(b) that the amount of loans or advances so made and outstanding at any time will not be less than the outstanding amount of the loans or advances obtained by it from the Bank;

(13) the opening of an account with an office outside India of any bank, including a bank incorporated in India or the making of an agency agreement with, and the acting as an agent or correspondent of, any bank incorporated outside India, or the principal currency authority of any country under the law for the time being in force in that country or any international or regional bank or financial institution formed by such principal currency authorities or foreign governments, and the investing of the funds of the Bank in the shares and securities of any such international or regional bank or financial institution or of any other foreign institution as may be approved by the Central Board in this behalf;

(13-A) participation in any arrangement for the clearing and settlement of any amounts due from, or to any person or authority on account of the external trade of India with any other country or group of countries or of any remittances to, or from; that country or group of countries, including the advancing, or receiving of any amount in any currency in connection therewith, and, for that purpose, becoming, with the approval of the Central Government, a member of any international or regional clearing union of central banks, monetary or other authorities, or being associated with any such clearing arrangements, or becoming a member of any body or association formed by central banks, monetary or other similar authorities, or being associated with the same in any manner;

(14) the borrowing of money for a period not exceeding one month for the purposes of the business of the Bank, and the giving of security for money so borrowed:

Provided that no money shall be borrowed under this clause from any person in India other than a scheduled bank or from any person outside India other than a bank which is the principal currency authority of any country under the law for the time being in force in that country:

Provided further that the total amount of such borrowings from persons in India shall not at any time exceed the amount of the capital of the Bank;

(15) the making and issue of bank notes subject to the provisions of this Act;

(15-A) the exercise of powers and functions and the performance of duties entrusted to the Bank under this Act or under any other law for the time being in force;

(15-B) the providing of facilities for training in banking and for the promotion of research, where, in the opinion of the Bank, such provision may facilitate the exercise by the Bank of its powers and functions, or the discharge of its duties;

(16) generally, the doing of all such matters and things as may be incidental to or consequential upon the exercise of its powers or the discharge of its duties under this Act.

18. Power of Direct Discount

When, in the opinion of the Bank a special occasion has arisen making it necessary or expedient that action should be taken under this section for the purpose of regulating credit in the interests of Indian trade, commerce, industry and agricultural, the Bank may, notwithstanding any limitation contained in Section 17,—

(1) purchase, sell or discount any bill of exchange or promissory note though such bill or promissory note is not eligible for purchase or discount by the Bank under that section; or

[* * * * *]

(3) make loans or advances to—

(a) a State co-operative bank, or

(b) on the recommendation of a State co-operative bank, to a co-operative society registered within the area in which the State co-operative bank operates, or

(c) any other person.

repayable on demand or on the expiry of the fixed periods, not exceeding ninety days, on such terms and conditions as the Bank may consider to be sufficient.

18-A. Validity of loan or advance not to be questioned

Notwithstanding anything to the contrary contained in any other law for the time being in force,—

(a) the validity of any loan or advance granted by the Bank in pursuance of the provisions of this Act shall not be called in question merely on the ground of non-compliance with the requirements of such other law as aforesaid or of any resolution, contract, memorandum, articles of association or other instrument:

Provided that nothing in this clause shall render valid any loan or advance obtained by any company or co-operative society where such company or co-operative society is not empowered by its memorandum to obtain loans or advances;

(b) where a loan or advance has been granted under clause (3-A) or under clause (3-B) of Section 17 or a loan or advance granted under clause (3) of Section 18 by the Bank to any person has been applied by such person, wholly or in part, in making a loan or advance to any borrower, any sum received—

(i) by the borrowing bank on account of bills of exchange in respect of which the declaration under clause (i) of the proviso to clause (3-A) of Section 17 has been furnished or in repayment or,realisation of the outstanding loans and advances referred to in clause (*ii*) of the said proviso or in the proviso to clause (3-B) of the said section, or

(ii) by the borrowing bank or any other person in repayment or realisation of loans and advances granted to a borrower out of funds obtained by it or by him from the Bank under Section 18,

shall be utilised only for the repayment by the borrowing bank or other person, as the case may be, of the amounts due to be repaid by it or by him to the Bank, and shall be held by it or by him in trust for the Bank, until such time as the amounts are so repaid.

19. Business Which the Bank May Not Transact

Save as otherwise provided in Sections 17, 18,42 and 45, the Bank may not—

(1) engage in trade or otherwise have a direct interest in any commercial, industrial, or other undertaking except such interest as it may in any way acquire in the course of the satisfaction of any of its claims: provided that all such interests shall be disposed of at the earliest possible moment;

(2) purchase the shares of any banking company or of any other company, or grant loans upon the security of any such shares;

(3) advance money on mortgage of, or otherwise on the security of, immovable property or documents of title relating thereto, or become the owner of immovable property, except so far as is necessary for its own business premises and residences for its officers and servants;

(4) make loans or advances;

(5) draw or accept bills payable otherwise than on demand;

(6) allow interest on deposits or current accounts.

III. CENTRAL BANKING FUNCTIONS

20. Obligation of the Bank to Transact Government Business

The Bank shall undertake to accept monies for account of the Central Government and to make payments up to the amount standing to the credit of its account, and to carry out its exchange, remittance and other banking operations, including the management of the public debt of the Union.

21. Bank to Have the Right to Transact Government Business in India

(1) The Central Government shall entrust the Bank, on such conditions as may be agreed upon, with all its money, remittance, exchange and banking transactions in India, and, in particular, shall deposit free of interest all its cash balances with the Bank:

Provided that nothing in this sub-section shall prevent the Central Government from carrying on money transactions at places where the Bank has no branches or agencies, and the Central Government may hold at such places such balances as it may require.

(2) The Central Government shall entrust the Bank, on such conditions as may be agreed upon, with the management of the public debt and with the issue of any new loans.

(3) In the event of any failure to reach agreement on the conditions referred to in this section the Central Government shall decide what the conditions shall be.

(4) Any agreement made under this section shall be laid, as soon as may be after it is made before Parliament.

[******]

21-A. Bank to transact Government business of States on agreement

(1) The Bank may by agreement with the Government of any state undertake—

(a) all its money, remittance, exchange and banking transactions in India, including in particular, the deposit, free of interest, of all its cash balances with the Bank; and

(b) the management of the public debt of, and the issue of any new loans by, that State.

(2) Any agreement made under this section shall be laid, as soon as may be after it is made, before Parliament.

21-B. Effect of agreements made between the Bank and certain States before the 1st November, 1956

(1) Any agreement made under Section 21 or Section 21-A between the Bank and the Government of a State specified in the *Explanation* below and in force immediately before the 1st day of November, 1956, shall, as from that day have effect as if it were an agreement made on that day under Section 21-A between the Bank and the Government of the corresponding State subject to such modifications, if any being of a character not affecting the general operation of the agreement, as may be agreed upon between the Bank and the Government of the corresponding State, or in default of such agreement, as may be made therein by order of the Central Government.

Explanation.—In this sub-section "corresponding State" means,—

(a) in relation to the agreement between the Bank and the State of Andhra, the State of Andhra Pradesh;

(b) in relation to the agreement between the Bank and any other Part A State as it existed before the 1st day of November, 1956, the State with the same name; and

(c) in relation to the agreement between the Bank and the Part B State of Mysore or Travancore-Cochin as it existed before the 1st day of November, 1956, the State of Mysore or Kerala respectively.

(2) Any agreement made under Section 21-A between the Bank and the Government of the Part B State of Hyderabad, Madhya Bharat or Saurashtra shall be deemed to have terminated on the 31 st day of October, 1956.

22. Right to Issue Bank Notes

(1) The Bank shall have the sole right to issue bank notes in India, and may, for a period which shall be fixed by the Central Government on the recommendation of the Central Board, issue currency notes of the Government of India supplied to it by the Central Government, and the provisions of this Act applicable to bank notes shall, unless a contrary intention appears, apply to all currency notes of the Government of India issued either by the Central Government or by the Bank in like manner as if such currency notes were bank notes, and references in this Act to bank notes shall be construed accordingly.

(2) On and from the date on which this Chapter comes into force the Central Government shall not issue any currency notes.

23. Issue Department

(1) The issue of bank notes shall be conducted by the Bank in an Issue Department which shall be separated and kept wholly distinct from the Banking Department, and the assets of the Issue Department shall not be subject to any liability other than the liabilities of the Issue department as hereinafter defined in Section 34.

(2) The Issue Department shall not issue bank notes to the Banking Department or to any other person except in exchange for other bank notes or for such coin, bullion or securities as are permitted by this Act to form part of the Reserve.

[******]

24. Denominations of Notes

(1) Subject to the provisions of sub-section (2) bank notes shall be of the denominational values of two rupees, five rupees, ten rupees, twenty rupees, fifty rupees, one hundred rupees, five hundred rupees, one thousand rupees, five thousand rupees and ten thousand rupees or of such other denominational values, not exceeding ten thousand rupees, as the Central Government may, on the recommendation of the Central Board, specify in this behalf.

(2) The Central Government may, on the recommendation of the Central Board, direct the on-issue or the discontinuance of issue of bank notes of such denominational values as it may secify in this behalf.

25. Form of Bank Notes

The design, form and material of bank notes shall be such as may be approved by the Central Governmcnt after consideration of the recommendations made by the Central Board.

26. Legal Tender Character of Notes

(1) Subject to the provisions of sub-section (2), every bank note shall be legal tender at any place in India in payment or on account for the amount expressed therein, and shall be guaranteed by the Central Government.

(2) On recommendation of the Central Board the Central Government may, by notification in the Gazette of India, declare that, with effect from such date as may be specified in the notification, any series of bank notes of any denomination shall cease to be legal tender save at such office or agency of the Bank and to such extent as may be specified in the notification.

26-A. Certain Bank Notes to Cease to be Legal Tender

Notwithstanding anything contained in Section 26, no

bank note of the denominational value of five hundred rupees, one thousand rupees or ten thousand rupees issued before the 13th day of January, 1946, shall be legal tender in payment or on account for the amount expressed therein.

27. Re-issue of Notes

The Bank shall not re-issue bank notes which are torn, defaced or excessively spoiled.

28. Recovery of Notes Lost, Stolen, Mutilated or Imperfect

Notwithstanding anything contained in any enactment or rule of law to the contrary, no person shall of right be entitled to recover from the Central Government or the Bank, the value of any lost, stolen, mutilated or imperfect currency note of the Government of India or bank note:

Provided that the Bank may, with the previous sanction of the Central Government, prescribe the circumstances in and the conditions and limitations subject to which the value of such currency notes or bank notes may be refunded as of grace and the rules made under this proviso shall be laid on the table of Parliament.

[******]

28-A. Issue of Special Bank Notes and Special One Rupee Notes in Certain Cases

(1) For the purpose of controlling the circulation of bank notes without India, the Bank may, notwithstanding anything contained in any other provision of this Act, issue bank notes of such design, form and material as may be approved under sub-section (3) (hereinafter in this section referred to as special bank notes) of the denominational values of five rupees, ten rupees and one hundred rupees.

(2) For the purpose of controlling the circulation of

Government of India one rupee notes without India, the Central Government may, notwithstanding anything contained in any other provision of this Act or in the Currency Ordinance, 1940 (Ord. 4 of 1940), issue Government of India notes of the denominational value of one rupee of such design, form and material as may be adopted under sub-section (3) (hereinafter in this section referred to as special one rupee notes).

(3) The design, form and material of the special bank notes shall be such as may be approved by the Central Government after consideration of the recommendations made by the Governor and of the special one rupee notes shall be such as the Central Government may think fit to adopt

(4) Neither the special bank notes nor the special one rupee notes shall be legal tender in India.

(5) The special one rupee note shall be deemed to be included in the expression "rupee coin" for all the purposes of this Act except Section 39, but shall be deemed not to be a currency note for any of the purposes of this Act.

(6) Where a special bank note is on its face expressed to be payable at a specified office or branch of the Bank, the obligation imposed by Section 39 shall be only on the specified office or branch and. further, shall be subject to such regulations as may be made under this section.

(7) The Bank may, with the previous sanction of the Central Government, make regulations to provide for all matters for which provision is necessary or convenient for the purpose of giving effect to the provisions of this section, and, in particular, the manner in which, and the conditions or limitations subject to which —

(*i*) bank notes and one rupee notes in circulation in any country outside India may be replaced by special notes issued under this section;

(II) any such special notes may be exchanged for any other bank notes or one rupee notes.

29. Bank Exempt from Stamp Duty on Bank Notes

The Bank shall not be liable to the payment of any stamp duty under the Indian Stamp Act, 1899 (2 of 1899), in respect of bank notes issued by it.

30. Powers of Central Government to Supersede Central Board

(1) If in the opinion of the Central Government the Bank fails to carry out any of the obligations imposed on it by or under this Act the Central Government may, by notification in the Gazette of India, declare the Central Board to be superseded, and thereafter the general superintendence and direction of the affairs of the Bank shall be entrusted to such agency as the Central Government may determine, and such agency may exercise the powers and do all acts and things which may be exercised or done by the Central Board under this Act.

(2) When action is taken under this section the Central Government shall cause a full report of the circumstances leading to such action and of the action taken to be laid before Parliament at the earliest possible opportunity and in any case within three months from the issue of the notification superseding the Board.

31. Issue of Demand Bills and Notes

(1) No person in India other than the Bank, or, as expressly authorized by this Act the Central Government shall draw, accept, make or issue any bill of exchange,

hundi, promissory note or engagement for the payment of money payable to bearer on demand, or borrow, owe or take up any sum or sums of money on the bills, hundis or notes payable to bearer on demand of any such person:

Provided that cheques or drafts, including hundis, payable to bearer on demand or otherwise may be drawn on a person's account with a banker, shroff or agent.

(2) Notwithstanding anything contained in the Negotiable Instrument Act, 1881 (26 of 1881), no person in India other than the Bank or, as expressly authorised by this Act, the Central Government shall make or issue any promissory note expressed to be payable to the bearer of the instrument.

32. [*Penalty*.]

Rep. by the Reserve Bank of India (Amendment) Act. 1974 (51 of 1974), S. 9.

33. Assets of the Issue Department

(1) The assets of the Issue Department shall consist of gold coin, gold bullion, foreign securities, rupee coin and rupee securities to such aggregate amount as is not less than the total of the liabilities of the Issue Department as hereinafter defined.

(2) The aggregate value of the gold coin, gold bullion and foreign securities held as assets and the aggregate value of the gold coin and gold bullion so held shall not at any time be less than two hundred crores of rupees and one hundred and fifteen crores of rupees, respectively.

[(3) The remainder of the assets shall be held in rupee coin, Government of India rupee securities of any maturity, promissory notes drawn by the National Bank for any loans or advances under clause (4-E) of Section 17 and such bills of exchange and promissory notes payable in India as are eligible for purchase by the Bank under sub-clause *(a)* sub-clause *(b)* or sub-clause *(bb)* of clause (2) of Section 17 or under clause (1) of Section 18.]

(4) For the purposes of this section, gold coin and gold bullion shall be valuated at [a price not exceeding the international market price for the time being obtaining], rupee coin shall be valued at its face value, and securities shall be valued at rates not exceeding the market rates for the time being obtaining.

(5) Of the gold coin and gold bullion held as assets, not less than seventeen-twentieths shall be held in India, and all gold coin and gold bullion held as assets shall be held in the custody of the Bank or its agencies:

> Provided that gold belonging to the Bank which is in any other bank or in any mint or treasury or in transit may be reckoned as part of the assets.

(6) For the purposes of this section, the foreign securities which may be held as part of the assets shall be—

- (i) securities of the following kinds payable in the currency of any foreign country which is a member of the International Monetary Fund, namely:—
  - (a) balances with the bank which is the principal currency authority of that foreign country and any other balances, or securities in foreign currency maintained with or issued by the International Monetary Fund, the International Bank for Reconstruction and Development, the International Development Association or the International Finance

Corporation or Asian Development Bank or the Bank for International Settlements or any banking or financial institution [approved] by the Central. Government in this behalf, provided that they are repayable within a period of ten years;

(b) bills of exchange bearing two or more good signatures and drawn on and payable at any place in that foreign country and having a maturity not exceeding ninety days; and

(c) Government securities of that foreign country maturing within ten years;

(ii) any drawing rights representing a liability of the International Monetary Fund.

34. Liabilities of the Issue Department

(1) The liabilities of the Issue Department shall be an amount equal to the total of the amount of the currency notes of the Government of India and bank notes for the time being in circulation.

[******]

[******]

35. [*Initial Assets and Liabilities.*]

Rep. by Act 62 of 1948, Section 7 and Sch. (w.e.f. 1-1-1949).

36. [*Method of Dealing with Fluctuations in Rupee Coin Assets*]

Rep. *by Act 55 of 1963, Section 3 (w.e.f. 1-2-1964).*

37. Suspension of assets requirements as to foreign securities

Notwithstanding anything contained in the foregoing provisions, the Bank may, with the previous sanction of the Central Government, for periods not exceeding six months in the first instance, which may, with the like sanction, be extended from time to time by periods not exceeding three months at a time, hold as assets foreign securities of less amount in value than that required by sub-section (2) of Section 33:

[******]

38. Obligations of Government and the Bank in Respect of Rupee Coin

The Central Government shall undertake not to put into circulation any rupees, except through the Bank, and the Bank shall undertake not to dispose of rupee coin otherwise than for the purposes of circulation.

39. Obligation to Supply Different Forms of Currency

(1) The Bank shall issue rupee coin on demand in exchange for bank notes and currency notes of the Government of India, and shall issue currency notes or bank notes on demand in exchange for coin which is legal tender under the Indian Coinage Act, 1906 (3 of 1906).

(2) The Bank shall, in exchange for currency notes or bank notes of two rupees or upwards, supply currency notes or bank notes of lower value or other coins which are legal tender under the Indian Coinage Act, 1906 (3 of 1906), in such quantities as may, in the opinion of the Bank, be required for circulation; and the Central Government shall supply such coins to the Bank on demand. If the Central Government at any time fails to supply such coins, the Bank shall be released from its obligations to supply them to the public.

[40. Transactions in Foreign Exchange

The Bank shall sell to or buy from any authorized person who makes a demand in that behalf at its office in

Bombay, Calcutta, Delhi or Madras or at such of its branches as the Central Government may, by order, determine, foreign exchange at such rates of exchange and on such conditions as the Central Government may from time to time by general or special order determine, having regard so far as rates of exchange are concerned to its obligations to the International Monetary Fund:

Provided that no person shall be entitled to demand to buy or sell foreign exchange of a value less than two lakhs of rupees.

Explanation.—In this section "authorized person" means a person who is entitled by or under the Foreign Exchange Regulation Act, [1973 (46 of 1973)] to buy, or as the case may be, sell, the foreign exchange to which his demand relates.]

41-A. [*Obligation to Provide Remittance between India and Burma.*]

Rep. by Act 11 of 1947, Section 22 (w.e.f. 1-4-1947).

42. Cash Reserves of Scheduled Banks to be Kept with the Bank

(1) Every bank included in the Second Schedule shall maintain with the Bank an average daily balance the amount of which shall not be less than three per cent of the total of the demand and time liabilities in India of such bank as shown in the return referred to in sub-section (2):

Provided that the Bank may, by notification in the Gazette of India, increase the said rate to such higher rate as may be specified in the notification so however that the rate shall not be more than [twenty per cent] of the total of the demand and time liabilities.

Explanation.—For the purposes of this section,—

(a) "average daily balance" shall mean the average of the balances held at the close of business on each day of a [fortnight];

[(b) 'fortnight' shall mean the period from Saturday to the second following Friday, both days inclusive;]

(c) "liabilities" shall not include—

(i) the paid-up capital or the reserves or any credit balance in the profit and loss account of the bank;

(ii) the amount of any loan taken from the bank or from the Development Bank [or from the Exim Bank] [or from the Reconstruction Bank] [or from the National Housing Bank] or from the [National Bank] [or from the Small Industries Bank];

(iii) in the case of a State co-operative bank, also any loan taken by such bank from a State Government [or from the National Co-operative Development Corporation established under the National Co-operative Development Corporation Act, 1962 (26 of 1962)] and any deposit of money with such bank representing the reserve fund or any part thereof maintained with it by any co-operative society within its area of operation;

(iv) in the case of a State co-operative bank, which has granted an advance against any balance maintained with it, such balance to the extent of the amount outstanding in respect of such advance;

[(v) in the case of a Regional Rural Bank, also any loan taken by such bank from its Sponsor Bank;]

(d) the aggregate of the "liabilities" of a scheduled

bank which is not a State co-operative bank, to,—

(i) the State Bank;

(ii) a subsidiary bank as defined in Section 2 of the State Bank of India (Subsidiary Banks) Act, 1959 (38 of 1959);

(iii) a corresponding new bank constituted by Section 3 of the Banking Companies (Acquisition and Transfer of Undertakings) Act, 1970 (5 of 1970);

[(iiia) a corresponding new bank constituted by Section 3 of the Banking Companies (Acquisition and Transfer of Undertakings) Act, 1980 (40 of 1980);]

(iv) a banking company as defined in clause *(c)* of Section 5 of the Banking Regulation Act, 1949 (10 of 1949);

(v) a cooperative Bank; or

(vi) any other financial institution notified by the Central Government in this behalf.

shall be reduced by the aggregate of the liabilities of all such banks and institutions to the scheduled bank;

(e) the aggregate of the "liabilities" of a scheduled bank which is a State co-operative bank, to,-

(i) the State Bank;

(ii) a subsidiary bank as defined in Section 2 of the State Bank of India (Subsidiary Banks) Act, 1959 (38 of 1959);

(iii) a corresponding new bank constituted by Section 3 of the Banking Companies (Acquisition and Transfer of Undertakings) Act, 1970 (5 of 1970);

[(iiia) a corresponding new bank constituted by Section 3 of the Banking Companies (Acquisition and Transfer of Undertakings) Act, 1980 (40 of 1980);]

(iv) *a* banking company as defined in clause *(c)* of Section 5 of the Banking Regulation Act, 1949 (10 of 1949); or

(v) any other financial institution notified by the Central Government in this behalf,

shall be reduced by the aggregate of the liabilities of all such banks and institutions to the State co-operative bank.

(1-A) Notwithstanding anything contained in sub-section (1), the Bank may, by notification in the Gazette of India, direct that every scheduled bank shall, with effect from such date as may be specified in the notification, maintain with the Bank; in addition to the balance prescribed by or under sub-section (1), an additional average daily balance the amount of which shall not be less than the rate specified in the notification, such additional balance being calculated with reference to the excess of the total of the demand and time liabilities of the bank as shown in the return referred to in sub-section (2) over the total of its demand and time liabilities at the close of business on the date specified in the notification as shown by such return so however, that the additional balance shall, in no case, be more than such excess:

[Provided that the bank may, by a separate notification in the Gazette of India, specify different dates in respect of a bank subsequently, included in the Second Schedule.]

(1-AA) Notwithstanding anything contained in sub-section (1) or sub-section (1-A), it shall not be necessary for any scheduled bank to maintain with the Bank any balance which shall be more than [twenty per cent] of the total of its demand and time liabilities as shown in the return referred to in sub-section (2).

(1-B) Where any scheduled bank maintains, in pursuance of a notification issued under the proviso to sub-section (1) or under sub-section (1-A), any balance with the Bank the amount of which is not less than that required to be maintained by such notification, the Bank may pay to the scheduled bank interest at such rate or rates as may be determined by the bank from time to time on the amount by which such balance actually maintained is in excess of the balance which the scheduled bank would have to maintain, if no such notification was issued:

Provided that no interest shall be payable on any such amount actually maintained as is in excess of the balance required to be maintained by or under sub-section (1) or under sub-section (1-A):

Provided further that where the Bank does not, "under sub-section (5), demand the payment of the penalty imposed by sub-section (3), it may pay interest at such rate or rates as may be determined by the Bank from time to time on the amount actually maintained with it by the scheduled bank, notwithstanding that such amount is less than the balance required to be maintained in pursuance of a notification issued under the proviso to sub-section (1) or under sub-section (1-A).

[(1-C) The Bank may, for the purposes of this section, specify from time to time with reference to any transaction or class of transactions that such transaction or transactions shall be regarded as liability in India of a scheduled bank, and if any question arises as to whether any transaction or class of transactions shall be regarded, for the purposes of this section, as liability in India of a scheduled bank, the decision of the Bank thereon shall be final.]

(2) Every scheduled bank shall send to the Bank a return signed by two responsible officers of such bank showing—

(a) the amount of its demand and time liabilities and the amount of its borrowings from banks in India, classifying them into demand and time liabilities,

[*****]

(b) the total amount of legal tender notes and coins held by it in India,

(c) the balance held by it at the Bank in India,

(d) the balances held by it at other banks in current account and the money at call and short notice in India,

(e) the investments (at book value) in Central and State Government securities including treasury bills and treasury deposit receipts,

(f) the amount of advances in India,

(g) the inland bills purchased and discounted in India and foreign bills purchased and discounted,

[at the close of business on each alternate Friday, and every such return shall be sent not later than seven days after the date to which it relates:]

Provided that the Bank may, by notification in the Gazette of India, delete or modify or add to any of the particulars specified in the foregoing clauses:

Provided further that where [such alternate] Friday is a public holiday under the Negotiable Instruments Act, 1881 (26 of 1881), for one or more offices of a scheduled bank, the return shall give the preceding working day's figures in respect of such office or offices, but shall nevertheless be deemed to relate to that Friday:

[Provided also that where the Bank is satisfied that the furnishing of a fortnightly return under this sub-section is impracticable in the case of any scheduled bank by reason of the geographical position of the bank and its branches, the Bank may allow such bank

(i) to furnish a provisional return for the fortnight within the period aforesaid to be followed by a final return not later than twenty days after the date to which it relates, or

(ii) to furnish in lieu of a fortnightly return a monthly return to be sent not later than twenty days after the end of the month to which it relates giving the details specified in this sub-section in respect of such bank at the close of business for the month.]

[(2-A) Where the last Friday of a month is not an alternate Friday for the purpose of sub-section (2), every scheduled bank shall send to the Bank, a special return giving the details specified in sub-section (2) as at the close of business on such last Friday or where such last Friday is a public holiday under the Negotiable Instruments Act, 1881 (26 of 1881), as at the close of business on the preceding working day and such return shall be sent not later than seven days after the date to which it relates.]

(3) If the average daily balance held at the Bank by a scheduled bank during any [fortnight] is below the minimum prescribed by or under sub-section (1) or sub-section (1-A), such scheduled bank shall be liable to pay to the Bank in respect of that [fortnight] penal interest at a rate of three per cent above the bank rate on the amount by which such balance with the Bank falls short of the prescribed minimum, and if during the next succeeding [fortnight] such average daily balance is still below the prescribed minimum, the

rates of penal interest shall be increased to a rate of five per cent above the bank rate in respect of that [fortnight] and each subsequent [fortnight] during which the default continues on the amount by which such balance at the Bank falls short of the prescribed minimum.

(3-A) When under the provisions of sub-section (3) penal interest at the increased rate of five per cent above the bank rate has become payable by a scheduled bank, if thereafter the average daily balance held at the Bank during the next succeeding [fortnight] is still below the prescribed minimum,—

(a) every director, manager or secretary of the scheduled bank, who is knowingly and wilfully a party to the default, shall be punishable with fine which may extend to five hundred rupees and with a further fine which may extend to five hundred rupees for each subsequent [fortnight] during which the default continues, and

(b) the Bank may prohibit the scheduled bank from receiving after the said [fortnight] any fresh deposit,

and, if default is made by the scheduled bank in complying with the prohibition referred to in clause *(b)*, every director and officer of the scheduled bank who is knowingly and wilfully a party to such default or who through negligence or otherwise contributes to such default shall in respect of each such default be punishable with fine which may extend to five hundred rupees and with a further fine which may extend to five hundred rupees for each day after the first on which a deposit received in contravention of such prohibition is retained by the scheduled bank.

Explanation.—In this sub-section "officer" includes a manager, secretary, branch manager, and branch secretary.

(4) Any, scheduled bank failing to comply with the provisions of sub-section (2) shall be liable to pay to the Bank a penalty of one hundred rupees for each day during which the failure continues.

(5) *(a)* The penalties imposed by sub-sections (3) and (4) shall be payable within a period of fourteen days from the date on which a notice issued by the Bank demanding the payment of the same is served on the scheduled bank, and in the event of failure of the scheduled bank to pay the same within such period, may be levied by a direction of the principal civil court having jurisdiction in the area where an office of the defaulting bank is situated, such direction to be made only upon an application made in this behalf to the court by the Bank;

(b) when the court makes a direction under clause *(a)*, it shall issue a certificate specifying the sum payable by the scheduled bank and every such certificate shall be enforceable in the same manner as if it were a decree made by the court in a suit;

(c) notwithstanding anything contained in this section, if the Bank is satisfied that the defaulting bank had sufficient cause for its failure to comply with the provisions of sub-section (1), (1-A) or (2), it may not demand the payment of the penal interest or the penalty, as the case may be.

(6) The Bank shall, save as hereinafter provided, by notification in the Gazette of India,

(a) direct the inclusion in the Second Schedule of any bank not already so included which carries on the business of banking in India and which

(i) has a paid-up capital and reserves of an aggregate value of not less than five lakhs of rupees, and

(ii) satisfies the Bank that its affairs are not being conducted in a manner detrimental to the interests of its depositors, and

(iii) is a State co-operative bank or a company as defined in Section 3 of the Companies Act, 1956 (1 of 1956), or an institution notified by the Central Government in this behalf or a corporation or a company incorporated by or under any law in force in any place outside India;

(b) direct the exclusion from that Schedule of any scheduled bank,

(i) the aggregate value of whose paid-up capital and reserves becomes at any time less than five lakhs of rupees, or

(ii) which is, in the opinion of the Bank after making an inspection under Section 35 of the Banking Regulation Act, 1949 (10 of 1949), conducting its affairs to the detriment of the interests of its depositors, or

(iii) which goes into liquidation or otherwise ceases to carry on banking business:

Provided that the Bank may, on application of the scheduled bank concerned and subject to such conditions, if any, as it may, impose, defer the making of a direction under sub-clause (*i*) or sub-clause (*ii*) of clause *(b)* for such period as the Bank considers reasonable to give the scheduled bank an opportunity of increasing the aggregate value of its paid-up capital and reserves to not less than five lakhs of rupees or, as the case may be, of removing the defects in the conduct of its affairs;

(c) alter the description in that Schedule whenever any scheduled bank changes its name.

Explanation.—In this sub-section the expression "value" means the real or exchangeable value and not the nominal value which may be shown in the books of the bank concerned; and if any dispute arises in computing the aggregate value of the paid-up capital and reserves of a bank, a determination thereof by the Bank shall be final for the purposes of this sub-section.

[(6-A) In considering whether a State co-operative bank or a regional rural bank should be included in or excluded from the Second Schedule, it shall be competent for the Bank to act on a certificate from the National Bank on the question whether or not a State co-operative bank or a regional rural bank, as the case may be, satisfies the requirements as to paid-up capital and reserves or whether its affairs are not being conducted in a manner detrimental to the interests of its depositors.]

(7) The Bank may, for such period and subject to such conditions as may be specified, grant to any scheduled bank such exemptions from the provisions of this section as it thinks fit with reference to all or any of its offices or with reference to the whole or any part of its assets and liabilities.

43. Publication of Consolidated Statement by the Bank

The Bank shall cause to be published each [fortnight] a consolidated statement showing the aggregate liabilities and assets of all the scheduled banks together, based on the returns and information received under this Act or any other law for the time being in force.

43-A. Protection of Action Taken in Good Faith

(1) No suit or other legal proceeding shall lie against the Bank or any of its officers for anything which is in good faith done or intended to be done in pursuance of

Section 42 or Section 43 or in pursuance of the provision of Chapter III-A.

(2) No suit or other legal proceedings shall lie against the Bank or any of its officers for any damage caused or likely to be caused by anything which is in good faith done or intended to be done in pursuance of Section 42 or Section 43 or in pursuance of the provisions of Chapter III-A.

44. [*Power to Require Returns from Co-operative Banks.*]

Rep. by the Banking Laws (Application to Co-operative Societies) Act, 1965 (23 of 1965), Section 7 (w.e.f. 1-3-1966).

[45. Appointment of Agents

(1) Unless otherwise directed by the Central Government with reference to any place, the Bank may, having regard to public interest, convenience of banking development and such other factors which in its opinion are relevant in this regard, appoint the National Bank, or the State Bank, or a corresponding new bank constituted under Section 3 of the Banking Companies (Acquisition and Transfer of Undertakings) Act, 1970 (5 of 1970), or a corresponding new bank constituted under Section 3 of the Banking Companies (Acquisition and Transfer of Undertakings) Act, 1980 (40 of 1980), or any subsidiary bank as defined in the State Bank of India (Subsidiary Banks) Act, 1959 (38 of 1959), as its agent at all places, or at any place in India for such purposes as the Bank may specify.

(2) When any bank is appointed by the Bank as its agent under sub-section (1) to receive on behalf of the Bank any payment required to be made into the Bank, or any bill, hundies or other securities required to be delivered into the Bank, under any law or rule, regulations or other instructions having the force of law, the same may be paid

or delivered into the bank so appointed as the agent of the Bank.]

III. A. COLLECTION AND FURNISHING OF CREDIT INFORMATION

45-A. Definitions

In this Chapter, unless the context otherwise requires,—

(a) "banking company" means a banking company as defined in Section 5 of the Banking Regulation Act, 1949 (10 of 1949), and includes the State Bank of India, any subsidiary bank as defined in the State Bank of India (Subsidiary Banks) Act, 1959 (38 of 1959), any corresponding new bank constituted by Section 3 of the Banking Companies (Acquisition and Transfer of Undertakings) Act, 1970 (5 of 1970), and any other financial institution notified by the Central Government in this behalf;

(b) "borrower" means any person to whom any credit limit has been sanctioned by any banking company, whether availed of or not, and includes—

(*i*) in the case of a company or corporation, as subsidiaries;

(*ii*) in the case of a Hindu undivided family, any member thereof or any firm in which such member is a partner;

(*iii*) in the case of a firm, any partner thereof or any other firm in which such partner is a partner; and

(*iv*) in the case of an individual, any firm in which such individual is a partner;

(c) "credit information" means any information relating to—

(i) the amounts and the nature of loans or advances and other credit facilities granted by a banking company to any borrower or class of borrowers;

(ii) the nature of security taken from any borrower or class of borrowers for credit facilities granted to him or to such class;

(iii) the guarantee furnished by a banking company for any of its customers or any class of its customers;

(iv) the means, antecedents, history of financial transactions and the creditworthiness of any borrower or class of borrowers;

(v) any other information which the Bank may consider to be relevant for the more orderly regulation of credit policy.

45-B. Power of Bank to Collect Credit Information

The Bank may—

(a) collect, in such manner as it may think fit, credit information from banking companies; and

(b) furnish such information to any banking company in accordance with the provisions of Section 45-D.

45-C. Power to Call for Returns Containing Credit Information

(1) For the purpose of enabling the Bank to discharge its functions under this Chapter, it may at any time direct any banking company to submit to it such statements relating to such credit information and in such form and

within such time as may be specified by the Bank from time to time.

(2) A banking company shall, notwithstanding anything to the contrary contained in any law for time being in force on in any instrument regulating the constitution thereof or in any agreement executed by it, relating to the secrecy of its dealings with its constituents, be bound to comply with any direction issued under sub-section (1).

45-D. Procedure for Furnishing Credit Information to Banking Companies

(1) A banking company may, in connection with any financial arrangement entered into or proposed to be entered into by it, with any person, make an application to the Bank in such form as the Bank may specify requesting it to furnish the applicant with such credit information as may be specified in the application.

(2) On receipt of an application under sub-section (1), the Bank shall, as soon as may be, furnish the applicant with such credit information relating to the matters specified in the application, as may be in its possession:

Provided that the information so furnished shall not disclose the names of the banking companies which have submitted such information to the Bank.

(3) The Bank may in respect of each application levy such fees, not exceeding twenty-five rupees, as it may deem fit for furnishing credit information.

45-E. Disclosure of Information Prohibited

(1) Any credit information contained in any statement submitted by a banking company under Section 45-C or furnished by the Bank to any banking company under Section 45-D, shall be treated as confidential and shall not,

except for the purposes of this Chapter, be published or otherwise disclosed.

(2) Nothing in this section shall apply to—

(a) the disclosure by any banking company, with the previous permission of the Bank, of any information furnished to the Bank under Section 45-C;

(b) the publication by the Bank, if it considers necessary in the public interest so to do, of any information collected by it under Section 45-C, in such consolidated form as it may think fit without disclosing the name of any banking company or its borrowers.

(c) the disclosure or the publication by the banking company or by the Bank of any credit information to any other banking company or in accordance with the practice and usage customary among bankers or as permitted or required under any other law:

Provided that any credit information received by a banking company under this clause shall not be published except in accordance with the practice and usage customary among bankers or as permitted or required under any other law.

(3) Notwithstanding anything contained in any law for the time being in force, no court, tribunal or other authority shall compel the Bank or any banking company to produce or to give inspection of any statement submitted by that banking company under Section 45-C or to disclose any credit information furnished by the Bank to that banking company under Section

45-D.

45-F. Certain Claims for Compensation Barred

No person shall have any right, whether in contract or otherwise, to any compensation for any loss incurred by reason of the operation of any of the provisions of this Chapter.

45-G [*Penalties.*]

Rep. by the Reserve Bank of India (Amendment) Act, 1974 (51 of 1974), S. 15.

III-B. PROVISIONS RELATING TO NON BANKING INSTITUTIONS RECEIVING DEPOSITS AND FINANCIAL INSTITUTIONS

45-H. III-B Not to Apply in Certain Cases

The provisions of this Chapter shall not apply to the State Bank or banking company as defined in Section 5 of the Banking Regulation Act, 1949 (10 of 1949) or [a corresponding new bank as defined in clause *(da)* of Section 5 of that Act or a subsidiary bank as defined in the State Bank of India (Subsidiary Banks) Act, 1959 (38 of 1959) or a Regional Rural Bank or a co-operative bank or a primary agricultural credit society or a primary credit society:

Provided that for the purposes of this Chapter, the Tamil Nadu Industrial Investment Corporation Limited shall not be deemed to be a banking company.

45-I. Definitions

In this Chapter, unless the context otherwise requires,—

(a) "company" means a company as defined in Section 3 of the Companies Act, 1956 (1 of 1956) and includes a foreign company within the meaning of Section 591 of that Act:

(b) "corporation" means a corporation incorporated by an Act of any legislature;

[(bb) 'deposit' includes and shall be deemed always to have included any receipt of money by way of deposit or loan or in any other form, but does not include,—

(i) amounts raised by way of share capital;

(ii) amounts contributed as capital by partners of a firm;

(iii) amounts received from a scheduled bank or a co-operative bank or any other banking company as defined in clause (c) of Section 5 of the Banking Regulation Act, 1949 (10 of 1949);

(iv) any amount received from,—

(a) the Development Bank,

(b) a State Financial Corporation,

(c) any financial institution specified in or under Section 6-A of the Industrial Development Bank of India Act, 1964 (18 of 1964), or

(d) any other institution that may be specified by the Bank in this behalf;

(v) amounts received in the ordinary course of business, by way of—

(a) security deposit,

(b) dealership deposit,

(c) earnest money, or

(d) advance against ordeers for goods, properties or services

(vi) any amount received from an individual or a firm or an association of individuals not being a body corporate, registered under any enactment relating to money lending which is for the time being in force in any State; and

(vii) any amount received by way of subscriptions in respect of a chit.

Explanation I.—'Chit' has the meaning assigned to it in clause *(b)* of Section 2 of the Chit Funds Act, 1982 (40 of 1982).

Explanation II.—Any credit given by a seller to a buyer on the sale of any property (whether movable or immovable) shall not be deemed to be deposit for the purposes of this clause;]

(c) "financial institution" means any non-banking institution which carries on as its business or part of its business any of the following activities, namely:—

(i) the financing, whether by way of making loans or advances or otherwise, of any activity other than its own;

(ii) the acquisition of shares, stock, bonds, debentures or securities issued by a Government or local authority or other marketable securities of a like nature;

(iii) letting or delivering of any goods to a hirer under a hire-purchase agreement as defined in clause *(c)* of Section 2 of the Hire-Purchase Act, 1972 (26 of 1972);

(iv) the carrying on of any class of insurance business;

(v) managing, conducting or supervising, as foreman, agent or in any other capacity, of chits or kuries as defined in any law which is for the time being in force in any State, or any business, which is similar thereto;

(vi) collecting, for any purpose or under any scheme or arrangement by whatever name called, monies in lumpsum or otherwise, by way of subscriptions or by sale of units, or other instruments or in any other manner and awarding, prizes or gifts, whether in cash or kind, or disbursing monies in any other way, to persons from whom monies are collected or to any other person,

but does not include any institution, which,—

(i) is an industrial concern as defined in clause (c) of Section 2 of the Industrial Development Bank of India Act, 1964 (18 of 1964), or

(ii) carries on as its principal business,—

(a) agricultural operations; or

(b) the purchase or sale of any goods (other than securities) or the providing of any services; or

(c) the purchase, construction or sale of immovable property, so, however, that no portion of the income of the institution is derived from the financing of purchases, constructions or sales of immovable property by other persons;

(d) "firm" means a firm as defined in the Indian Partnership Act, 1932 (9 of 1932) [***];

(e) "non-banking institution" means a company, corporation [or co-operative society].

45-J. Bank to Regulate or Prohibit Issue of Prospectus or Advertisement Soliciting Deposits of Money

The Bank may, if it considers necessary in the public interest so to do, by general or special order,—

(a) regulate or prohibit the issue by any non-banking institution of any prospectus or advertisement soliciting deposits of money from the public; and

(b) specify the conditions subject to which any such prospectus or advertisement, if not prohibited, may be issued.

45-K. Power of Bank to Collect Information from Non-Banking Institutions as to Deposits and to Give Directions

(1) The Bank may at any time direct that every non-banking institution shall furnish to the Bank, in such form, at such intervals and within such time, such statements, information or particulars relating to or connected with deposits received by the non-banking institution, as may be specified by the Bank by general or special order.

(2) Without prejudice to the generality of the power vested in the Bank under sub-section (1), the statements, information or particulars to be furnished under sub-section (1), may relate to all or any of the following matters, namely, the amount of the deposits, the purposes and periods for which, and the rates of interest and other terms and conditions on which, they are received.

(3) The Bank may, if it considers necessary in the public interest so to do, give directions to non-banking institutions either generally or to any non-banking institution or group of non-banking institutions in particular, in respect of any matters relating to or connected with the receipt of deposits, including the rates of interest payable on such deposits, and the periods for which deposits may be received.

(4) If any non-banking institution fails to comply with any direction given by the Bank under sub-section (3), the

Bank may prohibit the acceptance of deposits by that non-banking institution.

[* * * *]

(6) Every non-banking institution receiving deposits shall, if so required by the Bank and within such time as the Bank may specify, cause to be sent at the cost of the non-banking institution a copy of its annual balance-sheet and profit and loss account or other annual accounts to every person from whom the non-banking institution holds, as on the last day of the year to which the accounts relate, deposits higher than such sum as may be specified by the Bank.

45-L. Power of Bank to Call for Information from Financial Institutions and to Give Directions

(1) If the Bank is satisfied for the purpose of enabling it to regulate the credit system of the country to its advantage it is necessary so to do, it may—

(a) require financial institutions either generally or any group of financial institutions or financial institution in particular, to furnish to the Bank in such form, at such intervals and within such time, such statements, information or particulars relating to the business of such financial institutions or institution, as may be specified by the Bank by general or special order;

(b) give to such institutions either generally or to any such institution in particular, directions relating to the conduct of business by them or by it as financial institutions or institution.

(2) Without prejudice to the generality of the power vested in the Bank under clause (a) of sub-section (1), the

statements, information or particulars to be furnished by a financial institution may relate to all or any of the following matters, namely, the paid-up capital, reserves or other liabilities, the investments whether in Government securities or otherwise, the persons to whom, and the purposes and periods for which, finance is provided and the terms and conditions, including the rates of interest, on which it is provided.

(3) In issuing directions to any financial institution under clause *(b)* of sub-section (1), the bank shall have due regard to the conditions in which, and the objects for which, the institution has been established, its statutory responsibilities, if any, and the effect the business of such financial institution is likely to have on trends in the money and capital markets.

45-M. Duty of Non-banking Institutions to Furnish Statements etc., Required by Bank

It shall be the duty of every non-banking institution to furnish the statements, information or particulars called for, and to comply with any direction given to it, under the provisions of this chapter.

45-MA. Powers and Duties of Auditors

(1) It shall be the duty of an auditor of a non-banking institution to inquire whether or not the non-banking institution has furnished to the Bank such statements, information or particulars relating to or connected with deposits received by it, as are required to be furnished under this Chapter, and the auditor shall, except where he is satisfied on such inquiry that the non-banking institution has furnished such statements, information or particulars, make a report to the Bank giving the aggregate amount of such deposits held by the non-banking institution.

(2) Where, in the case of a non-banking institution, being a company, the auditor has made, or intends to make, a report to the Bank under sub-section (1), he shall include in his report under sub-section (2) of Section 227 of the Companies Act, 1956 (1 of 1956), the contents of the report which he has made, or intends to make, to the Bank.

45-N. Inspection

(1) The Bank may, at any time, cause an inspection to be made by one or more of its officers or employees or other persons (hereafter in this section referred to as the inspecting authority)—

(i) of any non-banking institution, including a financial institution, for the purposes of verifying the correctness or completeness of any statement, information or particulars furnished to the Bank or for the purpose of obtaining any information or particulars which the non-banking institution has failed to furnish on being called upon to do so; or

(ii) of any non-banking institution being a financial institution, if the Bank considers it necessary or expedient to inspect that institution.

(2) It shall be the duty of every director or member of any committee or other body for the time being vested with the management of the affairs of the non-banking institution or other officer or employee thereof to produce to the inspecting authority all such books, accounts and other documents in his custody or power and to furnish that authority with any statements and information relating to the business of the institution as that authority may require of him, within such time as may be specified by that authority.

(3) The inspecting authority may examine on oath any director or member of any committee or body for the time being vested with the management of the affairs of the non-banking institution or other officer or employee thereof, in relation to its business and may administer an oath accordingly.

45-NA. Deposits Not to be Solicited by Unauthorised Persons

No person shall solicit on behalf of any non-banking institution either by publishing or causing to be published any prospectus or advertisement or in any other manner deposits of money from the public unless—

(a) he has been authorised in writing by the said non-banking institution to do so and specifics the name of the institution which has so authorised him, and

(b) the prospectus or advertisement complies with any order made by the Bank under Section 45-J and with any other provision of law for the time being in force, applicable to the publication of such prospectus or advertisement.

45-O. [*Penalties.*]

Rep. by the Reserve Bank of India (Amendment) Act, 1974 (51 of 1974), S. 22.

45-P. [*Cognizance of Offences.*]

Rep. by S. 22, ibid.

45-Q. III-B to Override Other Laws

The provisions of this Chapter shall have effect notwithstanding anything inconsistent therewith contained in any other law for the time being in force or any instrument having effect by virtue of any such law.

III-C. PROHIBITION OF ACCEPTANCE OF DEPOSITS BY UNINCORPORATED BODIES

45-R. Interpretation

The words and expressions used in this Chapter and defined in III-B shall have the meanings respectively assigned to them therein.

45-S. Deposits Not to be Accepted in Certain Cases

(1) No person, being an individual or a firm or an unincorporated association of individuals shall, at any time, have deposits from more than the number of depositors specified against each, in the table below:—

TABLE

(i)	Individual	Not more than twenty-five depositors excluding depositors who are relatives of the individual.
(ii)	Firm	Not more than twenty-five depositors per partner and not more than two hundred and fifty depositors in all, excluding, in either case, depositors who are relatives of any of the partners.
(iii)	Unincorporated association of individuals	Not more than twenty-five depositors per individual and not more than two hund red and fifty depositors in all, excluding, in cither case, depositors who are relatives of any of the individuals constituting the association.

(2) Where at the commencement of Section 10* of the Banking Laws (Amendment.) Act, 1983 (1 of 1984), the deposits held by any such person are not in accordance with sub-section (1), he shall, before the expiry of a period of two years from the date of such commencement, repay such of the deposits as are necessary for bringing the number of depositors within the relative limits specified in

---

* February 15. 1984.

that sub-section.

Explanation.—For the purposes of this section,—

(a) a person shall be deemed to be a relative of another if, and only if,—

(i) they are members of a Hindu undivided family; or

(ii) they are husband and wife; or

(iii) the one is related to the other in the manner indicated in the List of relatives below:—

LIST OF RELATIVES

1.	Father	12.	Son's daughter
2.	Mother (including step-mother)	13.	Son's daughter's husband
3.	Son (including step-son)	14.	Daughter's husband
4.	Son's wife	15.	Daughter's son
5.	Daughter (including step-daughter)	16.	Daughter's son's wife
6.	Father's Father	17.	Daughter's daughter
7.	Father's mother	18.	Daughter's daughter's husband
8.	Mother's mother	19.	Brother (including step brother)
9.	Mother's Father	20.	Brother's wife
10.	Son's son	21.	Sister (including step-sister)
11.	Son's son's wife	22.	Sister's husband

(b) a person in whose favour a credit balance is outstanding for a period not exceeding six months in any account relating to mutual dealings in the ordinary course of trade or business shall not, on account of such balance alone, be deemed to be a depositor.

45-T. Power to Issue Search Warrants

(1) Any court having jurisdiction to issue a search

warrant under the Code of Criminal Procedure, 1973 (2 of 1974) may, on an application by an officer or of the State Government authorised in this behalf stating his belief that certain documents relating to acceptance of deposits in contravention of the provisions of Section 45-S are secreted in any place within the local limits of the jurisdiction of such court, issue a warrant to search for such documents.

(2) A warrant issued under sub-section (1) shall be executed in the same manner and shall have the same effect as a search warrant issued under the Code of Criminal Procedure, 1973 (2 of 1974).]

IV. GENERAL PROVISIONS

46. Contribution by Central Government to the Reserve Fund

The Central Government shall transfer to the Bank rupee securities of the value of five crores of rupees to be allocated by the Bank to the Reserve Fund.

[46-A. Contribution to National Rural Credit (Long Term Operations) Fund and National Rural Credit (Stabilisation) Fund

The Bank shall contribute every year such sums of money as it may consider necessary and feasible to do so, to the National Rural Credit (Long Term Operations) Fund and the National Rural Credit (Stabilisation) Fund established and maintained by the National Bank under Sections 42 and 43, respectively, of the National Bank for Agriculture and Rural Development Act, 1981.]

46-C. National Industrial Credit (Long Term Operations) Fund

(1) The Bank shall establish and maintain a Fund to be known as the National Industrial Credit (Long Term Operations) Fund to which shall be credited—

(a) an initial sum often crores of rupees by the Bank;

(b) such further sums of money as the Bank may contribute every year:

Provided that the annual contribution during each of the five years commencing with the year ending on the 30th day of June, 1965 shall not be less than five crores of rupees;

Provided further that the Central Government may, if the circumstances so require, authorise the Bank to reduce the said sum of five crores of rupees in any year.

(2) The amount in the said fund shall be applied by the Bank only to the following objects, namely:—

(a) the making to the Development Bank of loans and advances for the purpose of the purchase of, or subscription to, stocks, shares, bonds or debentures issued by the Industrial Finance Corporation of India a State Financial Corporation or any other financial institution which may be notified by the Central Government in this behalf, or for the purposes of any other business of the Development Bank;

(b) the purchasing of bonds and debentures issued by the Development Bank.

[(c) the making to the Exim Bank [or the Reconstruction Bank [or the Small Industries Bank] as the case may be] of loans and advances for the purposes of any business of the Exim Bank;

(d) the purchasing of bonds and debentures issued by the Exim Bank [or the Reconstruction Bank [or the Small Industries Bank], as the case may be].

[46-D. National Housing Credit (Long Term Operations) Fund

(1) The Bank shall establish and maintain a Fund to be known as the National Housing Credit (Long Term Operations) Fund to which shall be credited every year such sums of money as it may consider necessary.

(2) The amount in the said Fund shall be applied by the Bank only to the following objects, namely:—

(a) the making to the National Housing Bank of loans and advances for the purpose of any business of the National Housing Bank;

(b) the purchasing of bonds and debentures issued by the National Housing Bank.]

47. Allocation of Surplus Profits

After making provision for bad and doubtful debts, depreciation in assets, contributions to staff and superannuation funds and for all other matters for which provision is to be made by or under this Act or which are usually provided for by bankers, the balance of the profits shall be paid to the Central Government.

48. Exemption of Banks from Income-Tax and Super-Tax

(1) Notwithstanding anything contained in the Income-tax Act, 1961 (43 of 1961), or any other enactment for the time being in force relating to income-tax or super-tax, the bank shall not be liable to pay income-tax or super-tax on any of income, profits or gains.

[* * * * *]

49. Publication of Bank Rate

The Bank shall make public from time to time the standard rate at which it is prepared to buy or re-discount bills of exchange or other commercial paper eligible for purchase under this Act.

50. Auditors

(1) Not less than two auditors shall be appointed, and their remuneration fixed, by the Central Government.

(2) The auditors shall hold office for such term not exceeding one year as the Central Government may fix while appointing them, and shall be eligible for re-appointment.

51. Appointment of Special Auditors by Government

Without prejudice to anything contained in Section 50, the Central Government may at any time appoint the Comptroller and Auditor-General to examine and report upon the accounts of the Bank.

52. Powers and Duties of Auditors

(1) Every auditor shall be supplied with a copy of the annual balance-sheet, and it shall be his duty to examine the same, together with the accounts and vouchers relating thereto; and every auditor shall have a list delivered to him of all books kept by the Bank, and shall at all reasonable times have access to the books, accounts and other documents of the Bank, and may, at the expense of the Bank, employ accountants or other person to assist him in investigating suc] accounts and may, in relation to such accounts, examine any Director or officer of the Bank.

(2) The auditors shall make a report to the Central Government upon the annual balance-sheet and accounts, and in every such report they shall state whether, in their

opinion, the balance-sheet is a full and fair balance-sheet containing all necessary particulars and properly drawn up so as to exhibit a true and correct view of the state of the Bank's affairs, and, in case they have called for any explanation or information from the Central Board, whether it has been given and whethef it is satisfactory.

53. Returns

(1) The Bank shall prepare and transmit to the Central Government a weekly accounts of the Issue Department and of the Banking Department in such form as the Central Government may, by notification in the Gazette of India, prescribe. The Central Government shall cause these accounts to be published in the Gazette of India at such intervals and in such modified form as it may deem fit.

(2) The Bank shall also, within two months from the date on which the annual accounts of the Bank are closed, transmit to the Central Government a copy of the annual accounts signed by the Governor, the Deputy Governors and the Chief Accounting Officer of the Bank, and certified by the auditors, together with a report by the Central Board on the working of the Bank throughout the year, and the Central Government shall cause such accounts and report to be published in the Gazette of India.

[54. Rural Credit and Development

The Bank may maintain expert staff to study various aspects of rural credit and development and in particular it may,—

(a) tender expert guidance and assistance to the National Bank;

(b) conduct special studies in such areas as it may consider necessary to do so for promoting integrated rural development.]

54-A. Delegation of Powers

(1) The Governor may, by general or special order, delegate to a Deputy Governor, subjects to such conditions and limitations, if any, as may be specified in the order, such of the powers and functions exercisable by him under this Act or under any other law for the time being in force as he may deem necessary for the efficient administration of the functions of the Bank.

(2) The fact that a Deputy Governor exercises any power or does any act or thing in pursuance of this Act shall be conclusive proof of his authority to do so.

54-AA. Power of Bank to Depute Its Employees to Other Institutions

(1) The Bank may, notwithstanding anything contained in any law, or in any agreement, for the time being in force, depute any member of its staff for such period as it may think fit,—

(a) to any institution which is wholly or substantially owned by the Bank;

(b) to the Development Bank, so, however, that no such deputation shall continue after the expiration of thirty months from the commencement of Section 5 of the Public Financial Institutions Laws (Amendment) Act, 1975;

(c) to the Unit Trust, so, however, that no such deputation shall continue after the expiration of thirty months from the date notified by the Central Government under sub-section (1) of Section 4-A of the Unit Trust of India Act, 1963 (52 of 1963);

and thereupon the person so deputed shall, during the period of his deputation, render such service to the institution to which he is so deputed as that institution may require.

(2) Where a person has been deputed to an institution under sub-section (1), he shall not be entitled to claim any salary, emoluments and other terms and conditions of service which he would not have been entitled to claim if he had not been so deputed.

(3) Nothing contained in this section shall empower the Bank to depute any member of its staff to any institution on any salary, emoluments or other terms and conditions which is or are less favourable to him than that or those to which he is entitled immediately before such deputation.

(4) For the purposes of this section, an institution shall be deemed to substantially owned by the Bank if in the capital of the institution the Bank has not less than forty per cent share.

Explanation.—The word "capital" means, in relation to the Unit Trust, the initial capital of that Trust.

55 and 56. *[Reports by the Bank, Power to Require Declaration as to Ownership of Registered Shares.]*

Rep. by Act 62 of 1948, S. 7 and Sch. (w.e.f. 1-1-1949).

57. Liquidation of the Bank

(1) Nothing in the Companies Act, 1956 (1 of 1956) shall apply to the Bank and the Bank shall not be placed in liquidation save by order of the Central Government and in such manner as it may direct.

58. Power of the Central Board to Make Regulations

(1) The Central Board may, with the previous sanction of the Central Government, [by notification in the Official Gazette] make regulations consistent with this Act to provide for all matters for which provision is necessary or convenient for the purpose of giving effect to the provisions of this Act.

(2) in particular and without prejudice to the generality of the foregoing provision, such regulations may provide for all or any of the following matters, namely: —

(f) the manner in which the business of the Central Board shall be transacted, and the procedure to be followed at meetings thereof;

(g) the conduct of business of Local Boards and the delegation to such Boards of powers and functions; .

(h) the delegation of powers and functions of the Central Board to Deputy Governors, Directors or officers of the Bank;

(i) the formation of Committees of the Central Board, the delegation of powers and functions of the Central Board to such Committees, and the conduct of business in such Committees;

(j) the constitution and management of staff and superannuation funds for the officers and servants of the Bank;

(k) the manner and form in which contracts binding on the Bank may be executed;

(l) the provision of an official seal of the Bank and the manner and effect of its use;

(m) the manner and form in which the balance-sheet of the Bank shall be drawn up, and in which the accounts shall be maintained;

(n) the remuneration of Directors of the Bank;

(o) the relations of the scheduled banks with the Bank and the returns to be submitted by the scheduled banks to the Bank;

(p) the regulation of clearing-houses for [banks (including post office savings banks)];

(q) the circumstances in which, and the conditions and limitations subject to which, the value of any lost, stolen, mutilated or imperfect currency note of the Government of India or bank note may be refunded; and

(r) generally, for the efficient conduct of the business of the Bank.

(3) Any regulation made under this section shall have effect from such earlier or later date as may be specified in the regulation.

(4) Every regulation shall, as soon as may be after it is made by the Central Board, be forwarded to the Central Government and that Government shall cause a copy of the same to be laid before each House of Parliament, while it is in session, for a total period of thirty days which may be comprised in one session or in two or more successive sessions and if, before the expiry of the session immediately following the session or the successive sessions aforesaid, both Houses agree in making any modification in the regulation, or both Houses agree that the regulation should not be made, (the regulation shall, thereafter, have effect only in such modified form or be of no effect, as the case may be; so, however, that any such modification or annulment shall be without prejudice to the validity of anything previously done under that regulation.

(5) Copies of all regulations made under this section shall be available to the public on payment.

58-A. Protection of Action Taken in Good Faith

(1) No suit, prosecution or other legal proceeding shall lie against the Central Government or the Bank or any other person in respect of anything which is in good faith done or intended to be done under this Act or in pursuance

of any order, regulation or direction made or given thereunder.

(2) No suit or other legal proceeding shall lie against the Central Government or the Bank for and damage caused or likely to be caused by anything which is in good faith done or intended to be done under this Act or in pursuance of any order, regulation or direction made or given thereunder.

V. PENALTIES

58-B. Penalties

(1) Whoever in any application, declaration, return, statement, information or particulars made, required or furnished by or under or for the purposes of any provisions of this Act, or any order, regulation or direction made or given thereunder or in any prospectus or advertisement issued for or in connection with the invitation by any person, of deposits of money from the public wilfully makes a statement which is false in any material particular knowing it to be false or wilfully omits to make a material statement shall be punishable with imprisonment for a term which may extend to three years and shall also be liable to fine.

(2) If any person fails to produce any book, account or other document or to furnish any statement, information or particulars which, under this Act or any order, regulation or direction made or given thereunder, it is his duty to produce or furnish or to answer any question put to him in pursuance of the provisions of this Act or of any order, regulation or direction made or given thereunder, he shall be punishable with fine which may extend to two thousand rupees in respect of each offence and if he persists in such failure or refusal, with further fine which may extend to one hundred rupees for every day, after the first during

which the offence continues.

(3) If any person contravenes the provisions of Section 31, he shall be punishable with fine which may extend to the amount of the bill of exchange, hundi, promissory note or engagement for payment of money in respect whereof the offence is committed.

(4) If any person discloses any credit information, the disclosure of which is prohibited under Section 45-E, he shall be punishable with imprisonment for a term which may extend to six months, or with fine which may extend to one thousand rupees, or with both.

(5) If any person—

(a) receives any deposit in contravention of any direction given or order made under III-B; or

(b) issues any prospectus or advertisement otherwise than in accordance with Section 45-NA or any order made under Section 45-J, as the case may be,

he shall be punishable with imprisonment for a term which may extend to three years and shall also be liable to fine which may extend,—

(i) in the case of a contravention falling under clause *(a)*, to twice the amount of the deposit received; and

(ii) in the case of a contravention falling under clause *(b)*, to twice the amount of the deposit called for by the prospectus or advertisement.

[(5-A) If any person contravenes any provision of Section 45-S, he shall be punishable with imprisonment for a term which may extend to two years, or with fine which may extend to twice the amount of deposit received by such person in contravention of that section, or two thousand rupees, whichever is more, or with both:

Provided that in the absence of special and adequate reasons to the contrary to be mentioned in the judgment of the court, the imprisonment shall not be less than one year and the fine shall not be less than one thousand rupees.

(5-B) Notwithstanding anything contained in Section 29 of the Code of Criminal Procedure, 1973 (2 of 1974), it shall be lawful for a Metropolitan Magistrate or a Judicial Magistrate of the first class to impose a sentence of fine in excess of the limit specified in that section on any person convicted under sub-section (5-A).]

(6) If any other provision of this Act is contravened or if any default is made in complying with any other requirement of this Act or of any order, regulation or direction made or given or condition imposed thereunder, any person guilty of such contravention or default shall be punishable with fine which may extend to two thousand rupees and where a contravention or default is a continuing one, with further fine which may extend to one hundred rupees for every day, after the first, during which the contravention or default continues.

58-C. Offences by Companies

(1) Where a person committing a contravention or default referred to in Section 58-B is a company, every person who, at the time the contravention or default was committed, was in charge of, and was responsible to, the company for the conduct of the business of the company, as well as the company, shall be deemed to be guilty of the contravention or default and shall be liable to be proceeded against and punished accordingly:

Provided that nothing contained in this sub-section

shall render any such person liable to punishment if he proves that the contravention or default was committed without his knowledge or that he had exercised all due diligence to prevent the contravention or default.

(2) Notwithstanding anything contained in sub-section (1), where an offence under this Act has been committed by a company and it is, proved that the same was committed with the consent or connivance of, or is attributable to any neglect on the part of, any director, manager, secretary, or other officer or employee of the company, such director, manager, secretary, other officer or employee shall also be deemed to be guilty of the offence and shall be liable to be proceeded against and punished accordingly.

Explanation 1.—Any offence punishable under this Act shall be deemed to have been committed at the place where the registered office or the principal place of business, as the case may be, in India, of the company is situated.

Explanation II.—For the purpose of this section,—

(a) "a company" means any body corporate and includes a corporation, a non-banking institution, a firm, a co-operative society or other association of individuals;

(b) "director", in relation to a firm, means a partner in the firm.

58-D. Application of Section 58-B Barred

Nothing contained in Section 58-B shall apply to, or in respect of, any matter dealt with in Section 42.

58-E. Cognizance of Offences

(1) No court shall take cognizance of any offence punishable under this Act except upon a complaint in writing made by an officer of the Bank, generally or specially

authorised in writing in this behalf by the Bank, and no court other than that of a Metropolitan Magistrate or a Judicial Magistrate of the first class or a court superior thereto shall try any such offence.

[Provided that in respect of any offence punishable under sub-section (5-A) of Section 58-B, a complaint in writing may also be made by an officer of the State Government, generally or specially authorised in writing in this behalf by that Government.]

(2) Notwithstanding anything contained in the Code of Criminal Procedure, 1973 (2 of 1974) a Magistrate may, if he sees reason so to do, dispense with the personal attendance of the officer of the Bank filing the complaint, but the Magistrate may in his discretion, at any stage of the proceedings, direct the personal attendance of the complainant.

58-F. Application of Fine

A Court imposing any fine under this Act may direct that the whole or any part thereof shall be applied in, or towards payment of, the costs of the proceedings.

59 to 61. ***[Amendment of Act 3 of 1906. Repeals. Amendment of Section 11, Act 7 of 1913.]***

Rep. by Act 20 of 1937, S. 3 and Sch. II.

THE FIRST SCHEDULE

(See Section 9)

1. The Western Area shall consist of the States of Goa, Gujarat, Madhya Pradesh, Maharashtra and the Union territories of Dadra and Nagar Haveli and Daman and Diu.

2. The Eastern Area shall consist of the States of

Arunachal Pradesh, Assam, Meghalaya, Mizoram, Nagaland, West Bengal, Bihar, Orissa, Manipur and Tripura and the Union territory of Andaman and Nicobar Islands.

3. The Northern Area shall consist of the States of Jammu and Kashmir, Punjab, Haryana, Himachal Pradesh, Rajasthan and Uttar Pradesh and the Union territories of Chandigarh and Delhi.

4. The Southern Area shall consist of the States of Andhra Pradesh, Karnataka, Tamil Nadu and Kerala and the Union territories of Pondicherry and Lakshadweep.

THE SECOND SCHEDULE

[See Section 42 and Section 2(e)] Scheduled Banks*

Abhyudaya Co-operative Bank Ltd., Bombay (18-8-1988 w.e.f. 19- 1-1988)

ABN Amro Bank N.V. (11-10-1991)

Adhiyaman Grama Bank', Dharmapuri (Tamil-Nadu) (27- 12- 1985)

Akola Gramin Bank, Akola (Maharashtra) (16- 10- 1983)

Alaknanda Gramin Bank, Pauri (U.P.) (31-8-1985)

Aligarh Gramin Bank, Aligarh (U.P.) (22-3-1981)

Allahabad Bank

Allahabad Kshetriya Gramin Bank, Allahabad (U.P.) (23-8-1980)

Alwar-Bharatpur Anchalik Gramin Bank, Bharatpur (Rajasthan) (21-2-1981)

Ambala-Kurukshetra Gramin Bank, Ambala City (Haryana) (18-1-1985)

---

* Publisher's Note: This list is for information only and no warranty is being given regarding the completeness or accuracy of this list. Kindly refer to relevant Gazette or publication of Reserve Bank. The date in brackets indicataes the date of notification.

American Express Bank Ltd.

Andhra Bank, Masulipatam

Andhra Pradesh State Co-operative Bank Ltd., Hyderabad (2-7-1966)

ANZ Grindlays Bank p.l.c. (25- 1 - 1990)

Aravali Kshetriya Gramin Bank, Sawaimadhopur (Rajasthan) (2-10-1981)

Arunachal Pradesh Rural Bank, Pasighat (Arunachal Pradesh) (30-11-1983)

Aurangabad- Jalna Gramin Bank, Aurangabad (Maharashtra) (6-12-1982)

Baitarani Gramya Bank, Baripada (Orissa) (23-6-1980)

Balasore Gramya Bank, Balasore (Orissa) (6-8-1980)

Ballia Kshetriya Gramin Bank, Ballia (25-12-1976)

Banaskantha-Mehsana Gramin Bank, Patan (Gujarat) (29-11-1981)

Bank of America National Trust and Savings Association (29-5-1964)

Bank of Bahrain and Kuwait B.S.C. (14-7-1986)

Bank of Baroda

Bank of Credit and Commerce International (Overseas) Ltd.

Bank of India

Bank of Karad Ltd., Karad (5-6-1968)

Bank of Madurai Ltd., Madurai

Bank of Maharashtra

Bank of Nova Scotia, Toronto (Canada) (31-5-1984)

Bank of Oman Ltd.

Bank of Punjab Limited (19-4-1995)

Bank of Rajasthan Ltd., Udaipur

Bank of Tamilnad Ltd. (22-11-1979)

Bank of Tokyo

Banque de 1' Indochine et de Suez (INDOSUEZ) (2-10-1981)

Banque National de Paris (1-7-1966)

Barabanki Gramin Bank, Barabanki

Bardhaman Gramin Bank, Burdwan, W.B. (25-11-1980)

Bareilly Corporation Bank Ltd., Bareilly

Bareilly Kshetriya Gramin Bank, Bareilly (U.P.) (27-9-1980)

Bassein Catholic Co-operative Bank Ltd., Papdy Vasai (Town) Thane District, Maharashtra (1-11-1990)

Bastar Kshetriya Gramin Bank, Jagdalpur (15-12-1979)

Basti Gramin Bank, Basti (U.P.) (1-8-1980)

Begusarai Kshetriya Gramin Bank, Begusarai (Bihar) (23-3-1985)

Benares State Bank

Bhagalpur-Banka Kshetriya Gramin Bank Bhagalpur (Bihar) (22-3-1985)

Bhagirath Gramin Bank, Sitapur (19-9-1976)

Bhandara Gramin Bank, Bhandara (Maharashtra)

Bharat Overseas Bank Ltd., Madras

Bhilwara-Ajmer Kshetriya Gramin Bank, Bhilwara (Rajasthan) (24-3-1984)

Bhojpur Rohtas Gramin Bank, Arrah (26-12-1975)

Bidur Gramin Bank, Bijnor (U.P.) (18-1-1983)

Bihar State Co-operative Bank Ltd., Patna (2-7-1966)

Bijapur Grameena Bank, Bijapur (Karnataka) (31-3-1983)

Bikaner Kshetriya Gramin Bank, Bikaner (Rajasthan) (25-3-1985)

Bilaspur-Raipur Kshetriya Gramin Bank, Bilaspur (20-10-1976)

Bolangir Anchalik Gramya Bank, Bolangir (10-4-1976)

Bombay Mercantile Co-operative Bank Ltd., Bombay (18-8-1988 w.e.f. 1-9-1988)

British Bank of the Middle East

Buldhana Gramin Bank, Buldhana (Maharashtra) (17-10-1985)

Bundelkhand Kshetriya Gramin Bank, Tikkamgarh

Bundi-Chittorgarh Kshetriya Gramin Bank, Bundi (Rajasthan) (23-3-1984)

Cachar Gramin Bank, Silchar (Assam) (31-3-1981)

Canara Bank

Catholic Syrian Bank Ltd., Trichur (18-8-1969)

Cauvery Grameena Bank, Mysore (2-10-1976)

Central Bank of India

Centurion Bank Limited (27-1 -1995)

Chaitanya Grameena Bank, Tenali (Guntur) (A.P.) (25-3-1983)

Chambal Kshetriya Gramin Bank, Morena (M.P.) (11-2-1984)

Champaran Kshetriya Gramin Bank, Motihari (21-3-1976)

Chandrapur Gadchiroli Gramin Bank, Chandrapur (Maharashtra) (4-2-1983)

Chartered Bank

Chase Manhattan Bank N.A. (7-12-1994)

Chhatrasal Gramin Bank, Orai (U.P.) (30-3-1982)

Chhindwara-Seoni Kshetriya Gramin Bank, Chhindwara (M.P.) (20-1-1983)

Chikmagalur-Kodagn Grameena Bank, Chikmagalur (Karnataka) (28-4-1984)

Chitradurga Gramin Bank, Chitradurga (Karnataka) (5-8-1981)

City Union Bank Ltd.

Citibank N.A.

Corporation Bank Ltd.

Cosmos Co-operative Bank Ltd., Pune (Maharashtra) (1-11-1990)

Credit Lyonnais (28-12-1989)

Cuttack Gramya Bank, Cuttack (11 -10-1976)

Damoh-Panna-Sagar Kshetriya Gramin Bank, Damoh (M.P.) (30-3-1981)

Dena Bank

Deutsche Bank A.G. (15-11-1980) (13-12-1986) (5-4-1988)

Development Co-operative Bank Ltd., Bombay (18-8-1988 w.e.f. 1-9-1988)

Devipatan Kshetriya Gramin Bank, Gonda (U.P.) (17-1-1981)

Dewas Shajapur Kshetriya Gramin Bank, Dewas (M.P.) (30-3-1982)

Dhanalakshmi Bank Ltd., Trichur

Dhenkanal Gramya Bank, Dhenkanal (Orissa) (12-8-1981)

Dungarpur-Banswara Kshetriya Gramin Bank, Dungarpur (Rajasthan) (25-3-1984)

Durg-Rajnandgaon Gramin Bank, Rajnandgaon (12-3-1980)

Ellaquai Dehati Bank, Srinagar (10-7-1979)

Emirates Commercial Bank Ltd. (6-3-1981)

Etah Gramin Bank, Etah (U.P.) (29-3-1981)

Etawah Kshetriya Gramin Bank, Etawah (U.P.) (18-3-1980)

European Asian Bank

Faizabad Kshetriya Gramin Bank, Faizabad (U.P.) (5-9-1980)

Faridkot Bhatinda Kshetriya Gramin Bank, Bhatinda (Punjab) (22-3-1986)

Farrukhabad Gramin Bank, Farrukhabad (29-3-1976)

Fatehpur Kshetriya Gramin Bank, Fatehpur (U.P.) (6-9-1980)

Federal Bank Ltd., Alwaye

Ganga Yamuna Gramin Bank, Dehradun (U.P.) (29-3-1985)

Gaur Gramin Bank, Malda (W.B.)

Giridih Kshetriya Gramin Bank, Giridih (Bihar) (30-6-1984)

Global Trust Bank Limited (11-10-1994)

Goa State Co-operative Bank Ltd. (15-12-1994)

Godavari Grameena Bank, Rajahmundry (A.P.) (11-4-1987)

Golconda Grameen Bank, Hyderabad (A.P.) (15-2-1985)

Gomti Gramin Bank, Jaunpur (U.P.) (30-3-1981)

Gopalganj Kshetriya Gramin Bank, Gopalganj (Bihar) (27-3-1981)

Gorakhpur Kshetriya Gramin Bank, Gorakhpur (30-9-1975)

Gujarat State Co-operative Bank Ltd., Ahmedabad (2-7-1966)

Gurdaspur Amritsar Kshetriya Gramin Vikas Bank, Gurdaspur (Punjab) (31-3-1983)

Gurgaon Gramin Bank, Gurgaon (28-3-1976)

Gwalior Datia Kshetriya Gramin Bank, Datia (M.P.) (19-9-1985)

HDFC Bank Ltd. (23-1-1995)

Hadoti Kshetriya Gramin Bank, Kotah (Rajasthan) (14-10-1982)

Hardoi-Unnao Gramin Bank, Hardoi (7-6-1977)

Haryana Kshetriya Gramin Bank, Bhiwani (Haryana)

Haryana State Co-operative Apex Bank Ltd., Ambala, at Chandigarh

Hazaribagh Kshetriya Gramin Bank, Hazaribagh (Bihar) (19-11-1984)

Himachal Gramin Bank, Mandi (23-12-1976)

Hindon Gramin Bank, Ghaziabad (U.P.) (28-3-1987)

Hissar-Sirsa Kshetriya Gramin Bank, Hissar (Haryana) (2-10-1984)

Hongkong and Shanghai Banking Corporation Limited (25-1-1990)

Howrah Grameen Bank, Howrah (W.B.) (12-6-1982)

Indian Bank

Indian Overseas Bank

Indore-Ujjain Kshetriya Gramın Bank, Ujjain (M.P.) (19-11-1984)

Jaipur Nagaur Aanchalik Gramin Bank, Jaipur (Rajasthan)

Jammu and Kashmir Bank Ltd., Srinagar (11-8-1971)

Jammu Rural Bank, Jammu (12-3-1976)

Jamnagar Gramin Bank, Jamnagar (26-12-1978)

Jamuna Gramin Bank, Agra (U.P.) (2-12-1983)

Janata Sahakari Bank Ltd., Pune (18-8-1988 w.e.f. 1-9-1988)

Jhabua-Dhar Kshetriya Gramin Bank, Jhabua (M.P.) (20-6-1980)

Junagadh Amreli Gramin Bank, Junagadh (Gujarat)

Ka Bank Nangkyndong Ri Khasi Jaintia (Meghalaya) (29-12-1981)

Kakathiya Grameena Bank, Warangal (A.P.) (28-6-1982)

Kalahandi Anchalika Gramya Bank, Bhawanipatna (Orissa) (26-5-1980)

Kalpatharu Grameena Bank, Tumkur (Karnataka) (31-3-1982)

Kalupur Commercial Co-operative Bank Ltd., Ahmedabad (18-8-1988 w.e.f. 1-9-1988)

Kamraz Rural Bank, Sopore (J & K) (16-6-1981)

Kanakadurga Grameena Bank, Gudivada (A.P.) (28-3-1986)

Kanpur Kshetriya Gramin Bank, Kanpur (27-2,1980)

Kapurthala Firozpur Kshetriva Gramin Bank, Kapurthala (Punjab) (30-3-1983)

Karbi N.C. Rural Bank, Diphu (Assam) (27-1-1982)

Karnataka Bank Ltd., Mangalore

Karnataka State Co-operative Apex Bank Ltd., Bangalore (2-7-1966)

Karur Vysya Bank

Kashi Gramin Bank, Varanasi (U.P.) (28-7-1980)

Kerala State Co-operative Bank Ltd., Trivandrum (2-7-1966)

Khasi Jaintia Rural Bank, Shillong (Meghalaya)

Kisan Gramin Bank, Budaun (U.P.) (19-5-1980)

Kolar Gramin Bank, Kolar (Karnataka) (16-2-1983)

Koraput-Panchabati Gramya Bank, Jeypore (13-11-1976)

Kosi Kshetriya Gramin Bank, Purnea (23-12-1976)

Krishna Grameena Bank, Gulbarga (1-12-1978)

Kshetriya Gramin Bank, Hoshangabad (20-1-1976)

Kshetriya Kisan Gramin Bank, Mainpuri (U.P.) (20-5-1980)

Kutch Gramin Bank, Bhuj (23-12-1978)

Lakhimi Gaonlia Bank, Golaghat (Assam) (29-7-1980)
Lakshmi Vilas Bank Ltd., Karur
Langpi Dehangi Rural Bank, Dhipu (Assam)
Lord Krishna Bank Ltd., Kodungallur (16-4-1971)
Madhubani Kshetriya Gramin Bank, Madhubani (31-3-1979)
Madhya Pradesh (Rajya Sahakari Maryadit), Jabalpur
Madhya Pradesh State Co-operative Bank Ltd., Jabalpur (2-7-1966)
Madras State Co-operative Bank Ltd., Madras (2-7-1966)
Magadh Gramin Bank, Gaya (10-11-1976)
Mahakaushal Kshetriya Gramin Bank, Narsinghpur (M.P.) (1-4-1984)
Maharashtra State Co-operative Bank Ltd., Bombay (Incorporating the Vidarbha Co-operative Bank Ltd.) (2-7-1966)
Malaprabha Grameena Bank, Dharwar (13-8-1976)
Mallabhum Gramin Bank, Bankura (9-4-1976)
Malwa Gramin Bank, Sangrur (Punjab) (27-2-1986)
Mandla-Balaghat Kshetriya Gramin Bank, Mandla (M.P.) (14-11-1982)
Manipur Rural Bank, Imphal (Manipur) (28-5-1981)
Manjira Grameena Bank, Songareddy (A.P.) (31-3-1982)
Marathwada Gramin Bank, Nanded (26-8-1976)
Marudhar Kshetriya Gramin Bank, Churu (29-3 -1979)
Marwar Gramin Bank, Pali (6-9-1976)
Mayurakshi Gramin Bank, Suri (16-10-1976)
Mercantile Bank Ltd.
Mewar Aanchalik Gramin Bank, Udaipur (Rajasthan) (25-1-1983)

Mithila Kshetriya Gramin Bank, Darbhanga (14-3-1980)

Mitsui Taiyo Kobe Bank Ltd.

Mizoram Rural Bank, Aizwal (Mizoram) (27-9-1983)

Monghyr Kshetriya Gramin Bank, Monghyr (12-3-1977)

Murshidabad Gramin Bank, Berhampore (W.B.) (17-11-1984)

Muzaffaranagar Kshetriya Gramin Bank, Muzaffarnagar (U.P.) (27-7-1984)

Mysore State Co-operative Apex Bank Ltd., Bangalore (2-7-1966)

Nadia Gramin Bank, Krishnagar (W.B.) (27-8-1980)

Nagaland Rural Bank, Kohima (Nagaland) (30-3-1983)

Nagarjuna Gramin Bank, Khammam (30-4-1976)

Nalanda Gramin Bank, Bihar Shariff (31-3-1979)

Nainital Almora Kshetriya Grameen Bank, Nainital (U.P.) (26-3-1983)

Nainital Bank Ltd.

Nedungadi Bank, Calicut

Netravati Grameena Bank, Mangalore (Karnataka) (11-10-1984)

New India Co-operative Bank Ltd., Bombay, Maharashtra (1-9-1990)

Nimar Kshetriya Gramin Bank, Khargone (M.P.) (26-6-1982)

North Malabar Gramin Bank, Cannanore (12-12-1976)

Oman International Bank S.A.O.G. (25-1-1990)

Oriental Bank of Commerce

Orissa State Co-operative Bank Ltd., Cuttack (2-7-1966)

Palamau Kshetriya Gramin Bank, Daltonganj (15-5-1980)

Panchmahal Gramin Bank, Godhra (Gujarat) (30-3-1982)

Pandyan Grameen Bank, Sattur (9-3-1977)

Parvatiya Gramin Bank, Chamba (H.P.) (2-11-1985)

Patliputra Gramin Bank, Patna (Bihar) (27-11-1984)

Pinakini Grameena Bank, Nellore (A.P.)

Pithoragarh Kshetriya Gramin Bank, Pithoragarh (U.P.) (27-3-1985)

Pragjyotish Gaonlia Bank, Nalbari (6-7-1976) .

Pratapgarh Kshetriya Gramin Bank, Pratapgarh (U.P.) (25-8-1980)

Prathama Bank, Moradabad (30-9-1975)

Punjab and Sind Bank, Amritsar

Punjab Co-operative Bank. Amritsar

Punjab National Bank

Punjab State Co-operative Bank Ltd., Chandigarh

Puri Gramya Bank, Pipli (25-2-1976)

Rae Bareli Kshetriya Gramin Bank, Rae Bareli (29-3-1976)

Raigarh Kshetriya Gramin Bank, Raigarh (M.P.) (31-1-1981)

Rajasthan State Co-operative Bank Ltd., Jaipur (2-7-1966)

Rajgarh Kshetriya Gramin Bank, Rajgarh (M.P.)

Rajgarh Sehore Kshetriya Gramin Bank, Biaora (Rajgarh) (M.P.) (23-3-1983)

Rajkot Nagrik Sahakari Bank Ltd., Bombay (18-8-1988 w.e.f. 1 -9-1988)

Ranchi Kshetriya Gramin Bank, Ranchi (Bihar) (21 -6-1980)

Rani Lakshmi Bai Kshetriya Gramin Bank, Jhansi (U.P.) (31-3-1982)

Ratlam Mandsaur Kshetriya Gramin Bank, Mandsaur (M.P.)

Ratnagiri Sindudurg Gramin Bank, Ratnagiri (Maharashtra) (19-11-1983)

Ratnakar Bank Ltd., Kolhapur

Rayalaseema Grameena Bank, Cuddapah (6-8-1976)

Rewa-Sidhi Gramin Bank, Rewa (20-12-1976)

Rupee Co-operative Bank Ltd., Pune (18-8-1988 w.e.f. 1-9-1988)

Rushikulya Gramya Bank, Berhampur (Orissa) (14-2-1981)

SBI Commercial and International Bank Limited (30-11-1993)

Sabarkantha-Gandhinagar Gramin Bank, Himatnagar (Gujarat) (9-8-1984)

Sagar Gramin Bank, Amtala (West Bengal) (24-9-1980)

Sahyadri Gramin Bank, Shimoga (Karnataka) (6-9-1984)

Samastipur Kshetriya Gramin Bank, Samastipur (12-5-1980)

Samyut Kshetriya Gramin Bank, Azamgarh (6-1-1976)

Sangameshwara Grameena Bank, Mahboobnagar (A.P.) (31-3-1982)

Sangli Bank

Sangli Urban Co-operative Bank Ltd., Sangli (18-8-1988 w.e.f. 1-9-1988)

Santhal Pargannas Gramin Bank, Dumka (30-3-1977)

Saran Kshetriya Gramin Bank, Chapra (Bihar) (28-3-1981)

Saraswat Co-operative Bank Ltd., Bombay (18-8-1988 w.e.f. 1-9-1988)

Sarayu Gramin Bank, Lakhimpur (U.P.) (9-8-1983)

Satar Bank of Mysore

Shahadol Kshetriya Gramin Bank, Shahadol (M.P.)

Shahjahanpur Kshetriya Gramin Bank, Shahjahanpur (U.P.) (24-3-1983)

Shamrao Vithal Co-operative Bank Ltd., Bombay (18-8-1988 w.e.f. 1-9-1988)

Sharda Gramin Bank Satna (31-3-1979)

Shekhawat Gramin Bank, Sikar (7-10-1976)

Shivalik Kshetriya Gramin Bank, Hoshiarpur, (Punjab) (30-3-1983)

Shivpuri-Guna Kshetriya Gramin Bank, Shivpuri (M.P.) (28-3-1981)

Shri Venkateswara Grameena Bank, Chittoor- (A.P.) (22-3-1981)

Singhbhum Kshetriya Gramin Bank, Chaibasa (31-3-1979)

Siwan Kshetriya Gramin Bank, Siwan (Bihar) (31-3-1981)

Solapur Gramin Bank, Solapur (Maharashtra) (21-1-1984)

Sonali Bank

South Indian Bank Ltd., Trichur

South Malabar Gramin Bank, Malappuram (11-12-1976)

Sravasthi Gramin Bank, Bahraich (4-3-1980)

Sree Anantha Grameena Bank, Anantapur (1-11-1979)

Sri Saraswati Grameena Bank, Adilabad (A.P.) (30-3-1982)

Sri Satavahana Grameena Bank, Karimnagar (A.P.) (28-3-1983)

Sri Visakha Grameena Bank, Srikakulam (30-9-1976)

Sriganganagar Kshetriya Gramin Bank, Sriganganagar (Rajasthan) (31-3-1984)

Srirama Grameena Bank, Nizamabad (A.P.) (21-2-1985)

Standard Chartered Bank

State Bank of Bikaner and Jaipur

State Bank of Hyderabad

State Bank of India

State Bank of Indore

State Bank of Mauritius Ltd. (12- 12-1994)

State Bank of Mysore

State Bank of Patiala

State Bank of Saurashtra, Bhavnagar

State Bank of Travancore

Subansiri Gaonlia Bank, North Lakhimpur (Assam) (30-3-1982)

Sultanpur Kshetriya Gramin Bank, Sultanpur (8-2-1977)

Surat Peoples Co-operative Bank Ltd., Surat (18-8-1988 w.e.f. 1-9-1988)

Surat-Bharuch Gramin Bank, Bharuch (Gujarat) (28-2-1984)

Surendranagar-Bhavnagar Gramin Bank, Surendranagar (Gujarat) (15-12-1983)

Surguja Kshetriya Gramin Bank, Ambikapur (M.P.) (24-10-1979)

Syndicate Bank

Tamil Nadu Mercantile Bank Ltd.

Tamil Nadu State Apex Co-operative Bank Ltd., Madras (25-5-1989)

Thane Gramin Bank, Thane (Maharashtra) (30-3- 1 986)

Thar Aanchalik Gramin Bank, Jodhpur (Rajasthan) (31-1-1983)

Tripura Gramin Bank, Agartala (21-12-1976)

Tulsi Gramin Bank, Banda (U.P.) (26-3-1981)

Tungabhadra Gramin Bank, Bellary (25-1-1976)

UCO Bank

Union Bank of India

United Bank of India

United Western Bank

Uttar Banga Kshetriya Gramin Bank, Cooch Bihar (7-3-1977)

Uttar Pradesh Co-operative Bank Ltd., Lucknow (2-7-1966)

Vaishali- Kshetriya Gramin Bank, Muzaffarpur (10-3-1977)

Vallalar Grama Bank, Cuddalore (Tamil Nadu) (19-6-1986)

Valsad-Dangs Gramin Bank, Bulsar (Gujarat) (23-2-1984)

Varada Grameena Bank, Kumta (Karnataka) (12-10-1984)

Vidisha-Bhopal Kshetriya Gramin Bank, Vidisha (M.P.) (31-3-1986)

Vidur Gramin Bank Bijnor (U.P.)

Vijaya Bank Ltd., Mangalore

Vindhyavasini Gramin Bank,. Mirzapur (U.P.) (30-3-1983)

Visveshwaraya Grameen Bhnk, Mandya (Karnataka) (27-3- 1985)

Vysya Bank Ltd., Bangalore City

West Bengal Provincial Co-operative Bank Ltd., Calcutta (2-7- 1966)

West Bengal State Co-operative Bank Ltd., Calcutta

Yavatmal Gramin Bank, Yavatmal (Maharashtra) (29-1-1985)

THE THIRD SCHEDULE

Rep. by Act 23 of 1955, S. 52 and Sch. III (w.e.f. 1.7.1995)

THE FOURTH SCHEDULE

Rep by Act 62 of 1948, S.7 anbd Sch. (w.e.f. 1.1.1949)

THE FIFTH SCHEDULE

Rep. by the M.O. 1937

INDEX

❑❑❑